THE FIGARO TRILOGY

PIERRE-AUGUSTIN CARON DE BEAUMARCHAIS was born in Paris in 1732. He was musical and inherited the practical skills of his father, a watchmaker, and to them added a talent for self-promotion. Still only 21, he perfected a new escapement mechanism which a rival attempted to pass off as his own. Caron defended himself with a brio which attracted royal favour and he gave music lessons to the king's daughters. In 1757 he married a widow and took the name of a small property she possessed. Now Caron de Beaumarchais, he became the associate of a wealthy financier, Pâris-Duverney. In 1764 he travelled to Spain, which would provide the atmosphere of his two most famous comedies. The first of his six plays was staged in 1767, and thereafter he filled his life with multifarious activities as entrepreneur, international go-between, secret agent, pamphleteer, playwright, self-appointed diplomat, publisher, and gun-runner. He made, spent, and lost large sums of money, was involved in highly publicized legal battles, carried out covert operations for the government, and shipped guns to the insurgents during the American War of Independence, while still finding time to write and stage *The Barber of Seville* (1775) and *The Marriage of Figaro* (1784). At times a popular hero, he also had many enemies who feared that Figaro's rebellious spirit would precipitate a national crisis. But in 1789 Beaumarchais's moderate political opinions and his grand lifestyle made him appear a lukewarm supporter of the Revolution. The new regime was as suspicious of him as the old, though in 1792 he was authorized to buy 60,000 'Dutch guns' for France, a protracted affair which cost him dear. In the same year *The Guilty Mother* was performed, to unenthusiastic audiences. In 1794, when his name was added to the list of émigrés, he fled the guillotine and did not return to France for two years. Thereafter he sought a political role, but without success. He died in his sleep in 1799.

DAVID COWARD is Emeritus Professor of French at the University of Leeds. He is the author of *A History of French Literature* (2002) and many translations, most recently Paul Morand, *Hecate and Her Dogs* (2009). For Oxford World's Classics he has edited nine novels by Alexandre Dumas and translated titles by Maupassant, Sade, Diderot, and Gaston Leroux. Winner of the 1996 Scott-Moncrieff Prize for translation, he reviews regularly for the *Times Literary Supplement*, *The New York Review of Books*, and other literary periodicals.

OXFORD WORLD'S CLASSICS

*For over 100 years Oxford World's Classics have brought
readers closer to the world's great literature. Now with over 700
titles—from the 4,000-year-old myths of Mesopotamia to the
twentieth century's greatest novels—the series makes available
lesser-known as well as celebrated writing.*

*The pocket-sized hardbacks of the early years contained
introductions by Virginia Woolf, T. S. Eliot, Graham Greene,
and other literary figures which enriched the experience of reading.
Today the series is recognized for its fine scholarship and
reliability in texts that span world literature, drama and poetry,
religion, philosophy and politics. Each edition includes perceptive
commentary and essential background information to meet the
changing needs of readers.*

OXFORD WORLD'S CLASSICS

BEAUMARCHAIS

The Figaro Trilogy

The Barber of Seville
The Marriage of Figaro
The Guilty Mother

Translated with an Introduction and Notes by
DAVID COWARD

OXFORD
UNIVERSITY PRESS

OXFORD
UNIVERSITY PRESS

Great Clarendon Street, Oxford OX2 6DP

Oxford University Press is a department of the University of Oxford.
It furthers the University's objective of excellence in research, scholarship,
and education by publishing worldwide in

Oxford New York

Athens Bangkok Buenos Aires Cape Town Chennai
Dar es Salaam Delhi Hong Kong Istanbul Karachi Kolkata
Kuala Lumpur Madrid Melbourne Mexico City Mumbai Nairobi
São Paulo Shanghai Taipei Tokyo Toronto

Oxford is a registered trade mark of Oxford University Press
in the UK and in certain other countries

Published in the United States
by Oxford University Press Inc., New York

First published as an Oxford World's Classics paperback 2003
Reissued 2008

British Library Cataloguing in Publication Data

Data available

Library of Congress Cataloging in Publication Data

Data available

ISB 978-0-19-953997-0

16

Typeset in Ehrhardt
by RefineCatch Limited, Bungay, Suffolk
Printed in Great Britain by
Clays Ltd, Elcograf S.p.A.

CONTENTS

CONTENTS

INTRODUCTION

Eighteenth-century Paris was stage-struck. Three officially licensed playhouses (the Comédie Française, the Opera, and the Théâtre Italien) were not enough to satisfy the appetite of theatregoers. Short plays and farces were also staged for the capital's two permanent fairs which, though they catered for a popular audience, drew established playwrights and attracted elements of the cultured, fashionable playgoing public. By the 1760s new fixed theatres were appearing on the Boulevards, attendances continued to rise, and the enthusiasm for amateur theatricals fuelled the vogue for intimate *théâtre de société* which turned salons in private houses into improvised stages. The royal court ordered command performances of successful plays, and Marie-Antoinette acted in productions of *The Barber of Seville* (she was a lively Rosine), Rousseau's *Le Devin du Village* (*The Village Soothsayer*), and others. Not to be outdone, nobles and wealthy bourgeois invited the stars of the professional stage into their mansions, but also encouraged authors to contribute short *parades*, not always tasteful comedies and farces in which they, their families, and their friends performed.

Yet history has treated eighteenth-century theatre very badly. Despite its central role in the cultural life of the Enlightenment, it left the most meagre legacy. Voltaire's tragedies, once so admired, and the socially conscious *drame bourgeois*, launched by Diderot, now have only an antiquarian interest and, curiously, novels like Diderot's *Le Neveu de Rameau*, Voltaire's *Candide*, and above all Laclos's *Les Liaisons dangereuses* have proved far more stageworthy. Only two playwrights remain theatrically viable: Marivaux, with his knack of being periodically rediscovered, and Beaumarchais, the only truly international theatre star the age produced.

Yet even his literary reputation is ambiguous. His fame rests upon *The Barber of Seville* (1775) and *The Marriage of Figaro* (1784), the only plays which his stage-mad century bequeathed to the permanent repertoire. But his success has been adulterated, for 'Beaumarchais' has long been a kind of brand name for a variable product reprocessed by Paisiello, Mozart, and Salieri in his century, by Rossini most famously in the nineteenth, and by Massenet and Milhaud

in the twentieth. A score of librettists and musicians have perpetu-
ated his plots, his characters, and his name, and in the process his
plays have regularly been betrayed. Rossini's Figaro is a busy, cheeky
valet, and Mozart, cutting the five acts of *The Marriage* to four,
demotes him after Act II, abandoning the subversive thrust of the
original in favour of the feelings of Almaviva and the Countess.
Beaumarchais's mixed posthumous fortunes have been coloured in
part by his annexation by others. But he has also been the victim of
his own enigmatic personality.

For many have wondered where his real loyalties lay. Was the
creator of Figaro on the side of the angels or simply president of
Beaumarchais Enterprises, a man who had his sticky fingers in many
pies? In his lifetime he was, to the great and the good, an upstart, and
kings and governments suspected his motives. The middle classes
envied his wealth and rejoiced at his failures, but nevertheless identified him as the embodiment of entrepreneurial energy and the
defender of the freedoms they claimed. Popular opinion, which he
manipulated expertly, hailed him as a hero until 1789, when the
adoring crowds spotted feet of clay and turned on him. He offered
his services to the Revolution but not with the required zeal, and was
denounced as a reactionary. Since his death in 1799, ambiguity has
continued to cling to him. His abilities are not in doubt. Here was a
man of infinite resource and resilience whose versatility was all-
encompassing. Yet he plied his many trades—watchmaker, musician,
international go-between, entrepreneur, secret agent, pamphleteer,
playwright, self-appointed diplomat, publisher, and gun-runner—
with brash, self-advertising, self-serving zeal.

But the most intriguing question of all has centred on his role as
catalyst of the French Revolution. Was his impertinent barber the
Sweeney Todd of the *ancien régime*, a rebel whose razor turned into a
guillotine blade? Louis XVI banned *The Marriage of Figaro*, observing that 'the Bastille would have to be pulled down before such a play
could be staged'. His estimate of the danger was confirmed on 14
July 1789 and subsequently by Danton, who declared that 'Figaro
killed off the nobility'. Napoleon, who saw *The Marriage* as 'the
Revolution in action', would have done what Louis XVI dared not
do and locked Beaumarchais up for everybody's good.

But however shop-soiled, dubious, or damnable his reputation
might be, it would be wrong to mistake Beaumarchais for Figaro.

There is no denying that they are related and that each was the product of his age. But Beaumarchais was a man of the theatre, and his characters are separate from him and have long since become the property of the greater world. Figaro and what he stands for have secured a place in the collective psyche; his true cousins are Hamlet, Don Quixote, or D'Artagnan, those mythical expressions of the human spirit.

The Life and Careers of Beaumarchais

Beaumarchais was born plain Pierre-Augustin Caron in Paris in 1732, the seventh of the ten children of a watchmaker. Home was happy and cultured, and it might seem that he had made a wise choice of parent. His century had discovered that the entire cosmos was a clock and cast God as the Great Clockmaker. A man could not be better placed to understand the mechanisms of nature and unravel the mysteries of the universe. But it the sense that really mattered, his birth counted against him. Grace and favour were distributed by a different kind of machine altogether, one which had served caste, kings, and God for centuries. Besides, Beaumarchais, though he was aware of the role of chance in human affairs, showed little interest in the mysteries of the universe, God, or the soul. From an early age, he was driven by an ambition to succeed.

He was given some schooling until he was 13, when he was apprenticed to his father, a genuinely good man who taught him a lasting respect for family values. He was musical, clever with his hands, and in 1753 he invented a new escapement mechanism which was appropriated by a colleague of his father. Burning with indignation, he wrote precociously clever letters to the Académie des Sciences, which ruled in his favour. The affair attracted attention at court and his future as a Watchmaker by Royal Appointment seemed assured. It was not enough.

His sudden fame had opened wide horizons. He was taken up by Louis XV's daughters and gave them music lessons. He improved his accent, read indispensable classics, and jotted down quotable Latin tags in a little book. Having his entrée at court, he also became a familiar at the home of Le Normant d'Étioles, husband of Madame de Pompadour, the king's mistress, and it was there that he staged the first of his *parades* which an odd inverted snobbery had made fashionable in a society bored with the regularity of the professional theatre. By 1759, having married a widow and taken the name of the estate which went with her, he cut a small dash as Caron de Beaumarchais, despised by blue blood and the old money, but already noticed by leaders of the new mercantile aristocracy. One of them, the immensely rich army supplier Pâris-Duverney, bought him an office at court and made him his associate. In 1764 he travelled to Madrid on matters of family and semi-official business. He failed to rescue his sister, Lisette, from the consequences of an unfortunate liaison, and had little more success with schemes, funded by Pâris-Duverney, for supplying the Spanish army, irrigating the Sierra Morena, and founding a French company to trade with Louisiana. But at least he had acquired a useful introduction to the international arena of finance and diplomacy. He was also a social success, and happily absorbed the Spanish atmosphere which added a touch of exoticism to the first two Figaro plays.

He returned to Paris, and in 1766 joined Pâris-Duverney in a scheme to exploit a timber concession at Chinon in the Loire Valley. The enterprise embroiled him in a legal wrangle which was merely a foretaste of battles to come. When Pâris-Duverney died in 1770, his estate passed to his nephew by marriage, the Comte de La Blache, who attempted to persuade the courts to annul the agreement of association which his uncle had signed. Threatened with financial ruin, Beaumarchais published his defence against La Blache (and soon the lawyer Goëzman) in a series of witty, saw-toothed *mémoires à consulter* which delighted the public, though it was not until 1778 that he finally won his case.

By then his pen had brought him fame in another quarter. Between 1757 and 1763 he had written a number of short *scènes* and *parades* for private *théâtres de société*. But with *Eugénie* (1767), he began his assault on the Paris stage. Like *Les Deux Amis* (1770), it was a *drame bourgeois*, sentimental in tone and earnest in its defence of middle-class values. *Eugénie* was a modest success, but *Les Deux Amis* was not well received. For his next venture Beaumarchais returned to the spirit of his *parades*. The result was *The Barber of Seville*. It was first offered to the Théâtre Italien in 1772 as a comic opera. When it was rejected he revised it in five acts and approached the Comédie Française, where it was accepted in 1773 and again in 1774. The delay was caused by a public altercation with the Duke de

Chaulnes, for which Beaumarchais was briefly jailed, and his witty, pungent *mémoires* against Goëzman which caught the imagination of the public but irritated the authorities. When the courts found in his favour in February 1774, his popularity reached new heights. But the judgement also censured him and deprived him of his civil rights. To earn his pardon he offered his services to the court, which sent him on secret missions to London, Amsterdam, and Vienna where he was briefly jailed. His orders were to buy off expatriate journalists who were threatening to make damaging revelations about Louis XV's relationship with Madame du Barry. Although Louis XV died at this point, his successor used Beaumarchais in a similar capacity. He returned in the summer of 1774 with his standing enhanced, and permission to stage his play was finally given. The first performance of *The Barber* on 23 February 1775 was a failure. Undaunted, Beaumarchais took three days to prune its five acts to four, and on 26 February it was enthusiastically applauded.

In 1775 he again travelled to England, this time to silence the Chevalier d'Éon who possessed documents potentially damaging to French interests. Beaumarchais compiled a report on the state of England which greatly interested the government, and he was rehabilitated in 1776. Louis XVI did not entirely trust a man whom he regarded as a gamekeeper who also poached. But by this time Beaumarchais had developed political views which greatly interested the new foreign minister, Vergennes.

Beaumarchais had visited Birmingham in 1775, and had there observed the Industrial Revolution in action. But he saw little future in industry. For him, Britain was a trading nation whose power depended on the wealth it drew from its colonies. When the American War of Independence broke out in 1776, he stopped being a minor emissary and began thinking like a statesman. If Britain lost the colonies, her economic power would be reduced; if the Americans won their freedom with French help, France stood to gain what Britain lost. The prospect tempted Louis and Vergennes. To avoid provoking open war with their mighty neighbour, they resolved to supply practical help to the Americans indirectly, in return for imported goods. Implementation of the policy was left to Beaumarchais in his capacity as a private citizen. It was thus that he furnished the insurgents with arms, including the guns which sealed the fate of Burgoyne at Saratoga in 1777.

He was only partly funded by the French Crown, and had to wait nearly ten years before Louis XVI repaid most of what was owed. The insurgents treated him even more shabbily. He had failed to obtain the ratification of the rebel government, which accpted his supplies but did not pay for them. When the war ended, the American Congress refused to reimburse him, although no Frenchman had done more for their cause, and the debt was not finally settled until 1835.

During the war Beaumarchais helped to shape the direction of France's foreign policy. But he also found time to shape public opinion through an influential periodical, *Le Courier de l'Europe*. He was a major shareholder, and the paper supported his political views, puffed his plays, and publicized his business ventures. But it also translated political articles from the English and American press and gave extensive coverage to House of Commons debates, a development which alarmed the British government. Among its readers was Vergennes, who found that the *Courier* kept him better informed of Britain's intentions than his own ambassador and intelligence service combined.

But in addition to publicizing the deliberations of the British parliament, the paper also showed its readers how the 'free' England lauded by Voltaire and Montesquieu worked in practice. As subjects of an absolute monarchy, the French had very limited opportunities to express their views of government policy. The *Courier* provided them with lessons in parliamentary procedure, demonstrated the novel principle of ministerial accountability, and explained the role of an official Opposition. In France such ideas were intriguing, and words like *amendement*, *constitutionnel*, *motion*, and *popularité* (not forgetting *comité*, of which Suzanne complains in *The Guilty Mother*, IV.4) were now redefined for French readers who thus acquired a linguistic framework which made *opposition* to absolutism psychologically possible and paved the way for the profound changes to come. 'Le Journal de Beaumarchais' offered them a weapon more lethal than an arsenal of guns: a vocabulary with which to fight the *ancien régime*. It was not the smallest of the hurts which he inflicted on the political establishment.

Throughout the war Beaumarchais was indefatigable. In addition to his political and commercial activities, he founded the Society of Dramatic Authors, campaigned against the monopolistic exploitation of literary property by the actors of the Comédie Française, and began a labour of love, the Kehl Edition of the works of Voltaire (1783–90), which ran to seventy-two volumes. He helped struggling playwrights, defended the rights of Protestants, began *The Marriage of Figaro* in 1778, and fought for six years against political and royal opposition before it was staged triumphantly in 1784. Its impact may be judged against the thirty performances rarely exceeded by even the most successful eighteenth-century plays: *The Marriage* was staged more than a hundred times. It inspired thirty or so imitations and parodies, and within two years had been turned into an opera by Mozart. But when Beaumarchais sought a musician to provide a score for *Tarare*, a libretto completed in 1784, he chose Antonio Salieri. *Tarare*, 'a drama with music' written to defend virtue against despotism, was performed thirty-three times in 1787.

But not all his ventures succeeded. Plans for raising money to rebuild the French fleet and found a charitable institution came to nothing and his involvement in a company set up to provide Paris with clean drinking-water made him enemies and brought him into open conflict with Mirabeau, a formidable opponent. The Kehl Edition of Voltaire, in which he invested much effort and money, failed to attract the required number of subscribers and proved to be a costly failure. Ill-advisedly as it turned out, he defended Mme Kornman, who had been abused by her powerful husband. He became interested in her case in 1781 and was drawn into a protracted legal battle which involved six lawsuits and a highly publicized exchange of *mémoires* with Kornman's lawyer, Bergasse, who proved a skilful and tenacious adversary. Although Bergasse finally lost the case early in 1789, he painted Beaumarchais in the blackest colours as an agent of debauchery, a disrupter of families, and the embodiment of oppression. Bergasse emerged as the champion of freedom, while Beaumarchais was insulted in the street and entered the Revolution under a cloud. It was a damaging outcome, and Beaumarchais took his revenge in *The Guilty Mother*, where Figaro's hypocritical adversary is immediately recognizable under the anagram 'Bégearss'.

The self-made, wealthy Beaumarchais compounded his fall from public favour by building a palace of looking-glass and marble opposite the Bastille, an unfortunate juxtaposition which was interpreted as a visible sign of his anti-revolutionary sympathies. When *Tarare* was revived in 1790, he added cautionary lines supporting constitutional monarchy and insisting that 'liberty means obeying the law', a point of view which clearly branded him as a moderate and confirmed growing doubts about his loyalties. He made generous donations to revolutionary causes (and ensured they received appropriate publicity), and when *The Guilty Mother* was accepted by the Comédie Française he withdrew it when the actors proved reluctant to apply the new laws governing literary property. Instead, it was performed to an unresponsive audience at the Théâtre du Marais on 26 June 1792. As a *drame*, its reliance on sentiment echoed the new taste for melodrama which grew after 1789. But its sentiments seemed anachronistic and unfashionably non-political. It belonged more to the old regime (it was begun in 1784), and reflected little of the new.

In June 1792 Louis XVI briefly considered making him his interior minister, but the plan came to nothing and Beaumarchais's troubles deepened. His house was ransacked by a mob believing it contained a store of arms, though they found only unsold copies of the works of Voltaire. He was arrested and sent to the Abbaye Prison, from which he emerged only days before the September Massacres, when another mob slaughtered 1,400 political prisoners. Meanwhile, he had become involved in a scheme to purchase 60,000 small arms seized by the Austrians after the failure of the revolt in Brabant. He travelled to Holland, where they were being stored, and thence to London. In his absence, fresh doubts about his loyalties were voiced and, to rebut them, he wrote a new series of self-justifying *mémoires* early in 1793. He was allowed to return to Paris and continued to work to secure the arms, which the nation desperately needed to resist the alliance of European powers ranged against it. But the 'Dutch guns' affair dragged on for years (the English finally acquired them in 1795), during which time he was accused of profiteering, saw the inside of jails in Paris and London, and was denounced as an émigré in 1794. It was a death sentence (his wife—his third—was obliged by law to divorce him), and he fled to Hamburg. There he lived in straitened circumstances, published new *mémoires* in his defence, and did not return to Paris until 1796, fat, deaf, but unbowed.

He remarried his wife and moved back into his grand house. *The Guilty Mother* was restaged in 1797 and played with gratifying success. He offered his services to the new government, believing that he could win Pitt's confidence. No one asked him to try, though ministers consulted him on a range of matters. Unavailingly, he asked Talleyrand to help with his appointment as ambassador to the United States. He published articles on the viability and usefulness of flying machines (he thought they might be called 'aerambules'), outlined the advantages of cutting a 'Nicaraguan canal' which would connect the Atlantic to the Pacific Ocean, and in April 1799 sent two letters on the subject of Christ to the *Journal de Paris*, his only overtly anti-religious writings. A month later, on 18 May, he died in his sleep, still dunned by the French authorities for their Dutch gun money.

Beaumarchais or Figaro?

Beaumarchais was perpetual motion, a facilitator who had charm, more than his fair share of talent, and the brash faults of the self-made man. He made many enemies and his own side sometimes questioned his good faith. The line between engaging *pícaro* and ruthless individualist is in his case particularly hard to draw.

In his defence are his well-documented loyalty to his family and its public face: his genuine, even idealistic, commitment to the public good. His theatre has a strongly 'committed', didactic side which defended the virtuous against the wicked and defined happiness in terms of family, love, friendship, loyalty, and honest dealing. Yet the case is far from clear. His idealism was genuine, but it was routinely pursued in a spirit of cheerful self-promotion. His *mémoires* against Goëzman may be exemplary models of self-defence, but self-defence is what they are: they plead not the cause of justice in general but the cause of Beaumarchais in particular. Moreover, he always took care to ensure that his acts of public service turned a profit, so that it is difficult not to suspect that what Almaviva says to Figaro in *The Marriage of Figaro* (III.5) might equally apply to his creator: 'Why is it that there's always something louche about everything you do?'

Ultimately, the best evidence on which to base an estimate of the man is provided by the plays. The *parades* which have survived show his sprightly, irreverent wit, and his ingenuity is clearly on show in *Eugénie* and *Les Deux Amis* which, within the requirements of the genre, are tightly plotted and verbally persuasive. Yet both his *drames* skirt contentious issues and are much less politically outspoken than those of, say, Sébastien Mercier, who raised serious social issues such as poverty. They do not make general points about society but operate within it, for the dangers which threaten the happiness of families do not derive from unjust laws but from circumstances and the personal callousness of individuals.

Beaumarchais's combative personality is much more clearly visible in the first scenes of *The Barber of Seville*, which turns the most hackneyed of comedy plots (young lovers, helped by servant, foil marriage plans of elderly guardian) into a dazzlingly crafted, exuberant celebration of youth and energy. If the situation was hardly new, the opening exchanges make it clear that Figaro is not just another insolent servant or licensed buffoon. His impertinence has an edge which makes it sound like a challenge—does Almaviva know many masters who would make adequate servants?—and his gift for manipulation turns defiance into a potential threat. His talents, for which he has the highest regard, have not brought him the reward they merit, and he demonstrates his quick-witted superiority by the ease with which he masterminds the aristocratic Almaviva's romance and outwits Bartholo, the bourgeois conservative and enemy of electricity, freedom of thought, the *Encyclopédie*, the *drame bourgeois*, and everything the progressive Enlightenment stood for. Beaumarchais offered more than satire. Figaro was the coming man, and he dared to say publicly what many were thinking privately.

Even so, Beaumarchais's outspoken defence of talent against privilege and the individual against the establishment is hardly central to the plot of *The Barber of Seville*. *The Marriage of Figaro*, in contrast, adds a more consistent dimension of provocative social criticism. It takes the *droit du seigneur*, which belonged more to legend than fact, as an excuse for highlighting the injustice of a system based on rank and privilege. Yet even here, Beaumarchais pulls his punches. Almaviva's power is absolute, yet he is approachable, more respected than feared, and does not conform to the standard image of the feudal tyrant who evicts widows and orphans and bleeds his serfs dry.

He is, however, prepared to abuse his authority. As master of Aguas-Frescas, he is free to subordinate love to sex, make Rosine unhappy, ruin Suzanne's reputation, and repay his faithful retainer by turning him into a cuckold. But his failings are personal, not those of his class. Neatly sidestepping any suggestion that his motive is political, Beaumarchais takes the edge off Almaviva's despotic behaviour by linking it to a form of oppression which could not be identified with the social hierarchy: Beaumarchais speaks up for women against men. He makes Almaviva's downfall very largely the work of women, and Marceline, who begins as a complaining pest, emerges as the victim of a society which condones male predatoriness. But Figaro too is a victim, and not only of the philandering of his new-found father, Bartholo, nor of what he mistakenly believes to be Suzanne's faithlessness. His long monologue in Act V sets out a more forthright libertarian case which denounces privilege and the abuse of power and demands the recognition of merit, the removal of obstacles to talent, freedom of expression, the reform of censorship, and an end to arbitrary justice. Here Figaro chafes much more openly against the prerogatives of privilege, and he is prepared to act. With the support of Almaviva's vassals, he stages a palace revolt. Though it is very polite as uprisings go, he nevertheless forces his master to stand by his promise to renounce the symbolic privilege of the *droit du seigneur*. It is not difficult to understand why the king banned the play for, as one contemporary wrote, 'persons of every condition' flocked to see Figaro 'as though to find consolation in laughing at the foolishness of those who are the cause of all their miseries'.

Yet it is far from clear that Figaro wants to change the world. After he asserts himself in Act I of *The Barber of Seville*, he is happy enough to help make the course of true love run smoothly, partly because he despises what Bartholo represents, but also because he sees an opportunity, at last, for 'making his fortune' (I.6). Almaviva abets his scheming with considerable plotting skills of his own, and once Bartholo is defeated he acts with honour and a proper respect for law: 'an upright magistrate', he declares, 'is the defender of all who are oppressed' (IV.8), a sentiment which Figaro could not dispute.

In *The Marriage of Figaro* the Count abuses his rank and privilege for his own sexual gratification, but for no other purpose. He is not a tyrant but a philanderer, and not a very effective one at that: it is difficult to imagine Valmont, the rake of Laclos's *Les Liaisons dangereuses* (1782), allowing his plans to be so easily derailed. Almaviva's designs on Suzanne apart, Figaro has no real criticism of his master, who is a just magistrate, a sound estate manager, and a pillar of a political system which is never itself openly challenged. The chateau of Aguas-Frescas is a hierarchical, liberal, constitutional, family-based but also well-heeled community, and it is in Figaro's interest to ensure that it stays that way. He readily admits that he fares badly when he is his own master. In this he is correct, for once he has his feet under a rich man's table he thrives, grumbling, plotting, but revelling in his role as the scourge of all who attempt to disrupt the settled order.

In *The Guilty Mother* Almaviva is a much more authoritarian figure. Yet his heartless treatment of Rosine and Leon, like his extreme fondness for Florestine, is motivated by his wife's guilty secret (and his own), not because he has reverted to type, turned into a feudal ogre, and hates Leon for being, as the cast list puts it, one of the 'ardent spirits of the new age'. On the contrary, he is happy to drop his title and proud to keep a bust of George Washington in his study. Indeed, Suzanne displays far more snobbish regard for the *ancien régime* than her betters when she complains that the Countess's practice of going out without her footman in livery means that the whole household will 'look the same as everybody else' (I.2). For his part, Figaro accepts the Count's moderate revolutionary sympathies without comment, and sets out once more to secure the victory of the non-aligned justice which he has always served. His plotting has no political dimension. In the same way, his opponent Bégearss is neither an enemy nor a friend of the people. Molière's Tartuffe hid his sordid ambitions under a cloak of official religion, but this 'new Tartuffe' makes no attempt to shelter behind its modern equivalent, false revolutionary zeal: his hypocrisy is personal, a tactic designed to line his pockets. Only as one last, desperate fling does he seek to turn Almaviva's admiration for Washington into a political weapon against him (V.7). It is because Bégearss is an embezzler and a disrupter of families that Figaro fights him, not because he is a political threat. The Count's house is a non-political zone, for although Leon makes a libertarian speech against forced celibacy, and the new law permitting divorce is evoked (both issues of concern to the happiness of individuals and families), it remains a community as insulated against the wider world as the chateau of Aguas-Frescas had been. To get the better of Bégearss, Figaro does not produce arguments drawn from the rights of man or any Revolutionary concept of virtue, but uses the same wits which had given him victory over Bartholo in *The Barber of Seville* and led (with help from Rosine and Suzanne) to the outbreak of peace and unity which ends *The Marriage of Figaro*.

The trilogy is thus entirely consistent in the way it expresses and deepens a philosophy which puts personal, family, and group harmony at the heart of a hierarchically structured society in which everyone has an honourable place and can be happy. It is a moral not a political position, and it had been Beaumarchais's from the start. Had not the callous seducer of his first play been convinced that true contentment lay in 'happiness with Eugénie, peace with myself, and the good opinion of honest people'? It is precisely this lesson which Almaviva at last learns at the end of *The Guilty Mother*. The final exchanges show master and servant in complete agreement, and each knows his place. When the Count observes that 'the time comes when good people forgive each other for the wrongs they did and the mistakes they once made', his words can be taken as an appeal to Revolutionary France as much as to the characters in the play. The same ambiguity attaches to Figaro's parting words. He who set out to make his fortune in *The Barber* and congratulated himself on ending up with three dowries in *The Marriage*, now refuses the Count's money and is content to be his servant. He does not reject his younger, embattled, combative self, but frankly admits that he is happy to live out his life in the house of a master whom he respects and who at last values his worth. For Almaviva has changed. He abandons the self which has made him unhappy and takes his place in the hierarchy as a benevolent, forgiving figure. Tyrants and hypocrites have been banished, the slate has been wiped clean ('Let's not worry too much if we've sometimes had our differences'), and the world has been returned to its rightful order. Figaro's last word ('Families are always well served when a troublemaker is shown the door') is a blessing on Almaviva's entire household. But it is also a piece of wisdom offered to the wider 'family' of a France divided by troublemaking dissent and conflict. To the end, Beaumarchais commends the spirit of reconciliation—of masters and servants, of men and women, of parents with children, and of all with life—which was celebrated by *The Marriage of Figaro*.

Of course, there is no denying that the Figaro of *The Barber* and *The Marriage* expresses views which are highly critical of the *ancien régime*. Yet he was no people's champion, for he belongs under his master's roof in the same way that Beaumarchais belonged to his century: in a state of opportunist connivance. The Enlightenment was less an age of abstract reasoning than of practical thinking, and the upwardly mobile Beaumarchais applied its lessons as much to social problems as he did to his own life. He believed that while Fate may deal the cards, every man must be free to play his own hand, just as society must be free to work out its own salvation through tolerance and the community spirit. It is to this kind of freedom that Figaro aspires, not to a victory over oppression and feudal slavery or the establishment of an egalitarian society. He may behave and sound like a popular hero, but he does not identify with 'the People'. Indeed, Beaumarchais portrays the lower classes in a most unflattering light: Old Youthful, Antonio, and Guillaume are stupid, incompetent, and need to be put right by their betters. But Almaviva the aristocrat also needs firm direction. The audience Beaumarchais had in his sights was the bourgeoisie, which had the flexibility and energy to make something of his version of the moral, social, and sentimental Enlightenment.

Both Figaro and his creator belong to the awkward squad. Like him, Beaumarchais was a radical opponent of arbitrary authority. He attacked injustice whatever its political colour, and had no more time for the tyranny of the People than for the oppression of Kings. Like Figaro, he was a bourgeois individualist, a champion of freedom, a radical, a rebel capable of reconciling patriotism and idealism with a career as profiteer and gun-runner.

But Beaumarchais was not free of self-doubt. *The Barber of Seville* expresses his dash, flair, and effectiveness at their carefree best. But *The Marriage of Figaro* has a darker tone which is nowhere more visible than in Figaro's celebrated monologue (V.3). As the trilogy advances, so Figaro's self-confidence and effectiveness diminish. In *The Barber* all his schemes work; in *The Marriage* he discovers he cannot control events, that chance works against him, and, when his master-plan fails, he is forced to improvise; in *The Guilty Mother* he is at his weakest and needs a great deal of authorial help to ensure his victory over Bégearss. Figaro is a *caractère* who grows in complexity, from the irrepressible barber who succeeds in all he attempts, to the self-doubting dupe of *The Marriage* where he fails, and finally to the ageing, vulnerable retainer of *The Guilty Mother*. It is a trajectory which reflects its maker's struggles. The truth about Beaumarchais is reflected less by the facts of his biography than by his life in literature.

The Figaro Plays

Beaumarchais was a man of the stage, and in many ways his life was theatrical. He may have kept his shadowy politico-business ventures firmly in the wings, but he fought his battles for survival in the arena of public opinion. He made his debut in 1743, when he first tasted adulation for the manner of his victory over Lepaute. Thereafter, whenever he found himself in difficulties, he stepped into the lime-light, stood centre-stage, and played directly to the gallery. His legal *mémoires* projected an engaging public persona which, though differ-ent in many respects from his private self, elicited applause, his best defence against the establishment which, before and after 1789, regarded him with suspicion. But he was not merely an instinctive practitioner of this form of real, live theatre. He also gave consider-able thought to how plays, playwrights, and players might be made to work more effectively for the collective good.

Even as he wrote his early comic *parades*, he was absorbing the arguments put forward by Diderot and others in favour of a new kind of theatre: the *drame bourgeois*. Tragedy, which had always dealt with great personages, had grown remote from everyday life, and comedy had become synonymous with satire of bourgeois attitudes. The new *drame* championed by Diderot and Sedaine set out to deal sympathetically with the problems of the wealthy middle class: love, marriage, and the family, and the financial, legal, and human mis-fortunes which threaten them. Beaumarchais believed theatre was not the school for vice which Rousseau had denounced in his *Lettre sur les spectacles* (1759), but a means of educating society in its civic and moral duties. His own *Essai sur le genre dramatique sérieux* (1767) replaced the terror of classical catharsis with pathos and argued against the traditional view that mockery corrects people and man-ners. Instead, he required authors to move their audiences (to tears preferably), for only when their emotions are genuinely engaged are they receptive.

In the long run, the *drame bourgeois* achieved its objectives. By 1830 both tragedy and comedy as distinct genres had disappeared and European theatre explored its emphasis on moral, social, and eventually psychological issues: Dumas *fils*, Ibsen, Shaw, and the 'problem play' of the twentieth century were its descendants. But in its primitive form the *drame* was too dull to survive the enthusiasm of its begetters. Earnest sentiments make stodgy literature, and the *genre sérieux* failed because it dealt not with humanity at large, but with its middle-class manifestation, and did so with cloying sentiment which anchors it firmly in its period. Beaumarchais's two *drames* are good examples of the genre. In *Eugénie* the virtue and honour of its melting heroine and her family are threatened by a rake who is brought to see the error of his ways and returns to the fold. *Les Deux Amis* are merchants who are prepared to face financial ruin rather than betray their friendship. Both project a stagy humanitarianism and have dated badly. Yet Beaumarchais never lost faith in the *drame*. Bartholo's elderly dismissal of 'these modern plays . . . in the new style' (*Barber*, I.3) is a glancing attack against its enemies. Marceline's tearful reunion with her lost Emmanuel is just one echo of it in *The Marriage*, and although *The Guilty Mother* has the structure of a traditional comic plot, Beaumarchais called it a *drame* and used it as a peg on which to hang not laughter or satire but the triumph of good. His two 'Spanish' comedies, he said, had merely been a preparation for the undoing of Bégearss and the shabby self-interest which threatens all that is decent and honourable. Nor was it to be his last word. When he died, he was planning a sequel no less didactic: 'The Revenge of Bégearss, or the Marriage of Leon.'

But Beaumarchais's commitment to the *drame* was only one strand of his concept of theatre. In the substantial prefaces he wrote for his Figaro plays, he defended the broader comic strokes of his *parades*. Molière, founding father of French comedy, had combined observation of men and manners with earthy, even farcical, humour. But his successors had eliminated the laughter and concentrated on psychological studies of *caractères* who defined vanity or ambition. The result was a series of portraits which, though patiently compiled and sometimes acute, were sober and static. Beaumarchais reverted to the older tradition and reinstated plot, an art that seemed lost, made dialogue the vehicle of the action, and maintained the tension with injections of pace and wit. This was what he meant when he said that he set out to restore to the stage the *franche gaieté* which it had lost. At first his ebullience got the better of him. The first performance of *The Barber of Seville* failed because, as his friend Gudin observed, it 'seemed long' because it wearied the audience with its 'superabundance of wit'. But by trimming it from five acts to four, Beaumarchais found a style which was irresistible.

At the outset he had no plans for a series of connected plays. Both sequels to *The Barber of Seville* were written in response to the curiosity of his enthusiastic public. But in the event, the Figaro plays constitute a trilogy of a highly original kind. The farcical tradition had long been prepared to give audiences more of what they liked, and stock or syndicated characters like Harlequin resurfaced regularly. But they were one-dimensional, different but always the same, for they were merely required to repeat the foolishness which was their only interesting feature. Beaumarchais was the first major playwright to use a set of recurring characters who remain recognizable but change and grow over a period of time, as would happen later in the fictional sequences of Balzac, Dumas, and Zola. There are occasional lapses. In *The Barber* Figaro has a 'little girl' who is never mentioned again, and the Bartholo of *The Marriage of Figaro* has lost his sharpness. But Figaro and Almaviva, Rosine and Suzanne, mature satisfactorily and Beaumarchais sustains them with remarkable consistency. Yet as a triptych, the plays illuminate more than the deepening psychology of the characters. Taken together, they chronicle the slide of the *ancien régime* into revolution and chart the growth of Beaumarchais's humanitarianism.

But although the whole is in this sense more than the sum of its parts, each play has its own distinct character. *The Barber of Seville* is a mountain brook, all unstoppable pace and twists, studded with stinging one-liners. Behind the good humour and helter-skelter inventiveness of the infinitely more complex *Marriage of Figaro* lie more sombre moods of self-questioning, which are resolved by an optimistic closure of general reconciliation. *The Guilty Mother* is not a comedy at all (though as a comic valet Guillaume would not have been out of place in the earlier episodes), but a drama which looks back both to the 'serious' manner of Molière (after all, it features a 'new Tartuffe') and to the anguished, effusive *drames bourgeois* which had opened Beaumarchais's career.

All three depend heavily on well-worn theatrical conventions. Each is structured around the old master–servant relationship and the unavoidably bumpy course of true love. The plots are driven by misdirected letters, disguises, misunderstandings, mistaken identity, indiscreet servants, illegitimate children, and go-betweens who may be double agents—like Figaro in *The Barber*, where he has two masters, or Suzanne in *The Guilty Mother*, who spies on Bégearss for

Figaro. Many of the satirical targets too have a solidly traditional cut: medicine (Bartholo is a doctor and Figaro a barber-surgeon), the law (in the figure of the stammering Brid'oison), and, despite Marceline's defence of her sex, a measure of anti-feminism. Beaumarchais does not emancipate wedlocked women (Marceline is happy enough to marry the gruesome Bartholo) any more than he liberates Figaro from the feudal yoke. For all must learn to respect the social order which, like marriage and the family, has its proper division of labour and responsibilities.

Beaumarchais was well aware that the ingredients he used were not new, and admitted that his basic situations (goodness and love under attack from the stratagems of the wicked) were the stuff of many kinds of theatre: tragedy, comedy, the *drame bourgeois*, and farce. It was only in their treatment, and especially in the *caractères* who acted them out, that they could take a particular form. His solution was to combine the spirit of the *parade* with the mood of the *genre sérieux*. It was not always an easy mixture, and over time the 'serious' loomed larger.

His characterization is fresh, there are bravura passages (Bazile's praise of slander, for example, or Figaro's views on the English language), moments of farce, and above all a determination to keep the tension high. To this end, Beaumarchais subordinates the psychological to the physical. He does not often pause to allow his characters time to agonize about their feelings, but hurries them through a rapid succession of events which ensures that the action remains fast and furious. The large number of separate scenes (forty-four in *The Barber*, ninety-three in *The Marriage*, seventy-one in *The Guilty Mother*) is a measure of this aesthetic of speed. On occasions his comic inventiveness gets the better of him. He allows some scenes (particularly in *The Marriage*) to run on, and jokes are sometimes indulged for their own sake: Bazile is detained in *The Barber* (I.11) for no other purpose than to allow him to mangle proverbs.

But as the trilogy advances, the *dramiste*, absent from *The Barber*, asserts himself. In *The Marriage* Marceline's defence of women (III.16) is a distraction and was cut in performance. Both Figaro's very long autobiographical monologue (V.3) and Almaviva's anguished reading of Rosine's letter in *The Guilty Mother* (II.1) slow the action. In her final incarnation, Rosine, like Leon, is more tears

INTRODUCTION

than smiles, and the mood is neither comic nor tragic, merely sombre: drama has turned into melodrama.

But Beaumarchais's plot-lines are simplicity itself. Will Almaviva marry Rosine? Will Figaro stop Bégearss? For *The Marriage* he devises a parallel structure, the one dependent on the other: will Figaro marry Suzanne and will Rosine win back her husband? The action is littered with stumbling-blocks which are removed one by one. Antonio, Marceline, and Bartholo are neutralized until only the desires of the Count, finally defeated by a concerted pincer movement, remain. It was not for nothing that Beaumarchais was a watchmaker: his plots run like clockwork.

He delights in multiplying obstacles, and gives Figaro very tough opponents. In *The Barber*, Bartholo is no soft target but cunning and alert, and Figaro has to work very hard to outwit him. In *The Marriage* his plotting is undone at every turn. Antonio is hostile, Marceline threatens his wedding plans, Bartholo undermines him, and Suzanne and Rosine go behind his back. But Almaviva, several times outflanked by Bartholo in *The Barber*, is also pushed on to the defensive in *The Marriage*. His vassals, prompted by Figaro, present him with a *fait accompli*, the ubiquitous Cherubin is a constant irritation, Marceline turns into Figaro's mother and cannot become his wife, and Rosine counterattacks so effectively that he must surrender. In *The Guilty Mother* Bégearss is unstoppable until the last act, when Figaro finally acquires—for ready money—the letter which exposes his villainy. Beaumarchais might leave us in no doubt that right will triumph in the end (the ability to reassure is not the least of his talents), but on the way he generates a sense of danger which adds a *frisson* of genuine suspense to his comedy.

The first two plays breathe an air of cheerful unreality. The costumes evoke exotic Spain and the music maintains the comic-opera mood with which Beaumarchais began in 1772. He uses songs not as freestanding interludes but as springs of the plot. Figaro's cheerful ditty (*The Barber*, I.2) established his character, and Lindor and Rosine communicate their feelings through a recitative 'in the Spanish style' (III.4), as does Cherubin in *The Marriage* (II.4), which ends 'not in tears but song'. The result of so much buoyant good cheer is to make us forget that the day packed so full of 'follies' is unnaturally long. 'Gaiety' and 'madness' combine to foster an easy generosity of spirit which, like the songs, is much missed in the more sober setting of *The Guilty Mother*.

There Beaumarchais largely abandons the light touch of the *parade*, and its heavy moralizing emphasizes uncomfortable realities which were disguised by the exuberance of its predecessors. For while his principal characters are fundamentally good, they do not always behave well. Figaro may be the scourge of Bartholo, Almaviva, and Bégearss, but he has always cut corners, is grudging with the truth, and never repays the rent money he owed Bartholo. But he is no womanizer. On the other hand, Marceline and Bartholo manage to produce a child out of wedlock. Indeed, for someone who defends virtue, marriage, and the family so staunchly, Beaumarchais allows his characters a great deal of sexual latitude. The Rosine who told lies to Bartholo, and has unwifely feelings for Cherubin which lead her to betray her husband and her marriage vows, seems to bear out Figaro's view of woman as a 'weak, deceitful creature'. The Count graduates very quickly from sighing lover to libertine. He lusts after Suzanne and Fanchette, and Florestine is his illegitimate daughter, fathered out of wedlock at about the same time as Leon was born. But although Rosine knows she is a 'guilty mother', Beaumarchais insists that she is fully redeemed by her saintly penitence. Almaviva is treated even more indulgently. He is far from being a hardened rake. His pursuit of Suzanne in *The Marriage* is half-hearted from the start ('if it was all simple and uncomplicated, I wouldn't want her anywhere near as much': III.4) and he is disarmed by Rosine's letter to Cherubin, of whom he thinks well; and the sincerity of his love for his wife may be judged by his jealousy and anger.

Beaumarchais goes out of his way to ensure that we take a lenient view of their shortcomings. While Bartholo and Bégearss are dyed-in-the-wool villains, he insists that Figaro, the Count, and the Countess err by temperament and that their faults are not intentional. What they do does not affect what they are, for they are as much victims of their feelings as of the shabby motives of others. Moreover, they benefit from unusually explicit written instructions about how they should be played. At a time where the theatre director had yet to be invented and playwrights had little say in how their work was staged, Beaumarchais's attempts to control his work were exceptional. His detailed stage directions were designed to ensure that the actors projected his own indulgent view of his characters. In part, these were aimed at the amateur performers of the *théâtre de société*. But he was clearly aware that his comedies depended for their sparkle on the way they were staged. He makes detailed recommendations governing sets, costumes, and stage business. He provides thumbnail sketches which define his characters and gives the actors detailed instructions which show how they are to behave and play a scene: they must be 'taken aback', 'furious', and respond 'quickly'—a constant reminder to keep the pace up. The note on the 'nominal ranking' of the actors in *The Marriage* indicates on which characters the dramatic spotlight should fall, and he even insists that the group in Act II scene 4 be arranged to resemble a print of Vanloo's painting *The Spanish Conversation*.

Beaumarchais's control, which helps to disguise certain inconsistencies and contradictions, is reinforced by much cheerful sleight-of-hand and his brilliantly inventive dramatic technique. *The Marriage* shows him at his most versatile, for it displays elements of many different theatrical styles: the comedy of character, action, and intrigue; the play of social and political comment; the *drame* (to which Marceline belongs), farce, melodrama, and comic opera. His dramatic skills are matched by the sheer exuberance of his dialogue. When to all this is added the atmosphere of spectacle, we are left with a dramatic mixture as heady as it is agreeable.

Of Beaumarchais's six plays, only two are now remembered. But *The Barber of Seville* and *The Marriage of Figaro* are masterpieces of skill, invention, and tolerant, civilizing values. They have never been far from the public's consciousness, and for a century their example helped to shape the direction of French theatre. They prefigure the melodramas of Scribe, the 'socially useful' Romantic theatre of 1830, the 'well-made play' of Dumas *fils*, the 'thesis-play' of Henri Becque, and the farces of Feydeau.

But while in theatrical terms Beaumarchais belonged to the future, his values make him a man of the Enlightenment. Like the *philosophes*, he was not interested in exploring human psychology in general terms but concentrated on human needs. Unfortunately, what individuals need to be happy and what governments are prepared to allow, rarely coincide. It is therefore not surprising that many have thought his plays to be dangerous. For their opera *Le nozze di Figaro*, Mozart and Da Ponte removed everything which might be construed as politically controversial. After 1800, revivals of *The Marriage of Figaro* were pruned to avoid giving offence. Until 1870 and even beyond, *The Marriage* was regarded as a subversive play, for there was always a dominant group who would not make half-decent valets and did not care to have the fact made public. During the Occupation of France *The Barber of Seville* was revived, but the Germans refused to allow *The Marriage of Figaro* to be staged in Paris, and Mussolini banned it in Italy. On this evidence, history has supplied Beaumarchais with unimpeachable liberal credentials.

But whether or not Beaumarchais was a devout capitalist, the begetter of the Revolution, or the most hands-on practitioner of Enlightenment tolerance has long ceased to matter. For while the particular battles he fought are now forgotten, the same war goes on—against officialdom, the corporate cosiness of privilege, the constraints on freedom, and the abuse of power. Beaumarchais does not mock with the corrosive comedy of derision but with a 'gaiety' rooted in the exhilarating spirit of joyful reconciliation which crowns *The Marriage*. His voice is unmistakable: pugnacious but vulnerable, embattled yet endlessly engaging, and still able to hit nails squarely on the head.

NOTE ON THE TEXT

The text used for this translation is the standard edition of Beaumarchais's *Oeuvres* published by Pierre and Jacqueline Larthomas (see Select Bibliography), which includes the *parades*, the *mémoires*, all six plays, and the prefaces which accompany them.

Beaumarchais was translated into English before he became famous. A free adaptation of *Eugénie* was published in 1769 by Elizabeth Griffiths as *The School for Rakes, a comedy*. Mrs Griffiths also published the first English version of *The Barber of Seville* in 1776. *The Marriage of Figaro* was translated (as *The Follies of a Day*) by Thomas Holcroft, for performance at Drury Lane on 14 December 1784. An anonymous version of *The Guilty Mother* appeared as *Frailty and Hypocrisy* in 1804. Since then Figaro has been given an English voice by numerous translators, and most recently by John Wells, whose eminently speakable versions were broadcast on BBC Radio 3 in 1984. They were published, together with the major prefaces and much helpful comment besides, by John Leigh, as *The Figaro Plays* (London: J. M. Dent, 1997).

SELECT BIBLIOGRAPHY

Editions

Oeuvres, ed. Pierre and Jacqueline Larthomas (Paris: Gallimard, Bibliothèque de la Pléiade, 1988).

Théâtre: Le Barbier de Séville, Le Mariage de Figaro, La Mère coupable, ed. Maurice Rat (Paris: Garnier, 1950).

Théâtre de Beaumarchais, présenté par René Pomeau (Paris: Garnier-Flammarion, 1965).

Théâtre, présenté par J.-P. de Beaumarchais (Paris: Garnier, 1980).

Le Barbier de Séville, ed. Louis Allen (London: Harrap, 1951).

Le Mariage de Figaro, ed. Louis Allen (London: Harrap, 1952).

Le Mariage de Figaro, ed. Malcolm Cook (London: Bristol Classical Press, 1992).

Le Barbier de Séville, ed. Malcolm Cook (London: Bristol Classical Press, 1994).

Le Mariage de Figaro, ed. Gérard Kahn, *Studies on Voltaire and the Eighteenth Century*, vol 12 (Oxford: The Voltaire Foundation, 2002).

For the Good of Mankind: Pierre-Augustin de Beaumarchais, Political Correspondence relative to the American Revolution, trans. Antoinette Shewmake (Lanham: University Press of America, 1987).

Gunnar and Mavis Von Proschwitz (eds.), *Beaumarchais et 'Le Courier de l'Europe'*, in *Voltaire Studies*, nos. 273–4 (Oxford: The Voltaire Foundation, 1992).

Beaumarchais: Correspondance, ed. Brian Norton (Paris: Nizet, 1969–).

Biographies

Gudin de la Brenellerie, *Histoire de Beaumarchais* (1809), ed. M. Tourneux (1888).

Philippe Van Tieghem, *Beaumarchais par lui-même* (Paris: Éditions du Seuil, 1960).

Frédéric Grendel, *Beaumarchais ou la calomnie* (Paris: Flammarion, 1973); trans. R. Greaves as *The Man Who Was Figaro* (New York: Crowell, 1977).

J.-P. de Beaumarchais, *Beaumarchais, le voltigeur des lumières* (Paris: Gallimard, 1996).

Critical Studies

Jacques Schérer, *La Dramaturgie de Beaumarchais* (Paris: Nizet, 1954).

René Pomeau, *Beaumarchais, l'homme et l'oeuvre* (Paris: Hatier-Boivin, 1956).

J. B. Ratermanis and W. R. Irwin, *The Comic Style of Beaumarchais* (Seattle: University of Washington Press, 1961).

E.-J. Arnould, *La Génèse du 'Barbier de Séville'* (Paris: Minard 1965).

Robert Niklaus, *Beaumarchais: The Barber of Seville* (London: Edward Arnold, 1968).

A. R. Pugh, *Beaumarchais: The Marriage of Figaro. An Interpretation* (London: Macmillan, 1970).

Maurice Descotes, *Les Grand Rôles du théâtre de Beaumarchais* (Paris: Presses Universitaires de France, 1974).

Robert Niklaus, *Beaumarchais: The Marriage of Figaro* (London: Grant & Cutler, 1983).

G. Conesa, *La Trilogie de Beaumarchais* (Paris: Presses Universitaires de France, 1985).

René Pomeau, *Beaumarchais ou la bizarre destinée* (Paris: Presses Universitaires de France, 1987).

Brian N. Morton and Donald C. Spinelli, *Beaumarchais: A Bibliography* (Ann Arbor: Olivia and Hill Press, 1988).

John Dunkley, *Beaumarchais: The Barber of Seville* (London: Grant & Cutler, 1991).

R. A. Francis, 'Figaro in changing times: Beaumarchais' *La Mère coupable*', in *British Journal for Eighteenth Century Studies*, 18: 1 (1995) 19–31.

W. D. Howarth, *Beaumarchais and the Theatre* (London and New York: Routledge, 1995).

—— *French Theatre in the Neo-classical Era, 1550–1789* (Cambridge: CUP, 1997).

Philip Robinson, *Beaumarchais et la chanson: Musique et dramaturgie des comédies de Figaro* (Oxford: The Voltaire Foundation, 1999).

—— (ed), *Beaumarchais, homme de lettres, homme de société* (Bern: Peter Lang, 2000).

Further Reading in Oxford World's Classics

Diderot, Denis, *Jacques the Fatalist*, trans. and ed. David Coward.

Five Romantic Plays 1768–1821, ed. Paul Baines and Edward Burns.

Laclos, Choderlos de, *Les Liaisons dangereuses*, trans. and ed. Douglas Parmée.

Rousseau, Jean-Jacques, *Confessions*, trans. Angela Scholar, ed. Patrick Coleman.

A CHRONOLOGY OF BEAUMARCHAIS

1732   Birth in Paris of Pierre-Augustin Caron, seventh of the ten children of André-Charles Caron (b. 1698), a watchmaker.

1745   Apprenticed to his father, he invents a new escapement mechanism which allowed smaller and slimmer watches to be made.

1751   Commencement of the publication of *L'Encyclopédie*, edited by Diderot and D'Alembert.

1753   He shows his new invention to Lapaute, who presents it to the Academy of Sciences as his own work. 13 November: Pierre-Augustin writes to the Academy, enclosing evidence to back his case

1754   23 February: the Academy finds in his favour. The affair attracts public attention. Pierre-Augustin receives orders from the court and is presented to Louis XV and the Queen.

1755   9 November: purchases a court position from Franquet, who dies, leaving a widow.

1756   27 November: marries Mme Franquet.

1757   Adopts the title Caron de Beaumarchais, after an estate belonging to his wife, who dies at the end of September. For legal reasons Beaumarchais does not inherit her property and finds himself in debt. Meets Le Normant d'Étioles, husband of Mme de Pompadour. Publication of Diderot's *Entretiens* on his play, *Le Fils naturel*, which, with his *Discours sur la poésie dramatique* (1758), set out the case for the *drame bourgeois*.

1759   Teaches music to the king's daughters. Meets the wealthy Pâris-Duverney.

1760   Using his influence at court, Beaumarchais obliges Pâris-Duverney who, in return, accepts him as an associate and helps to make his fortune.

1761   Persuades his father to retire from his business and, with funds supplied by Pâris-Duverney, purchases a court office which confers nobility. Henceforth he is officially Caron de Beaumarchais. Continues to write *parades*, which are performed at the home of Le Normant.

1763   Purchases a second court position and considers marriage with Pauline Le Breton.

1764   18 May: arrives in Madrid, where he fails to rescue his sister
        from a damaging entanglement, attends to semi-official gov-
        ernment business, and makes unsuccessful efforts to promote
        ventures funded by Pâris-Duverney. But he is a social success.

1765   22 March: leaves Madrid. In May he sells his court office.

1766   Summer: travels to the Loire Valley where, with Pâris-
        Duverney, he buys woodland at Chinon. The purchase is made
        in the name of his lackey, Lesueur.

1767   First performance of *Eugénie*. The text is prefaced by an *Essai
        sur le genre dramatique sérieux*. Legal problems with Lesueur,
        who claims all the income from the sale of the timber.

1768   11 April: marries Geneviève-Madeleine Wattebled (1731–70).
        14 December: birth of Augustin de Beaumarchais.

1770   13 January: first performance of *Les Deux Amis*. 7 March:
        birth of Aimable-Eugénie, who does not live. 1 April: signs an
        agreement with Pâris-Duverney to formalize their association.
        17 July: death of Pâris-Duverney, whose estate passes to the
        Comte de La Blache, his nephew by marriage. 20 November:
        death of Mme de Beaumarchais.

1771   Further legal arguments over Chinon timber are followed by
        La Blache's attempt to end the arrangement his uncle had
        made with Beaumarchais.

1772   February: following his *Mémoire* against La Blache, Beaumar-
        chais wins his case. October: death of Augustin.

1773   February: following an altercation with the Duke de Chaulnes
        over an actress, Beaumarchais is sent to prison, where he
        remains until May. 6 April: La Blache's appeal, led by the
        lawyer Goëzman, is successful, and Beaumarchais faces ruin.
        September–December: publication of three *Mémoires* against
        Goëzman.

1774   10 February: publication of the fourth *Mémoire* against Goëz-
        man, which leads to a ban on the staging of *The Barber of
        Seville*. 26 February: the court rules against Beaumarchais.
        Around this time he begins a liaison with Marie-Thérèse de
        Willer-Mawlas. May–June: travels to Flanders and London to
        negotiate with Théveneau de Morande. 10 May: death of
        Louis XV, who is succeeded by Louis XVI. June–September:
        further missions to London, where Beaumarchais purchases
        the silence of another journalist, and thence to Vienna, where
        he is imprisoned.

1775   16 January: publication of a *Mémoire* against La Blache. 23 February: first performance of *The Barber of Seville*. April: first dealings with the Chevalier d'Éon in London. Start of correspondence with Vergennes, the foreign minister, which continues until 1787.

1776   Start of American War of Independence. 10 June: receives 1 million livres from Vergennes to finance ships and munitions destined for the American insurgents. 23 June: first issue in London of *Le Courier de l'Europe*, of which Beaumarchais is part-owner. 6 September: a decree of the Paris *Parlement* over-turns the judgement of 26 February 1774.

1777   5 January: birth of Eugénie de Beaumarchais. Organizes a campaign against the actors of the Comédie Française, whom he accuses of abusing its monopoly. His views on foreign policy impress Vergennes, and Beaumarchais helps to direct France's conduct in the American war.

1778   Continues his war work. His feud with the Comédie Française ends successfully in December. Writes *The Marriage of Figaro* 21 July: finally wins his case against La Blache.

1779   15 January: a letter from the United States Congress sets out an account of moneys owed to Beaumarchais which, despite numerous reminders, were never repaid in his lifetime. Begins planning the publication of an edition of the complete works of Voltaire.

1781   January: publication of the prospectus for the Kehl Edition of Voltaire (72 vols., 1783–90). 29 September: *The Marriage of Figaro* is accepted by the Comédie Française. October: Beaumarchais takes an interest in the case of Mme Kornman (see Introduction, p. xiii).

1782   Publishes a letter to the lieutenant of police setting out his defence of *The Marriage of Figaro*, which had displeased the king. The official censor delivers an unfavourable judgement (July). Becomes principal shareholder in a company set up to supply Paris with drinking-water. Launches an appeal for rebuilding the French fleet after its defeat in April. September: first performance of Paisiello's opera, *The Barber of Seville*, at St Petersburg in the presence of Catherine the Great

1783   End of the American War of Independence. 12 February: revival of *Les Deux Amis*. Spring: receives 900,000 livres from Vergennes, as part settlement of moneys disbursed on the government's behalf during the American war. Further payments are made, the last in 1786. 13 June: *The Marriage of Figaro* is banned by Louis XVI. 26 September: *The Marriage of Figaro* is performed in the house of the Comte de Vaudreuil.

1784   27 April: first public performance of *The Marriage of Figaro.* The preface to the published text indicates that Beaumarchais had already begun work on *The Guilty Mother.* 12 August: writes to the *Journal de Paris* proposing the creation of a charitable foundation. The libretto of *Tarare* is accepted by the Royal Academy of Music.

1785   8–13 March: jailed at Saint-Lazare for his criticism of those who had attempted to ban *The Marriage of Figaro.* Beaumarchais defends himself and is allowed to publish the text. A royal order bans the Voltaire volumes which had appeared. He is embroiled in a public quarrel with Mirabeau over the Water Company in which both are involved.

1786   8 March: marries Marie-Thérèse de Willer-Mawlas, his third wife. 1 May: first performance in Vienna of Mozart's *The Marriage of Figaro.*

1787   February: death of Vergennes, his most powerful ally at court. 20 February: Bergasse's *Mémoire* in defence of Kornman, first of an acrimonious exchange which lasts until the spring of 1789. 8 June: first performance of *Tarare.* 26 June: buys a plot of land near the Bastille, on which he builds a magnificent town house into which he moves in the spring of 1791. Beginning of a liaison with Amélie Houret de La Marinaie.

1789   2 April: the courts find against Kornman and Bergasse, but public opinion is hostile to Beaumarchais. August: made responsible for overseeing the demolition of the Bastille. His loyalties are questioned and he is temporarily excluded from meetings of his District's revolutionary council.

1790   Makes generous donations to revolutionary causes and adds a new libertarian conclusion for the revival of *Tarare* (3 August). Takes up *The Guilty Mother,* which he finishes in January 1791. The Kehl Edition of Voltaire's works attracts only 2,000 subscribers (of the 15,000 needed), and is a commercial failure.

1791   February: *The Guilty Mother* is accepted by the Comédie Française, but is withdrawn in December when the actors refuse to apply the new laws governing literary property. Autumn: considers travelling to the United States to pursue his claims, and explores the possibility of supplying France with desperately needed small arms.

1792   March–April: beginning of the 'Dutch guns' affair. Beaumar-
        chais learns through a Belgian bookseller that 60,000 muskets
        are available in Holland. He agrees to act as agent for their
        purchase on behalf of the French government. June: the king
        considers making Beaumarchais minister of the interior. 26
        June: first of fourteen performances of *The Guilty Mother* at
        the Théâtre du Marais. August: Beaumarchais's house is
        searched, he is arrested, jailed briefly at the Abbaye Prison, and
        narrowly escapes the September Massacres. September: in the
        months when a French Republic is declared, he leaves France
        for Holland to negotiate the purchase of the Dutch guns. In his
        absence new accusations are made against him. At the end of
        the year he is arrested in London and jailed for debt. There he
        writes his six *Époques* to prove his innocence.

1793   19 January: execution of Louis XVI. March: Beaumarchais
        returns to France and defends himself successfully. He con-
        tinues his travels in hopes of finalizing the Dutch guns
        business.

1794   14 March: his name is added to the list of émigrés and his wife,
        who is saved from the guillotine by the fall of Robespierre in
        July, divorces him, as the law requires. He moves to Hamburg.

1795   Beaumarchais and his ex-wife and daughter campaign for his
        return to France. June: the Dutch guns are finally bought by
        the English.

1796   June: his name is removed from the list of émigrés and he
        returns to Paris (5 July).

1797   January: a commission investigates Beaumarchais's role in the
        Dutch guns affair. April: he remarries Marie-Thérèse and they
        return to their house in early May. 5 May: the first of six
        performances of *The Guilty Mother* at the Comédie Française
        receives a rapturous reception.

1798   Continuing difficulties with the commission investigating his
        affairs.

1799   1 January: a new report finds that Beaumarchais owes money to
        the government. 7 February: writes to Talleyrand, asking him
        to intervene on his behalf. 18 May: Beaumarchais dies in his
        sleep, aged 67.

1816   Death of Mme de Beaumarchais. First performance, in Rome,
        of Rossini's *The Barber of Seville*.

1822   Beaumarchais's remains are transferred to the cemetery of Père
        Lachaise, Paris.

THE BARBER OF SEVILLE

or,

The Pointless Precaution

A Prose Comedy in Four Acts

*First performed and came to grief 23 February 1775
at the Comédie Française**

And I was a father, and could not die!
(*Zaïre*, Act II*)

CHARACTERS

COUNT ALMAVIVA, *a Spanish nobleman, secret admirer of Rosine*
BARTHOLO, *a doctor, Rosine's guardian*
ROSINE, *a young woman of noble family, ward of Bartholo*
FIGARO, *barber at Seville*
DON BAZILE, *organist, and singing-teacher to Rosine*
OLD YOUTHFUL, *Bartholo's ancient servant*
WAKEFUL, *another servant of Bartholo, a slow-witted boy, usually half-asleep*
NOTARY
ALCALDE (*or* MAGISTRATE)
ALGUAZILS (*or* CONSTABLES), *and* SERVANTS *carrying torches*

The costumes worn by the actors should be in the old Spanish style.

COUNT ALMAVIVA. A Spanish grandee, Rosine's unknown admirer, appears in Act I dressed in a satin coat and breeches under a Spanish cape, or ample brown cloak; he wears a black hat with the brim turned down and a coloured ribbon circling the crown. In Act II he has a cavalryman's uniform, a false moustache, and riding boots. In Act III he is dressed as a student: hair in a fringe, wide ruff around his neck, jacket, breeches, stockings, and an ecclesiastical cloak. In Act IV he is dressed sumptuously in the Spanish style, with a rich cape over which he keeps the ample brown cloak closely wrapped.

BARTHOLO. A doctor and Rosine's guardian: a short black coat with buttons; a full wig; ruff and turned-back cuffs; a black waistband; and, for going out, a long scarlet cloak.

ROSINE. A young woman of noble family and Bartholo's ward: dressed in the Spanish style.

FIGARO. Barber at Seville, dressed like a Spanish dandy. On his head he wears a *redecilla*, or Spanish snood, and a white hat with a coloured ribbon around the crown. He has a loosely knotted silk scarf around his neck; a waistcoat and breeches, both satin, with buttons and buttonholes worked with silver thread; a wide silk waistband; garters fastened by tassels which swing around his calves; a contrasting coat with lapels the same colour as his waistcoat; white stockings and grey shoes.

DON BAZILE. Organist, and Rosine's singing-teacher. He wears a black, low-crowned felt hat, a short clerical gown, and a long cloak, but no ruff or cuffs.

OLD YOUTHFUL. Bartholo's ancient servant.

WAKEFUL. Another of Bartholo's servants, a slow-witted boy, usually half-asleep. Both are dressed like Galician peasants: pigtail, tan waistcoat, wide leather belt fastened by a buckle; knee-length blue breeches and matching coat with sleeves which, being open at the shoulder to accommodate the arms, hang down at the back.

NOTARY.

ALCALDE or MAGISTRATE, who carries a long white staff in his hand.

Various ALGUAZILS or CONSTABLES, and SERVANTS carrying torches.

The action takes place in Seville, in the street under ROSINE's *windows in Act I and thereafter in the house of* DOCTOR BARTHOLO

ACT I

A street in Seville. The windows of all the houses are barred

SCENE 1

The COUNT, *alone*

COUNT [*he wears a brown cloak and a wide-brimmed hat pulled down over his eyes. As he walks, he takes out his pocket-watch*]. It's not as late as I thought. It's hours before the time she usually appears on her balcony. Never mind. Better be early than miss the moment when I can see her. If my fashionable friends at court had any idea I was here, a hundred leagues from Madrid, hanging around every morning under the window of a girl I'd never spoken to, they'd think I was a throwback, a Don from ye olden days of Queen Isabella.* And why not? Everyone wants happiness and I've found mine in the heart of Rosine. Still, following a woman to Seville when Madrid and the court are awash with so many available pleasures... But that's what I'm trying to get away from. I'm tired of easy conquests served up by self-interest, stale habit, and vanity. It's wonderful to be loved for yourself! If I could only be sure that with this disguise... Damn, who's this?

SCENE 2

FIGARO *and the* COUNT, *who is hidden*

FIGARO [*he has a guitar on his back which hangs from a wide strap slung round his neck. He is singing a lively song to himself and is holding paper and a pencil*].

(NO. I)*

Let's banish dull care,
Let's put it to flight,
For deprived of good cheer
To make our step light

> We languish, we pine.
> A man without wine
> Would be dull as a fly
> And shortly would die...

So far so good. It's not bad, not bad at all.

> And shortly would die...
> Wine and sweet ease
> Compete for my heart.

That's wrong. They don't compete, they get along famously together.

> Co-exist... in my heart

Can you say 'co-exist'? Heigh-ho, the people who write comic operas don't worry about little things like that. These days what's not worth saying gets set to music. [*Sings*]

> Wine and sweet ease
> Co-exist in my heart

Now, for my finish I need something clever, brilliant, with a sparkle to it, something that sounds as if it might be profound.

> [*He puts one knee on the ground and writes as he sings*

> Co-exist in my heart.
> They blow like the breeze
> And make sorrow depart.

Ugh! That's awful! That's not it. I need a contrast, an antithesis:

> I... drink one... to the lees
> And make the other...

That's it! Got it!

> And make the other my art!

Brilliant, Figaro! [*He writes as he sings*]

> Wine and sweet ease
> Co-exist in my heart.
> I drink one to the lees
> And make the other my art,

And make the other my art,
And make the other my art.

With an accompaniment to go with it, we'll see, critics or no critics, if I know what I'm doing... [*He notices the* COUNT] I've seen that reverend gent somewhere before.

[*He stands up*

COUNT [*aside*]. That man is not unknown to me.

FIGARO. Hold on, that's no reverend gent. That haughty, aristocratic air...

COUNT. Those ridiculous clothes...

FIGARO. I'm not wrong: it's Count Almaviva!

COUNT. I do believe it's that rogue Figaro!

FIGARO. The very same, your Lordship.

COUNT. Oaf! if you say one word...

FIGARO. Ah so I was right: it is you. The same kind words you always honoured me with.

COUNT. I didn't know you. You've grown so fat and sleek...

FIGARO. Heigh-ho, your Lordship, it's the poverty that does it.

COUNT. You poor devil! But what are you doing in Seville? I gave you a reference for a job with the ministry ages ago.

FIGARO. I got it, your Lordship, and my gratitude...

COUNT. Call me Lindor. Can't you see I'm in disguise? I don't want to be recognized.

FIGARO. I'll be off then.

COUNT. On the contrary. I'm waiting here for a reason and two men talking together are less suspicious than one man loitering on his own. So let's look as if we're deep in conversation. Go on, what about this job?

FIGARO. The minister, having due regard to your Lordship's reference, immediately appointed me assistant apothecary.

COUNT. To the hospitals of the military?

FIGARO. No. To the stud-farms of Andalusia.

COUNT [*laughing*]. A brilliant start!

FIGARO. It wasn't a bad job as jobs go. I was in charge of bandages and medicines and so I was often able, for a consideration, to pass on pills intended for horses to suffering humanity...

COUNT. Which killed off his Majesty's subjects in droves!

FIGARO. There's no such thing as a cure for everything, but they did sometimes work on Catalans and peasants of that ilk.

COUNT. So why did you leave the job?

FIGARO. Me leave it? It left me. Somebody informed on me to the authorities: 'Ah Envy, hook-clawed, green-eyed ghoul, how oft...'*

COUNT. Spare me, please! So you've taken up poetry too? I saw you down on one knee scribbling and singing. Isn't it a little early in the day for that sort of thing?

FIGARO. Ah, now there you have the cause of my downfall. When the minister was told that I dashed off verses to the ladies—and very prettily even if I say so myself—sent puzzles to the newspapers, and had ditties of my composition on everyone's lips—in other words, when he found out that I was a published author—he took the tragic view and had me kicked out on the grounds that love of literature and a head for business go together like oil and water.

COUNT. Powerfully argued. I imagine you put it to him that...

FIGARO. I was only too glad he forgot all about me, for I reckon that great persons treat us ordinary mortals well enough when they're not doing us actual harm.

COUNT. But you're not giving the full story. As I recall, you were a bit of a rogue when you were in my service.

FIGARO. I ask you, sir, why is it that people assume that because a man's poor he should be pure as the driven snow?

COUNT. Idle, depraved...

FIGARO. Given the virtues required of servants, does your Lordship know many masters who would make a half-decent valet?

COUNT. That's not bad. Anyway, you moved here, to this place?

FIGARO. No, not straight away.

COUNT [*stopping him*]. Just a moment... I thought it was her... Go on with what you were saying. I'm still listening.

FIGARO. When I got back to Madrid, I thought I'd see where my literary talents would get me. I had the idea that the stage was my path to fame...

COUNT. Don't tell me...

FIGARO [*during his answer the* COUNT *keeps an attentive eye on the shuttered window*]. I honestly can't think why I wasn't a huge success. I'd packed the theatre with supporters. Hands like shovels, they had. I banned gloves and walking sticks, anything that muffles the applause. I tell you, before the curtain went up, the talk in the cafés seemed to be going entirely in my direction. But the claque did its worst...

COUNT. Oh dear, bribery and corruption. Behold, one failed author.

FIGARO. I'm not the first. Isn't that how bribery works? I was booed. But if I could get them together...

COUNT. You'd get even by boring them to death?

FIGARO. I still have it in for them, by God! Always will.

COUNT. Is that a fact? You know that in the law-courts you've only got twenty-four hours to be rude to your judges?*

FIGARO. It's different in the theatre: there you've got twenty-four years. But there aren't enough years in a life to smooth such badly ruffled feathers.

COUNT. You always cheer me up when you get angry! But you didn't say what made you leave Madrid.

FIGARO. Obviously my guardian angel, your Excellency, for here I am, happily reunited with my former employer. It soon dawned on me that literary society in Madrid was really a pack of wolves who prowl around with fangs bared for sinking into the nearest throat, beneath contempt with their ludicrous bitching, the lot of them—insects, mosquitoes, gnats, critics, horse-flies, back-biters, reviewers, publishers, censors, the whole tribe of parasites who infest the tender parts of struggling authors, and then chew them up and suck them dry of whatever small talent they are left with. I was tired of scribbling, bored with myself, nauseated by everyone else, up to my ears in debt and stony broke. In the end, I decided that the ready money I could earn by plying a razor was preferable to the unpaid honour of wielding a pen. So I left Madrid and set out with all my worldly goods strapped to my back, wandering philosophically through Castile, La Mancha, Estramadura, the Sierra Morena, and Andalusia, welcomed with open arms in one town, jailed in the next, and at all times taking events in my stride. Acclaimed by some and damned by others, prospering in good times and putting up with the bad, laughing at fools and defying the villains, indifferent to poverty and shaving all-comers, until at last you see me now, operating here in Seville, and available once more to serve your Lordship in whatever it pleases you to command.

COUNT. Where did you get such a cheerful view of things from?

FIGARO. Habitual misfortune. I make a point of laughing at life, because otherwise I'm afraid it would make me weep. Why do you keep looking up like that?

COUNT. We must go.

FIGARO. Why?

COUNT. Come on, you oaf! You'll ruin everything.

[*They hide*

SCENE 3

BARTHOLO, ROSINE

The first-floor shutter opens and BARTHOLO *and* ROSINE *appear at the balcony*

ROSINE. What a relief to breathe fresh air. This shutter is hardly ever opened.

BARTHOLO. What's that paper you've got there?

ROSINE. The words and music of a song from *The Pointless Precaution*. My singing-teacher gave it to me yesterday.

BARTHOLO. What's *The Pointless Precaution*?

ROSINE. It's a new comedy.

BARTHOLO. Not another one of these modern plays? Some piece of nonsense in the new style?[1]

ROSINE. I couldn't say.

BARTHOLO. Well the newspapers and the watch committee will soon put a stop to it. What a barbarous age we live in.

ROSINE. You're always complaining about the age we live in.

BARTHOLO. Pardon me for speaking! But what has it produced that people should say it's so wonderful? Nonsense of all sorts: freethinking, gravity, electricity, tolerance, inoculation, quinine, the *Encyclopedia*, and these new dramas.*

ROSINE [*the paper slips from her hand and drops into the street*]. Oh my music! My music fell while I was listening to you. Be quick, do hurry, or my song will blow away!

BARTHOLO. Dammit, when you're holding something you should keep a proper grip on it.

[*He leaves the balcony*

ROSINE [*she glances inside the room then signals to the street*]. Psst! [*The* COUNT *appears*] Quick, pick it up and go.

[*The* COUNT *steps out of his hiding place, snatches up the paper, and goes back into hiding*

BARTHOLO [*comes out of his front door and searches*]. Where the devil is it? I can't see it anywhere.

ROSINE. Look under the balcony, close to the wall.

BARTHOLO. The things I do for you! Did anybody pass this way?

[1] Bartholo did not like the new drama. Maybe, as a young man, he had written a tragedy.

ROSINE. I didn't see anyone.

BARTHOLO [*muttering*]. I must be all heart, rummaging around like this. Bartholo, you know what you are? An idiot! This will teach you never to open shutters that overlook the street.

[*He goes back into the house*

ROSINE [*still on the balcony*]. No one can blame me given the circumstances. Shut away with no one to turn to, persecuted by a horrible man, is it a crime to want to stop being a slave?

BARTHOLO [*reappearing on the balcony*]. Come in now, my dear. It's my fault you lost your music. But it won't happen again, that I guarantee.

[*He closes and locks the shutters*

SCENE 4

The COUNT *and* FIGARO *emerge cautiously from their hiding place*

COUNT. Now they've gone back indoors, let's take a look at this music. There's got to be more to this than meets the eye. It's a note!

FIGARO. And he wondered what a pointless precaution was!

COUNT [*reads eagerly*]. 'Your persistence makes me curious. My guardian has to go out. When he does, take the tune of this song which everyone knows and make it seem that you're singing it for no reason, but use words which tell me your name, who you are, and what you want so earnestly with a very unhappy Rosine.'

FIGARO [*imitating* ROSINE's *voice*]. Oooh! My music, I dropped my music. Be quick, do hurry! [*He laughs*] Ha ha ha! Women! If you want a sweet little girl to learn how to cheat and scheme, just keep locked her up!

COUNT. Rosine! My lovely Rosine!

FIGARO. Your Lordship doesn't have to tell me your reasons for this charade. This is wooing with a view.

COUNT. So now you know. But if you breathe one word...

FIGARO. Me? Breathe a word? I won't try to put your mind at rest by trotting out the usual guff about honour and dedication that rolls so easily off the tongue nowadays. All I'll say is this: if there's something in this for me, that's your guarantee. Judge everything by that principle and...

COUNT. All right, all right. This is the scenario. Six months ago, in the Prado,* I came across a girl, an absolute stunner!... That was her just now. I tried to trace her everywhere in Madrid but got nowhere. It's only in the last few days that I've learned that her name is Rosine, a duke's daughter. Both her parents are dead and she's married to an elderly doctor here, name of Bartholo.

FIGARO. A pretty bird in a gilded cage which won't be easy to open. Who told you she was married to the doctor?

COUNT. Everyone said so.

FIGARO. That's just a story he put about when he came here from Madrid, to put the local wolves off the scent and keep them from sniffing around his front door. She's still only his ward, but one of these days...

COUNT. That day won't dawn! Oh, this is wonderful news! I'd made up my mind to do the decent thing and leave. But now I learn that she's available! There's not a moment to lose. I must make her love me and save her from the gruesome marriage that's planned for her. I take it you know this guardian of hers?

FIGARO. Like my own mother.

COUNT. What's he like?

FIGARO. He's a well-favoured, well-upholstered, short young fogey, salt-and-pepper hair, sly, fly, faded, jaded, a watching, ferreting, scolding man who complains all the time.

COUNT. Yes, yes, I saw him. And his character?

FIGARO. A toad, mean with money, madly jealous, and in love with his ward who hates him like poison.

COUNT. So his attractiveness to women is...

FIGARO. Zero.

COUNT. Good. Is he honest?

FIGARO. Only as honest as it takes to keep him clear of the hangman's noose.

COUNT. Better and better. So we can punish a nasty piece of work and get our own way at the same time...

FIGARO. Defending the public good and promoting personal happiness—seems to me, that as schemes go this one, your Lordship, morally speaking, is masterly.

COUNT. You say he's afraid of the local competition and keeps his door locked?

FIGARO. No one gets in. If he could have it bricked up, he would.

COUNT. Damn! Still, there it is. You wouldn't happen to have a way of getting inside?

FIGARO. Do I know a way in? First, the house where I'm staying belongs to the doctor, who lets me live there for free...

COUNT. Interesting!

FIGARO. Yes. And in return I promise to pay him ten pistoles a year, also for free...

COUNT [*impatiently*]. You mean you're his tenant?

FIGARO. Not just that but also his barber, surgeon, and apothecary too. In that house there's not a razor, lancet, or enema-pump that moves unless the hand on it belongs to yours truly.

COUNT [*throwing his arms around him*]. Figaro, old friend, you are my salvation, my deliverer, the answer to my prayers!

FIGARO. Marvellous, isn't it. When I'm useful, social distinctions just vanish. That's what love does for you!

COUNT. Figaro, you're a lucky devil. You'll get to see her! You'll be seeing her! Have you any idea how fortunate that makes you?

FIGARO. Spoken like a man in love. But it's not me that's mad about her. Could we fix it so that you could go instead of me?

COUNT. If we could only get her jailers out of the way...

FIGARO. That's exactly what I'm thinking.

COUNT. Just for twelve hours!

FIGARO. If you keep people's minds focused on their own business, you can stop them poking their nose into other people's.

COUNT. True. And?

FIGARO. I'm wondering if my medicine chest might not help us come up with some innocent little diversion...

COUNT. That's immoral!

FIGARO. I don't intend to harm anybody. They all need my services at one time or another. I'll just have to arrange things so I treat them all together.

COUNT. But he's a doctor and might suspect something.

FIGARO. Then we'll have to move fast so that he won't have time to get suspicious. I've got an idea. The King's Own Regiment's arriving in town today.

COUNT. The colonel's a friend of mine.

FIGARO. Good. Turn up at the doctor's doorstep dressed like a cavalry officer. He'll have to billet you in his house. Then leave the rest to me.

COUNT. Excellent!

FIGARO. It would help if you behaved as if you'd had a drop to drink.

COUNT. What good would that do?

FIGARO. And come on a bit strong, as drunks do.

COUNT. Why?

FIGARO. So that he won't be suspicious and will assume you're more interested in getting a bed than in plotting under his roof.

COUNT. That's brilliant! But won't you be there?

FIGARO. But of course. We'll be lucky, though, if he doesn't see through the disguise, even though he's never set eyes on you before. But if he catches on, how would I get you in after that?

COUNT. You're right.

FIGARO. Perhaps you're not up to carrying it off. Not an easy part to sustain, a cavalryman, tight as a lord...

COUNT. You're joking. [*Acts drunk*] My good man, is this the house of Doctor Bartholo?

FIGARO. That's not bad. But maybe a bit more unsteady on your legs. [*Acts even drunker*] My good man, ish thish the housh...

COUNT. Dammit, that's how workmen behave when they're drunk.

FIGARO. It's the best way. You can tell they're enjoying it.

COUNT. Look, the door's opening.

FIGARO. It's our man. Let's fade into the background until he's gone.

SCENE 5

The COUNT *and* FIGARO *(in hiding),* BARTHOLO

BARTHOLO [*speaking into the open door*]. I shan't be long. Don't let anyone in. That was very stupid of me, coming down like that! I should have been suspicious the moment she asked me to. What's keeping Bazile? He was supposed to be seeing to the arrangements so that my marriage can go ahead in secret tomorrow, but there's not a word from him. I must go and find out what's holding him up.

[*He leaves*

SCENE 6

The COUNT, FIGARO

COUNT. Did I hear him right? He's going to marry Rosine tomorrow in secret!

FIGARO. Sir, the difficulty of succeeding merely makes the need to act boldly more urgent.

COUNT. Who's this Bazile who has a hand in the wedding?

FIGARO. A sorry specimen who teaches his ward music, about which he is mad, a dubious character who's always hard up and worships money and will be easy to manage, sir... [*Glancing up at the window*] Look, she's there!

COUNT. Who's where?

FIGARO. Behind the shutter, it's her! Don't look. Don't look!

COUNT. Why not?

FIGARO. Didn't she say in her note that you've got to make it appear as if you're singing for no reason? So sing as though you're singing... for no reason... at all. Yes, it's her all right.

COUNT. Since I've begun to make her curious about a man she doesn't know, I might as well go on using the name of Lindor by which people know me. All the better if she loves me without knowing who I am. [*He opens the sheet of paper which* ROSINE *dropped*] How am I supposed to put words to this music? I'm no good at making up lyrics.

FIGARO. Anything that comes to you, sir, will be fine. When people are in love, they don't tend to be overly critical... Here, you'd better take my guitar.

COUNT. What the devil am I do to with a guitar? I play very badly.

FIGARO. I thought a man like yourself could do everything. Use the back of the hand, thrum, thrum, thrum. In Seville, a man who sings without a guitar would stick out like a sore thumb and they'd soon be on to you.

> [FIGARO *stands under the balcony, with his back to the wall*

COUNT [*sings as he walks, accompanying himself on the guitar*].

(NO. 2)

> You said that my name should not be hidden.
> Without a name I dared to love thee.
> But naming may not bring felicity
> Yet I must do as I am bidden.

FIGARO [*whispers*]. Excellent start, sir, keep it going.

COUNT.

> They call me Lindor; 'tis but a humble name,
> And humble is my love—yet neither base nor flawed:
> Oh I could wish I were a noble lord
> To give you wealth and more than common fame.

FIGARO. Damn me, I couldn't do better myself, and I reckon I've got a gift for it.

COUNT.

> Here with sweetest voice I'll come each day
> And sing for you a song of hopeless love,
> Happy enough to see you stand and move:
> Will you hear or shall I be sent away?

FIGARO. Amazing! May I...?

> *[He approaches the* COUNT *and kisses the hem of his coat*

COUNT. Figaro!

FIGARO. Sir?

COUNT. Do you think she heard?

ROSINE [*inside the house, sings*].

> Fair Lindor's song suggests to me
> That I shall love him constantly...

> *[We hear a window being slammed shut*

FIGARO. Any doubts now about whether anyone was listening?

COUNT. She closed her window. Someone must have come into her room.

FIGARO. Poor, defenceless creature! How her voice trembled as she sung! She's hooked, sir.

COUNT. She used the same ploy she told me to use:

> Fair Lindor's song suggests to me
> That I shall love him constantly...

How delightful! How clever!

FIGARO. How scheming! It must be love!

COUNT. Do you think she really means it, Figaro?

FIGARO. She'd break through those bars rather than let you down.

COUNT. It's all settled, then. I am Rosine's... for ever and ever!

FIGARO. You're forgetting, sir: she can't hear you now.

COUNT. I've only one thing to say to you, Figaro: that girl is going to be my wife. And if you help with my plans by keeping my real name quiet... Am I making myself clear? You know me...

FIGARO. All right, I submit. So, Figaro, my lad, it's time to make your fortune.

COUNT. Let's not linger here. We don't want to arouse suspicion.

FIGARO [animatedly]. I shall go into that house and with a single wave of my wand put vigilance to sleep, awaken love, hoodwink jealousy, foil conspiracy, and overcome all obstacles. And you, sir, go to my house. You'll need uniform, billeting warrant, and money for your pockets.

COUNT. Money? Who for?

FIGARO. Money, for God's sake, and lots of it. Money makes the plots go round.

COUNT. No need to get mad, Figaro, I'll bring plenty.

FIGARO [as he leaves]. I'll see you there shortly.

COUNT. Figaro!

FIGARO. What?

COUNT. Your guitar.

FIGARO. Forgetting my guitar! I must be losing my grip.

[He makes to leave

COUNT. And the address? Do concentrate.

FIGARO [returns]. I'm definitely slipping! My shop's just round the corner, painted blue, mullioned windows, and a sign outside with three basins at the top above an eye in a hand* and, underneath, Consilio manuque—'A shrewd mind and a steady hand'—and the name FIGARO!

ACT II

ROSINE's *apartment. At the back of the stage is a large window closed up by a barred shutter*

SCENE 1

ROSINE, *alone*

ROSINE [*a candlestick in one hand, she takes a sheet of paper from the table and begins to write*]. Marceline's not well, all the servants are busy, and no one can see me writing. I don't know if the walls have eyes and ears or if my all-seeing guardian has some evil genie that tells him everything that goes on, but I can't say a word or make a move without him guessing what I'm up to... Oh Lindor! [*She seals the letter*] Might as well close my letter, though I don't know when or how I'm going to send it to him. I saw him through my shutter having a long talk with Figaro the barber. Now there's a nice man. Sometimes he seems quite sorry for me. If only I could have a brief word with him!

SCENE 2

ROSINE, FIGARO

ROSINE [*startled*]. Monsieur Figaro! I'm so glad to see you!

FIGARO. Are you well?

ROSINE. I could be better. I'm so bored!

FIGARO. I can believe it. Only imbeciles get fat on boredom.

ROSINE. Who were you talking to so earnestly in the street just now? I couldn't hear, but...

FIGARO. A young student, a relative of mine. We have great hopes for him. He has a way with words, he's sensitive, talented, and very handsome.

ROSINE. Oh, very. I couldn't agree more. What's his name?

FIGARO. Lindor. He hasn't a penny. But if he hadn't had to leave Madrid in such a hurry, he'd have found a good job there.

ROSINE [*gushingly*]. He'll find one, Monsieur Figaro. I'm sure he will. A young man such as you describe won't go unnoticed for long.

FIGARO [*aside*]. A good start. [*Aloud*] But he has one big failing which isn't going to help his career.

ROSINE. A failing, Monsieur Figaro! A failing! Are you sure?

FIGARO. He's in love.

ROSINE. In love? And you call that a failing?

FIGARO. It is, given the fact that he hasn't got any money.

ROSINE. Oh, life's so unfair! And has he mentioned the name of the girl? I'm being very inquisitive...

FIGARO. You're the last person I'd ever want to let into a secret like that.

ROSINE [*spiritedly*]. Why, Monsieur Figaro? I'm very discreet. This young man is a relative of yours, so naturally I want to know all about him... Go on, do tell.

FIGARO [*measuring her with a look*]. Picture the prettiest little creature—sweet natured, tender, graceful, fresh as a daisy and quite irresistible: dainty walk, willowy figure, tall, shapely arms, lips like rosebuds, and her hands! Her cheeks! Those teeth! And such eyes!...

ROSINE. And she lives here in Seville?

FIGARO. In this part of town.

ROSINE. In this very street perhaps?

FIGARO. She's standing not a million miles from me.

ROSINE. How marvellous... for your relative, I mean. And this person is...

FIGARO. Didn't I mention her name?

ROSINE. It's the only detail you left out, Monsieur Figaro. Go on, tell me and be quick. If anyone came in, I might never know...

FIGARO. You really insist? Well, the person in question is... your guardian's ward.

ROSINE. His ward?

FIGARO. Doctor Bartholo's legal ward, yes, Madame.

ROSINE [blushing]. Oh, Monsieur Figaro. I don't believe you. I really don't.

FIGARO. And what's more, he's dying to come and tell you himself.

ROSINE. You're making me feel scared, Monsieur Figaro.

FIGARO. Scared? Nonsense! That's no way to think, Madame. If you give in to the fear of consequences, you're already living with the consequences of fear. In any case I've managed to get all your jailers out of the way until tomorrow.

ROSINE. If he really loves me, he must prove it by keeping absolutely quiet about it.

FIGARO. Come, come, Madame! Can anybody who's in love stay quiet? I'm sorry for young people nowadays because they have a dreadful choice: either in love and no quiet, or a quiet life and no love.

ROSINE [lowering her eyes]. A quiet life without love... would seem...

FIGARO. Pretty miserable. When you think about it, love and no quiet looks like the better option. Speaking personally, if I were a woman...

ROSINE [embarrassed]. Of course, a young lady can't prevent a gentleman admiring her.

FIGARO. Quite. And my cousin admires you enormously.

ROSINE. But, Monsieur Figaro, if he were to do something silly, he'd ruin it all for both of us!

FIGARO [aside]. He'd ruin it all! [Aloud] But if you wrote a little letter telling him not to... A letter can be a powerful thing.

ROSINE [*giving him the letter she has just written*]. There isn't time to write this one again, but when you give it to him, say... you can tell him...

[*She listens*

FIGARO. There's nobody there.

ROSINE. That what I'm doing I do purely out of friendship.

FIGARO. Of course it is. Good lord, love is a another kettle of fish altogether.

ROSINE. Out of pure friendship. Have you got that? The only thing I'm afraid of is that if he's put off by all the difficulties, he...

FIGARO. ...might vanish like a will-o'-the-wisp? Don't forget: the wind that blows out a candle can also fan a fire into a blaze, and we men are like fires. Even when he's just talking about it, he breathes such flames that he almost conflagrated[1] me with his passion, and I'm just an onlooker.

ROSINE. Heavens! I can hear my guardian. If he were to find you here... Go out through the music room and down the stairs as quietly as you can.

FIGARO. Don't worry. [*Aside, with the letter in his hand*] This speaks louder than anything I can tell him.

[*He goes through the music room door*

SCENE 3

ROSINE, *alone*

ROSINE. I shan't stop worrying until he's outside. I really like Figaro, he's so kind and honest and so good to his cousin. Here comes the jailer. Where's my sewing?

[*She blows out the candle, sits down, and picks up her embroidery ring*

---

[1] This word 'conflagrated', which is not very good French, ruffled the feathers of the literary purists. I would not advise any gentleman to use it, but Figaro is a law unto himself!

SCENE 4

BARTHOLO, ROSINE

BARTHOLO [*he is furious*]. Damn! Damn! Blast that interfering, good-for-nothing, mad dog, Figaro! Can't a man leave his house for a few minutes without being certain that when he gets back...

ROSINE. What on earth has made you so angry?

BARTHOLO. It's that damned barber! He's put everyone in the house out of action at one fell swoop. He gave young Wakeful a sleeping concoction, and sneezing powder to Old Youthful. He bled Marceline by the toe and he's even had a go at my mule—he put a poultice over the eyes of a poor, blind animal! He owes me a hundred crowns, so he's bombarding me with bills. Just let him try it on, we'll see... And there's no one downstairs in the hall. Anyone could come up and march into this apartment as if it were a parade ground.

ROSINE. But who else would march in here, sir, except you?

BARTHOLO. I'd rather worry unnecessarily than leave myself vulnerable by not taking precautions. There are bold and resolute ruffians everywhere... Why, this very morning, somebody was quick enough to make off with your music while I was on my way down to retrieve it. Oh, I...

ROSINE. You read too much into everything. The wind could have taken it, or some passer-by, how should I know?

BARTHOLO. The wind! A passer-by! Listen, there was no wind and no one passed by. But there's always someone deliberately skulking about to pick up pieces of paper which women pretend to drop accidentally.

ROSINE. Pretend, sir?

BARTHOLO. Yes. Pretend.

ROSINE [*aside*]. The devious old fox!

BARTHOLO. But it won't happen again. I'm going to have the shutters nailed fast.

ROSINE. Why stop there? Why not brick up the windows? A prison or a dungeon, what's the difference?

BARTHOLO. Now that's not a bad idea, at least the ones that over-look the street. That barber hasn't been here, has he?

ROSINE. You don't you suspect him too?

BARTHOLO. I suspect everybody.

ROSINE. Well at least that's a frank answer.

BARTHOLO. Trust everybody and before you can look round you've got a loving wife who deceives you, best friends who run away with her under your nose, and loyal servants who help them do it.

ROSINE. So you don't even credit me with enough moral scruples not to resist Monsieur Figaro and his persuasive tongue?

BARTHOLO. I'm damned if anybody will ever understand how women's minds work! Moral scruples! How many times have I seen...

ROSINE [angrily]. If being a man is all it takes to turn a girl's head, why is it that I find you so very unattractive?

BARTHOLO [taken aback]. Why?... Why?... Look here, young lady, you still haven't answered my question about the barber.

ROSINE [incandescent]. Since you must know, yes, he was here. I saw him. I spoke to him. I won't even hide the fact that I found him very kind and understanding and I hope your suspicions choke you!

[She leaves

SCENE 5

BARTHOLO, alone

BARTHOLO. Oh! The heathen dogs! The curs! Damn those ser-vants! Old Youthful! Wakeful! Where's that blasted Wakeful!

SCENE 6

BARTHOLO, WAKEFUL

WAKEFUL [*enters yawning and still half asleep*]. Ooooah! Aaah!

BARTHOLO. Where were you, you brainless skiver, when the barber just walked into the house?

WAKEFUL [*yawning*]. Me sir? I was... Ooooah!

BARTHOLO. Up to no good, I dare say. Didn't you see him?

WAKEFUL. 'Course I seen him. Didn't he tell me to my face that I was ever so poorly? And he must have been right, 'cos I started havin' these pains in me arms and legs just with listening to him...

BARTHOLO [*imitating him*]. Just with listening to him! Where's Old Youthful, the good-for-nothing? Drugging the poor man without a prescription signed by me... there's got to be more to this than meets the eye.

SCENE 7

BARTHOLO, WAKEFUL, *and* OLD YOUTHFUL, *an elderly relic leaning on a walking stick, who sneezes several times*

WAKEFUL [*still yawning*]. Old Youthful?

BARTHOLO. You can sneeze on your day off.

OLD YOUTHFUL. This'll make fifty... in a moment... fi-fif-fifty times... [*He sneezes*] I'm fair shaken to bits.

BARTHOLO. Look here, I asked the pair of you if someone had been up to see Rosine, and neither of you said that the barber...

WAKEFUL [*still yawning*]. Do Monsieur Figaro count as someone? Aaaah!

BARTHOLO. I bet you're in cahoots with him, you crafty swine.

WAKEFUL [*weeping buckets*]. Me sir? In cahoots!

OLD YOUTHFUL [*sneezing*]. But sir, it's not fair. Where's the justice...

BARTHOLO. Justice! Ignorant clods like you can go on and on about justice. But I'm your master and that means I'm always right!

OLD YOUTHFUL [*sneezing*]. But if a thing is true...

BARTHOLO. If something's true! If I don't want a thing to be true, it isn't true by my say-so. If you let any Tom, Dick, or Harry be right, you'd soon see what's to become of authority and discipline!

OLD YOUTHFUL [*sneezing*]. I'd rather be given my notice. It's terrible working here. Hectic, that's what it is.

WAKEFUL [*in tears*]. A honest working man gets treated like a slave.

BARTHOLO. Be off with you, then, you honest working man! [*Mimicking them*] Atishoo! Aaaah! One sneezes in my face and the other yawns all over me.

OLD YOUTHFUL. I'll tell you one thing, sir, which is that without the young mistress there'd be nothing to make anybody want to stay in this house for.

[*Goes out sneezing*

BARTHOLO. A fine state Figaro has put them all in. But I can see what he's up to. The rogue wants to pay back my hundred crowns without opening his wallet...

SCENE 8

BARTHOLO, DON BAZILE, *and* FIGARO, *who is hidden in the music room but appears from time to time and listens*

BARTHOLO. Ah, Don Bazile. Were you on the way here to give Rosine her music lesson?

BAZILE. There's no hurry for that.

BARTHOLO. I called at your house but you weren't there.

BAZILE. I was out, on your business. I've some rather bad news.

BARTHOLO. Bad for you?

BAZILE. No, for you. Count Almaviva is here in town.

BARTHOLO. Keep your voice down. Is he the man who had people combing Madrid for Rosine?

BAZILE. He's taken a house on the main square and goes out every day in disguise.

BARTHOLO. You're absolutely right, this does concern me. What shall we do?

BAZILE. If he were just anyone, we'd get him out of the way without much trouble.

BARTHOLO. Yes. Lie in wait for him one night, armed to the teeth, chain-mail shirts and...

BAZILE. *Bone deus!* And compromise ourselves? Spread some nasty rumour, that's the way. And then, while the scandal is going the rounds, have him slandered by experts. QED.

BARTHOLO. Isn't that a peculiar way of getting rid of a man?

BAZILE. Slander, peculiar? You don't know what the word means if you can dismiss it so easily! I have seen the most decent, honest men brought virtually to their knees by it. Believe me, there's no downright lie, no tissue of horrors, no tittle-tattle so absurd that you can't get the crass, nosy population of any city to swallow if you set about it the right way, and here in Seville we have experts! It starts as a faint whisper, skimming the ground like a swallow before the storm, *pianissimo*. It whirrs and scatters, and as it spreads it shoots out poisoned barbs. A mouth catches one and, *piano*, *piano*, hooks it deftly into a convenient ear. The damage is done. It breeds, creeps, multiplies and, *rinforzando*, it hops like some fiend from mouth to mouth. Then suddenly, don't ask me how, you see Slander rear up, hissing, bulging, swelling as you watch. It takes flight, spreads its wings, swoops, swirls, enfolds, claws, seizes, erupts, and explodes and turns, God only knows how, into a general clamour, a public *crescendo*, a universal chorus of hate and condemnation. Is there a man alive who can survive it?

BARTHOLO. What do you mean by all this twaddle, Bazile? What's all this *piano* and *crescendo* nonsense got to do with me and my problem?

BAZILE. What's it got to do with you? All the methods anyone ever uses to deal with an enemy we must adopt to keep yours at arm's length.

BARTHOLO. At arm's length? I intend to marry Rosine before she even gets to know that this Count exists.

BAZILE. In that case, you haven't a moment to lose.

BARTHOLO. And who's to blame for that, Bazile? I asked you to look after all the details.

BAZILE. True, but you wanted the whole thing done on the cheap. Into the harmony that is order and conformity, a marriage between persons unequal in age, a wrongful decision of a court, an obvious miscarriage of justice, can all strike discordant notes. They must be anticipated and corrected by the perfect, golden chord that is money.

BARTHOLO [*giving him money*]. In that case, we'll have to do it your way. But sort it out quickly.

BAZILE. Now you're talking. It'll be all settled tomorrow. It's up to you to ensure that no one tells your ward today.

BARTHOLO. Leave it to me. Will you be coming back this evening, Bazile?

BAZILE. Don't count on it. Seeing to the arrangements for your marriage will keep me busy all day, so best not count on it.

BARTHOLO [*going to the door with him*]. Let me.

BAZILE. There's no need to bother, Doctor, I can let myself out.

BARTHOLO. It's no bother. I want lock the front door after you.

SCENE 9

FIGARO

FIGARO [*emerging from the music room*]. Carry on! Take all the precautions you want. You can lock the street door, but I shall unlock again it for the Count as I leave. This Bazile character is as slippery as they come. Fortunately, he is also a fool. If you're going to get anywhere with slander, you need to be somebody, have family connections, a name, a title, influence. That rules out Bazile. He could throw mud till he was blue in the face and nobody would pay any attention.

SCENE 10

ROSINE *running in*, FIGARO

ROSINE. What! Are you still here, Monsieur Figaro?

FIGARO. And it's lucky for you that I am. Your guardian and your singing-teacher thought they were alone and have just had the frankest heart-to-heart.

ROSINE. And you listened, Monsieur Figaro? Don't you know listening to other people's conversations is very wrong?

FIGARO. Wrong? But you don't hear anything unless you listen. There's something you should know: your guardian is planning to marry you tomorrow.

ROSINE. Oh my God!

FIGARO. Don't worry. We'll find so much to keep him busy that he won't have time to think about wedding bells.

ROSINE. He's coming back. Go out by the back stairs. You're scaring me to death.

[FIGARO *hurries off*

SCENE 11

BARTHOLO, ROSINE

ROSINE. Was there someone with you, sir?

BARTHOLO. Don Bazile. I've just seen him out—can't be too careful these days. Would you have preferred it to be Figaro?

ROSINE. I have no preference in the matter, I assure you.

BARTHOLO. I'm very curious to know what that damned barber had to tell you that was so urgent.

ROSINE. If you really want to know, he came to report on how Marceline is getting on—not too well, or so he said.

BARTHOLO. Came to report? I wouldn't mind betting he'd been paid to deliver some letter or other.

ROSINE. Who from, may I ask?

BARTHOLO. Who from? Someone women never put a name to. How should I know? Perhaps an answer to the piece of paper you dropped out of the window.

ROSINE [aside]. He never misses a trick! [Aloud] It would serve you right if that were were true.

BARTHOLO [examining ROSINE's hands]. But it is true. You've been writing.

ROSINE [disconcerted]. You're not serious? You're surely not proposing to force a confession out of me?

BARTHOLO [taking her right hand]. No need for that—there are traces of ink on your finger. What do you say to that, sly little minx!

ROSINE [aside]. Damn the man!

BARTHOLO [still holding her hand]. Women always think it's safe for them to do anything when they're by themselves.

ROSINE. Whatever you say. But is that your proof? Please let go, you're twisting my arm. I was doing some sewing too near the candle and burned myself. I was always told to dip a burn in ink and that's what I did.

BARTHOLO. You did that, did you? Well let's see if there's another piece of evidence to corroborate the first. I'm quite certain that there were six sheets of paper in this note-case. I know because I count them every morning and did so today.

ROSINE [to herself]. How could I be so careless!

BARTHOLO [counting]. Three, four, five...

ROSINE. The sixth...

BARTHOLO. I note that the sixth is missing.

ROSINE [*looking at the ground*]. The sixth? I used it to make a bag for some sweets I sent to Figaro's little girl.*

BARTHOLO. Figaro's little girl, eh? And how is it that this nib, which hadn't been used, is now black? Did it get that way when you used it to write the address of Figaro's little girl?

ROSINE [*aside*]. The man has a talent for jealousy. [*Aloud*] No, I used it to retrace a faded flower on the coat I'm embroidering for you.

BARTHOLO. I'm touched! But if you want people to believe you, my girl, you shouldn't blush each time you bury the truth a little deeper. But that's something you haven't learned yet.

ROSINE. Who wouldn't blush to see such a horrible interpretation put upon perfectly innocent actions?

BARTHOLO. Obviously I've got it wrong. You burn your finger, dip it in ink, make sweety-bags for Figaro's little girl, and draw flowers for my waistcoat on your embroidery frame, what could be more innocent than that? But what a mountain of lies to hide one simple fact... 'I am alone, no one can see me; I can lie all I want.' But the tip of your finger is inky, the nib of the pen is black, and there's a sheet of paper missing. You couldn't think of everything. But this you can be sure of, young lady. Whenever I go into town, I'll double-lock the front door! That'll cramp your style!

SCENE 12

The COUNT, BARTHOLO, ROSINE
The COUNT *is wearing a cavalry officer's uniform, looks as though he has been drinking, and is singing 'Let us awake her...'*

BARTHOLO. What does this man want? A soldier! Go to your room, Señora.

COUNT [*singing 'Let us awake her' and going up to* ROSINE]. Which of you two ladies goes by the name of Dr Barbaro. [*Whispers to* ROSINE] It's me, Lindor.

BARTHOLO. Bartholo!

ROSINE [*aside*]. He mentioned Lindor.

COUNT. Bartholo, Bartholas, Bartholat, Barbaro, Balustrado, it's all the same to me. All I want to know is which of you two ladies is... [*To* ROSINE, *holding out a letter*] Take this note.

BARTHOLO. Which lady! Can't you tell it's me? Ladies, indeed! Go to your room at once, Rosine. I do believe this man's been drinking

ROSINE. That's why I'm staying. You're all alone. Sometimes a woman can...

BARTHOLO. Get along with you, go. I'm not afraid.

[ROSINE *leaves*

SCENE 13

The COUNT, BARTHOLO

COUNT. Oh I recognized you straight off by the description they gave me.

BARTHOLO [*to the* COUNT, *who is still clutching the letter*]. What's that you're trying to hide in your pocket?

COUNT. I'm trying to hide it in my pocket so you won't know what it is.

BARTHOLO. It's my official particulars! The people who compile them always express themselves as if they thought everybody was in the army!

COUNT. You don't imagine drawing up your particulars was all that difficult, do you?

[*Sings*

> A nodding brow, a balding head,
> Eyes of green, a look of dread,
> Ferocious as ten wild Injuns,
> Short and fat, clothes too tight,
> Left arm shorter than the right.
> Face as mottled as a sturgeon's,
> Nose as big as three large pigeons.

> Bandy-legged, not one for jokes,
> Surly manner, voice that croaks:
> From his tongue may God protect us.
> Summing-up: a prince of doctors.[1]

BARTHOLO. What's all that supposed to mean? Did you come here to insult me? Get out of my house at once!

COUNT. Me, get out! Look here, you mustn't talk like that. Can you read, doctor... Gardyloo?

BARTHOLO. Got any more stupid questions?

COUNT. No need to feel bad about it, because I'm a medical man too and just as much a doctor as you are.

BARTHOLO. What are you talking about?

COUNT. I'm the regimental farrier. That's why they billeted me here deliberately on purpose—we're colleagues.

BARTHOLO. You can't compare a man who shoes horses with...

COUNT [speaks the first three lines and sings the last four to the tune: 'Long Live Wine'].

> I'm not saying that we doctors
> Are more skilful benefactors
> Than Hippocrates and the ancients.
> But to many, no hear me please,
> Your skill brings rest and ease:
> Though you may not cure disease
> At least you polish off the patients.

You can't say fairer than that.

BARTHOLO. What gives you, an ignorant horse-doctor, the right to denigrate the foremost, the greatest, the most beneficial of all the arts in this way?

COUNT. Tremendously beneficial—to those who practise it.

BARTHOLO. An art upon whose successes the sun is pleased to shine.

---

[1] Bartholo may cut short the description whenever he chooses.

COUNT. And whose blunders the earth is always pleased to bury.

BARTHOLO. You are a boor! It's quite obvious that you're only used to talking to horses.

COUNT. Talking to horses? Come, come, doctor. How can a clever man like yourself... Look, it's a well-known fact that a farrier always cures his patients without talking to them, while a doctor talks all the time to his patients...

BARTHOLO. Without curing them. Is that it?

COUNT. You said it, not me.

BARTHOLO. Who in hell landed this damned drunk on me?

COUNT. You say the sweetest things!

BARTHOLO. Look here, what do you want? What are you after?

COUNT [*pretending to be very angry*]. Right then, if you can lose your temper!... What am I after? Can't you tell what I'm after?

SCENE 14

ROSINE, *the* COUNT, BARTHOLO

ROSINE [*running in*]. Please, trooper, please don't lose your temper. [*To* BARTHOLO] Talk to him nicely. He doesn't know what he's saying.

COUNT. You're right. He doesn't know what he's talking about. But you and me, we know. Me dutiful, you beautiful... but that's enough of that. I'll be frank. You're the only person in this house I want to have anything to do with.

ROSINE. And how can I help, trooper?

COUNT. One small thing. But if what I say isn't clear...

ROSINE. I'll get your drift.

COUNT [*showing her the letter*]. No, stick to the letter of this letter. It just says... and I say this as an officer and a gentleman, that you've got to let me have a bed for the night.

BARTHOLO. Is that all?

COUNT. That's it. Here, read this tender epistle penned by my billeting officer.

[*He hides the letter and gives him another*

BARTHOLO. Let's have a look at this. [*Reads*] 'Doctor Bartholo will accommodate, feed, lodge, sleep...

COUNT [*underlining*]. ... in a bed...

BARTHOLO. '...for one night only, the above-mentioned Lindor, also known as Scholar, a cavalryman in the regiment of...

ROSINE. It's him! It's really him

BARTHOLO [*sharply, to* ROSINE]. What's that?

COUNT. Still say I've got it wrong, Doctor Barcarole?

BARTHOLO. Anyone would think the oaf gets some sort of perverted enjoyment from mangling my name in as many ways as he can. Just forget the Gardyloos and the Barcaroles and tell your impertinent officer that since my last trip to Madrid I've been exempted from having soldiers billeted on me.

COUNT [*aside*]. Damn! That's torn it!

BARTHOLO. Aha! That's put a spoke in your wheel, my friend! That's sobered you up. But you can clear off all the same.

COUNT [*aside*]. I thought I'd given the game away. [*Aloud*] Clear off? If you are exempt from billeting soldiers, are you also exempt from having a civil tongue? Clear off? Show me your certificate of exemption. I may not be able to read, but I'll soon see what's what.

BARTHOLO. Seeing it won't change anything. It's in this desk.

COUNT [*while* BARTHOLO *goes to the desk, he says, without moving from his place*]. Rosine! Lovely Rosine!

ROSINE. Are you really Lindor?

COUNT. Here, take this letter.

ROSINE. Be careful, he's watching us.

COUNT. Take out your handkerchief. I'll drop the note.

[*He takes a step towards her*

BARTHOLO. Hold it, soldier, not so fast. I don't like people staring at my wife from such close quarters.

COUNT. She's your wife?

BARTHOLO. And what of it?

COUNT. I thought you were her paternal, maternal, eternal great-grandfather. There must be at least three generations between her and you.

BARTHOLO [*reading a document*]. 'Pursuant to the sworn and faithful statements laid before us...'

COUNT [*he lunges at the documents, which cascade to the floor*]. I don't need any of that stupid drivel.

BARTHOLO. Do you realize, soldier, that if I call the servants I could have you dealt with here and now as you deserve?

COUNT. A fight! I'm your man. Fighting is my business and [*points to the pistol in his belt*] I've got what it takes to put the wind up them. Maybe you never saw a battle, Madame?

ROSINE. No, and I don't want to.

COUNT. But there's nothing more fun than a good battle. Picture the scene [*he pushes* BARTHOLO *out of the way*], the enemy is occupying one slope of the ravine and our side is on the other. [*To* ROSINE, *showing her the letter*] Get your handkerchief ready. [*He spits on the floor*]. That's the ravine, got it?

[ROSINE *gets out her handkerchief; the* COUNT *drops the letter between them*

BARTHOLO [*bends down and picks up the letter*]. Aha!

COUNT [*taking it from him*]. Well now, and just as I was about to tell you all my soldiering secrets... A virtuous wife, I must say. Isn't that a love letter that's just dropped out of her pocket?

BARTHOLO. Give it to me. Give it here.

COUNT. Easy does it, old man. What's private is private. What would you say if you'd dropped a prescription for senna pods?

ROSINE [*holding out her hand*]. It's all right, trooper, I know what it is.

[*She takes the letter and puts it in the pocket of her apron*

BARTHOLO. Are you going to leave?

COUNT. All right, all right, I'm going. Goodbye, Doctor, no hard feelings. My modest compliments, sweet lady. Pray that death forgets me for a few campaigns more. Life was never more dear to me.

BARTHOLO. Just go. If I had that sort of influence with Death...

COUNT. Influence? But you're a doctor. With all you do for Death, is there anything it could refuse you?

[*He goes*

SCENE 15

BARTHOLO, ROSINE

BARTHOLO [*watches him leave*]. There, he's gone at last. [*Aside*] I shall pretend to be nice.

ROSINE. Still, you must admit that he was very amusing for a soldier. Drunk he might have been, but you couldn't help noticing that he was really quite clever, and educated too.

BARTHOLO. I'm so relieved, my dear, that we managed to get rid of him. But aren't you just the tiniest bit curious for us to read the letter he gave you?

ROSINE. What letter?

BARTHOLO. The one he pretended to pick up so that he could hand it to you?

ROSINE. Oh, that! It's a letter from my cousin, the one in the army. It fell out of my pocket.

BARTHOLO. I had the impression he took it out of his.

ROSINE. I recognized it.

BARTHOLO. Where's the harm in just glancing at it?

ROSINE. I'm not sure what I've done with it.

BARTHOLO [*pointing to her pocket*]. You put it in there.

ROSINE. I must have done so without thinking.

BARTHOLO. Of course you did. It'll be some nonsense or other, you'll see...

ROSINE [*aside*]. Unless I make him lose his temper, I won't have any excuse for saying no.

BARTHOLO. Give it to me, my dear.

ROSINE. Do you have some reason for being so insistent? Is it because you still don't trust me?

BARTHOLO. Is there some reason why you won't show it to me?

ROSINE. I've already told you, sir. The letter is from my cousin, the one you gave me yesterday after you'd opened it. And since we're on the subject, let me say plainly that it's a liberty and I resent it intensely.

BARTHOLO. I don't follow you.

ROSINE. Do I open the letters that come for you? Why do you presume to interfere with those that are sent to me? If you do it because you are jealous, I think it's insulting. If you do it as a way of abusing your authority over me, I find it even more revolting.

BARTHOLO. What do you mean, revolting? You never talked to me like this before.

ROSINE. If I have never spoken out before now, it wasn't because I was prepared to let you walk all over me and never answer back.

BARTHOLO. Walk all over you? What do you mean?

ROSINE. It's intolerable that one persons thinks he has the right to open somebody else's letters.

BARTHOLO. Not even his wife's letters?

ROSINE. I'm not your wife yet. But why do you think it's all right to subject a wife to an indignity which you wouldn't inflict on anyone else?

BARTHOLO. You're just trying to confuse the issue so you can divert my attention from the letter, which is no doubt a message from your lover. But rest assured, see it I will!

ROSINE. You won't see it. If you come near me, I'll leave this house for good and ask the first person I meet to take me in.

BARTHOLO. No one will take you in.

ROSINE. We'll see about that.

BARTHOLO. Look, this isn't France, where women always get their own way. But I'll put a stop to all these silly notions: I'm going to lock the front door.

ROSINE [as he leaves]. Oh God! What shall I do?... Quick, switch the note for my cousin's letter, and make it easy, but not too easy, for him to find it.

[She makes the switch and leaves her cousin's letter protruding slightly from her pocket

BARTHOLO [returning]. And now I insist on reading it.

ROSINE. What gives you the right?

BARTHOLO. The oldest right in the world: the right of the strong.

ROSINE. If you want it, you'll have to kill me first.

BARTHOLO [stamping his foot]. Come, Madame!

ROSINE [collapses on to a chair and pretends to faint]. Oh! It's an outrage!

BARTHOLO. Give me the letter. Don't make me angry or I won't be responsible for the consequences!

ROSINE [prostrate]. I'm so unhappy!

BARTHOLO. Why, what's the matter with you?

ROSINE. What future is there for me?

BARTHOLO. Rosine!

ROSINE. I'm so angry I could choke!

BARTHOLO. She's really ill!

ROSINE. I feel faint! I think I'm dying!

BARTHOLO [*aside*]. Ah! the letter! I'll read it now and she'll never know.

[*He takes her pulse and reaches for the letter, turning slightly to one side as he tries to read it*

ROSINE [*still prostrate*]. I'm so miserable!

BARTHOLO [*releasing her wrist and muttering to himself*]. Why is it that we always insist on knowing what we most fear to learn?

ROSINE. Poor Rosine!

BARTHOLO. Using perfume... can bring on sudden attacks like this.

[*He reads the letter behind the chair as he takes her pulse.* ROSINE *raises her head slightly, looks at him out of the corner of her eye, gives a satisfied nod, and resumes her position without saying a word*

BARTHOLO [*aside*]. Oh no! It's her cousin's letter after all! I'm a fool to worry the way I do. How can I put things right with her now? At least, she mustn't know I've read it.

[*He makes a show of helping her to sit up and slips the letter back into her pocket*

ROSINE [*sighing*]. Oo–aah!

BARTHOLO. There, my dear, it was nothing. Just a touch of the vapours, that's all. Your pulse has stayed steady as a rock.

[*He goes to fetch a bottle from the sideboard*

ROSINE [*aside*]. He's put the letter back. My plan worked!

BARTHOLO. Rosine, my dear, try a sip of this brandy.

ROSINE. I don't want anything from you. Let me be.

BARTHOLO. I admit I may have got a little too worked up about the letter.

ROSINE. The letter's not important. It's the way you demand things that's so obnoxious.

BARTHOLO [*kneels*]. Please forgive me. I soon realized how utterly wrong I was. Look, I'm on my knees, begging for a chance to make amends.

ROSINE. Forgive you? When you still don't believe that the letter is from my cousin?

BARTHOLO. Whether it's from him or somebody else, I don't want to know.

ROSINE [*handing him the letter*]. You see, if you ask nicely, you can get me to do anything. Read it.

BARTHOLO. Your frankness would remove all my suspicions, if I was still foolish enough to have any.

ROSINE. Read it, sir. I insist.

BARTHOLO [*rising to his feet*]. God forbid I should ever offend you by doing any such thing.

ROSINE. A refusal will make me cross.

BARTHOLO. Take it as my penance, a mark of my complete trust in you. I'm going to see poor Marceline. Figaro, for some reason that's beyond me, bled her in the foot. Won't you come with me?

ROSINE. I'll come in a little while.

BARTHOLO. Since we've made peace, my dearest girl, give me your hand. If only you could love me, how happy you would be!

ROSINE [*looking at the floor*]. If only you could make me love you, oh how I would love you!

BARTHOLO. I will make you love me, I will! And I really mean it!

[*He leaves*

ROSINE [*watching him go*]. Oh, Lindor! He says he'll make me love him... But let's see what's in this note that caused all the fuss. [*She reads it, then exclaims*] Oh no! I should have read it sooner. He says I'm to pick a quarrel with my guardian and make it last. I had one, it was perfect, and now I've let it go. When he gave me the note, I felt my cheeks blush bright red. Oh, my guardian is right. I'm still a million miles from the sophistication which, so he tells

me, helps a woman to rise above any situation. But a man who's a
tyrant would turn the most innocent girl in the world into a
scheming, wicked woman!

ACT III

SCENE 1

BARTHOLO, *alone and dejected*

BARTHOLO. What's got into her! So unpredictable! I thought she'd calmed down... I wish someone would tell me who put it into her head that she wasn't going to have any more lessons from Don Bazile. She's found out he's got something to do with the marriage... [*There is a knock at the door*] You do everything to keep a woman's hat straight, but if you forget one little thing, just one... [*Another knock*] I'd better go and see who that is.

SCENE 2

BARTHOLO, *the* COUNT *wearing scholar's robes*

COUNT. Peace and joy to all who dwell beneath this roof from this day forth.

BARTHOLO [*crossly*]. A blessing which couldn't have come at a better time. What do you want?

COUNT. My name, sir, is Alonzo, student, graduate with honours...

BARTHOLO. I'm not in the market for private tutors.

COUNT. ... pupil of Don Bazile, organist at the Abbey, who is privileged to teach the art of singing to your...

BARTHOLO. Bazile? Organist? Is privileged? Ah yes, I know all about this.

COUNT [*aside*]. What an awful man! [*Aloud*] A sudden indisposition has confined him to bed and...

BARTHOLO. Bazile, confined to bed? I'm glad he let me know. I shall go round and see him at once.

COUNT [*aside*]. Damn! [*Aloud*] When I said bed, sir, what I really meant was... to his room.

BARTHOLO. Whatever's wrong with him, it's keeping him at home. Lead on, I'll follow.

COUNT [*floundering*]. Sir, I was asked to... Can anyone hear us?

BARTHOLO [*aside*]. He's up to something. [*Aloud*] Hear us? No. You're being very mysterious. You can speak plainly—if, that is, you're capable of it...

COUNT [*aside*]. Damn the old buzzard. [*Aloud*] Don Bazile asked me to tell you...

BARTHOLO. Speak up. I'm deaf in this ear.

COUNT [*raising his voice*]. Certainly. To tell you that Count Almaviva, who was living in rooms on the main square...

BARTHOLO [*alarmed*]. Keep your voice down! Not so loud!

COUNT [*even louder*]. ... moved out this morning. Since it was through me that he learned that Count Almaviva...

BARTHOLO. Please, not so loud.

COUNT [*as before*]. ... was in town, and as it was I who found out that Señora Rosine had written him a letter...

BARTHOLO. Written him a letter? Will you please stop shouting, my dear fellow! Look let's sit down and talk this over like good friends. You say you found out that Rosine...

COUNT [*proudly*]. I did indeed! Bazile was worried about the implications there were for you in this correspondence and asked me to show you the letter. But, given the way you're reacting...

BARTHOLO. There's nothing wrong with the way I'm reacting. But couldn't you possibly speak more quietly?

COUNT. Didn't you say you were deaf in one ear?

BARTHOLO. Look, Señor Alonzo, I'm sorry if I seemed suspicious and rude. But I am surrounded on all sides by plots and plotters...You'll admit, though, your appearance, your age, your manner...I am truly sorry. I apologize. Now, did you bring the letter?

COUNT. That's better. I'm glad that you're taking it so well. But I'm still worried someone might be listening.

BARTHOLO. Who is there who could listen? All my servants are laid up. Rosine's gone off in a huff and shut herself in her room. I don't know what's got into the place. But I'll go and check again.

[*Goes and quietly opens* ROSINE's *door*

COUNT [*aside*]. I've dug a hole for myself. How can I avoid letting him see the letter now? There's only thing to do: get out of here. I wish I'd never come... Still, perhaps I could show it to him. In fact, if I can warn Rosine, showing it to him would be pure genius!

BARTHOLO [*returning on tiptoe*]. She's sitting by the window, with her back to the door, rereading a letter from her cousin who's in the army. I opened it earlier. Now let's have a look at hers.

COUNT [*giving him* ROSINE's *letter*]. Here it is [*Aside*] That's my letter she's reading.

BARTHOLO [*reads*]. 'Ever since you told me your name and said who you were...' What!! of all the sly...! And it's her writing. I recognize it.

COUNT [*alarmed*]. Now it's your turn to keep your voice down.

BARTHOLO. My dear fellow, however can I repay you?

COUNT. When it's all over and if you still feel that I've been of assistance, that would be of course entirely up to you... According to enquiries which Don Bazile is pursuing with a lawyer...

BARTHOLO. A lawyer? He's consulting a lawyer about my marriage?

COUNT. Of course. He instructed me to inform you that everything will be ready by tomorrow. So, if she won't go along with it...

BARTHOLO. She won't.

COUNT [*tries to take the letter back but* BARTHOLO *grips it firmly*]. It's at that point that I can be of help. We'll show her the letter and, if it becomes necessary, [*conspiratorially*] I shall say I got it from another woman who'd been given it by the Count to prove his love to her. It's not hard to imagine in which direction the hurt, the shame, her outraged feelings will take her...

BARTHOLO [*laughing*]. Slander! My dear boy, now I know you really were sent by Bazile... But if all this is not to look as if it were all arranged in advance, wouldn't it be a good idea if she were to meet you beforehand?

COUNT [*restraining his delight*]. That was more or less what Don Bazile said. But how are we going to manage it? It's rather late... there's not much time left.

BARTHOLO. I'll say that you've come instead of him. You wouldn't mind giving her a lesson?

COUNT. I'd do anything you asked. But aren't you overlooking something? The bogus tutor-cum-singing-teacher ploy is pretty long in the tooth, a comedy cliché. What if she gets suspicious?

BARTHOLO. Suspicious of someone vouched for by me? Is that likely? You look much more like a lover in disguise than a helpful friend.

COUNT. You really think so? You think the way I look will help with the deception?

BARTHOLO. It would need someone with very sharp eyes to see through you. She's in a foul mood tonight. But if she just caught one glimpse of you, that would be enough for our purposes. Her harpsichord is in this room. Keep yourself amused while you wait. I'll try everything I can to persuade her to come.

COUNT. Whatever you do, don't mention the letter.

BARTHOLO. Before the crucial moment? That would spoil the whole effect. There's no need to tell me the same thing twice! So don't tell me the same thing twice!

[*He leaves*

SCENE 3

The COUNT, *alone*

COUNT. Saved! Phew! The old devil is so tricky to handle. Figaro was absolutely right about him. I could hear myself telling lies: I must have looked so stupid and shifty. And those eyes of his! I'll say this though: if it hadn't been for that sudden brainwave about the letter, I'd have been shown the door like a complete idiot. Oh Lord! They're quarrelling in there. What if she digs her heels in and refuses to come? Let's listen... She says she won't leave her room, which means that my cunning plan isn't going to get me anywhere. [*He listens again*] She's coming! Best not be around when she gets here.

[*He goes into the music room*

SCENE 4

The COUNT, ROSINE, BARTHOLO

ROSINE [*pretending to be angry*]. You can say what you like, sir, it won't do any good. I've made up my mind. I won't hear another word about singing lessons.

BARTHOLO. Listen, my dear, it's Señor Alonzo, a pupil and friend of Don Bazile who's chosen him to be one of our witnesses tomorrow. The music will calm you down, I guarantee it.

ROSINE. Me, sing this evening? You can put that idea out of your head at once... Anyway, where is this singing-teacher you seem too scared to send packing? I'll give him his marching orders, and Bazile too. It won't take long. [*She catches sight of the* COUNT *and gives a shriek*] Oh!

BARTHOLO. What is it?

ROSINE [*with both hands on her heart, in obvious distress*]. Oh my God, it's... Doctor Bartholo... Oh my God!

BARTHOLO. She's having a relapse... Señor Alonzo...

ROSINE. I'm not having a relapse. It's just when I turned... ouch!

COUNT. You twisted your ankle, Madame?

ROSINE. That's it, I turned on my ankle. And it hurt like anything.

COUNT. I could see that.

ROSINE [*looks the* COUNT *in the eye*]. I felt it here, in my heart.

BARTHOLO. A chair, a chair! Why aren't there any chairs here?

[*He goes out to get one*

COUNT. Oh Rosine!

ROSINE. You're mad to take such risks!

COUNT. There are so many absolutely vital things I must tell you.

ROSINE. He won't leave us alone together.

COUNT. Figaro's coming. He'll help us out.

BARTHOLO [*bringing a chair*]. Here, my sweet, sit down on this. Señor Alonzo, it doesn't look as if she'll be wanting a singing lesson this evening. We'll have to leave it for another day. Goodbye.

ROSINE [*to the* COUNT]. Don't go. The pain seems to be easing. [*To* BARTHOLO] I feel I behaved very badly to you. I'd like to follow your example and make amends here and now...

BARTHOLO. Ah, women are such sweet creatures underneath! But after what you've been through, my dear, you mustn't strain yourself. I won't hear of it. Goodbye, young man, goodbye.

ROSINE [*to the* COUNT]. Just one moment, please. [*To* BARTHOLO] Sir, I shall conclude that you aren't interested in what I want if you won't let me prove how truly sorry I am by having my lesson.

COUNT [*aside to* BARTHOLO]. If you want my opinion, you'd best let her have her way.

BARTHOLO. Very well, I won't insist, my sweet. And far from opposing whatever makes you happy, I shall stay here the entire time while you have your lesson.

ROSINE. Oh, there's no need for that, sir! I know you can't stand music.

BARTHOLO. I assure you that tonight it will have charms!

ROSINE [*aside to the* COUNT]. This is agony.

COUNT [*picking up a score from the music stand*]. Is this the piece you're going to sing, Madame?

ROSINE. Yes. It's rather nice. It's from *The Pointless Precaution*.

BARTHOLO. Not *The Pointless Precaution* again!

COUNT. It's the very latest thing. It captures the essence of spring-time in the most affecting way. If the young lady would care to try it?

ROSINE [*staring at the* COUNT]. With pleasure. The essence of springtime, it sounds divine. Spring, when nature becomes young again. As we emerge from winter, our hearts grow lighter—like the slave released from a long captivity who savours his new freedom.

BARTHOLO [*aside to the* COUNT]. Her head's still full of these silly notions.

COUNT [*whispering back*]. You do get the point, though?

BARTHOLO. Damned if I do.

[*He sits in the chair vacated by* ROSINE

ROSINE [*sings*].[1]

(NO. 3)

When love brings again
Fresh green to the plain,
Spring starts to sing,
Revives her domain
And gives life to each thing.
Her warmth she imparts
To flowers and hearts.
Flocks now abound
From hamlet to mound;
The hills all around

---

[1] This song, written in the Spanish style, was sung at the first Paris performance despite the jeers, booing, and the usual reaction of the pit in this age of crisis and confrontation. The actress was too frightened to sing it in later performances and the young theatre purists were loud in praise of her reticence. But if the dignity of the Comédie Française was the gainer, it must be admitted that *The Barber of Seville* was the loser. Which is why, when it is played in theatres where the occasional use of music does not rouse such high passions, we would encourage managers to include it, audiences to listen to it, critics to forgive the author, and all to bear in mind what kind of play this is and the enjoyment the piece will give to those who see it.

Echo with sound
Of lambs as they bound.
The sap starts to rise
And all multiplies.
Ewes are grazing
On flowers amazing,
While dogs ever faithful
Are constantly watchful.
But Lindor in bliss
Dreams only of this:
Will his sweet shepherdess
Bring a lover's caress?

Second verse

In her pretty Spring dress
Far from home roaming,
She sings in the gloaming
To where he lies waiting.
And so in this way
Love leads her astray.
But will singing dispel
That dangerous spell?
The sweet sound of pipes
The birdsong's delights,
The bloom and the sheen
Of a girl of sixteen—
All this excites her:
Her fate now invites her.
The poor girl's trembling.
Lindor, who's hiding,
Watches her coming.
As she draws near
See him appear!
Look, now he has kissed her,
And not like a sister!
But though she's not loth
She feigns a great wrath
And so her bold suitor
Must needs now placate her

Chorus

He gives her full measure
Of sighs and caresses,
And generous promises
Of sweetness and pleasure,
The whole range exhausting
Of pleasing and teasing.
And soon the young maid
Is no longer dismayed.
Should some jealous swain
Mar their happy refrain,
Our passionate pair
Would take every care...
To hide their emotion.
Yet love is not frightened,
For with every commotion
The pleasure is heightened.

As he listens, BARTHOLO *nods off. During the chorus, the* COUNT *reaches tentatively for* ROSINE's *hand and smothers it with kisses. The effect is to makes her sing more slowly, she falters and her voice breaks in the middle of her phrase at the words 'every care'. The orchestra, following her lead, also falters then stops when she does. The absence of the sounds which sent* BARTHOLO *to sleep, wakes him. The* COUNT *straightens up and* ROSINE *and the orchestra immediately resume and finish the song. If the chorus is to be repeated, it will be accompanied by the same stage business*

COUNT. Now that really is a most charming piece and Madame sang it with such intelligence, such...

ROSINE. You flatter me, sir. The credit is due entirely to you as my teacher.

BARTHOLO [*yawning*]. I must have dropped off for a moment during the performance. It was delightful. That's what having so many patients does for you. Dashing here, rushing there, always on the go. Then the minute I sit down, my poor legs...

[*He stands and pushes his chair back*

ROSINE [*whispers to the* COUNT]. Figaro hasn't come.

COUNT. We'll have to play for time.

BARTHOLO. Look here, young fellow, I've already asked old Bazile if there isn't a way of getting her to study something jollier than all these grand arias that go up high and then down low and have all those twiddly bits in between, hi hi, lo lo, oo-ah-oo, oo-ah-oo. They all sound like funeral dirges to me. You know, the sort of thing we used to sing when I was a lad, with tunes everybody could remember. There was one I used to know... how does it go?

While the accompaniment plays the introduction, he scratches his head for the words, snapping his fingers and dancing without moving his feet, the way old men do

> Won't you, sweetest Rosinette
> Cast your eye this way, my pet:
> A Prince of hubbies, that's what one is...

[*Turns to the* COUNT *and laughs*

It was Fanchonnette in the song, but I changed it and put Rosinette instead, so that it would be more fun for her and fit in with the present circumstances. Ha ha ha! Not bad, eh?

COUNT [*laughing*]. Ha ha ha! Marvellous! Wonderful!

SCENE 5

FIGARO, *at the back of the stage*, ROSINE, BARTHOLO, *the* COUNT

BARTHOLO [*sings*].

NO. 4

> Won't you, darling Rosinette
> Cast your eye this way, my pet:
> A Prince of hubbies, that's what one is,
> I may be no Adonis,
> But when it's night and black as pitch
> Then I'm at my handsomest.
> When lights are out, do not ask which

Cat is best,
For in the dark all cats are grey.

He repeats the last six lines, dancing as he sings. Behind him, FIGARO
imitates his movements

'I may be no Adonis...' [*Suddenly he sees* FIGARO] Ah! Enter, O
Prince of Barbers! Do come in! Still as charming as ever?

FIGARO [*bowing*]. Well, sir, that's exactly what my old mother always
used to say, though I've gone off a bit since those days. [*Aside to the*
COUNT] Well played, your Lordship.

For the rest of this scene, the COUNT *tries every way he can to speak to*
ROSINE *but is constantly thwarted by her guardian's alert and*
watchful eye. The result is a wordless pantomime which is carried on
among all the players, regardless of the dialogue between the
DOCTOR *and* FIGARO

BARTHOLO. Have you come to purge, bleed, drug, and put all my
servants on their backs again?

FIGARO. No one can live entirely for pleasure, sir. But setting aside
my routine duties, it will not have escaped your notice that whenever my services are required, my dedication does not wait upon
your orders.

BARTHOLO. Not wait upon my orders! If you're so dedicated, what
are you going to tell the poor devil who's walking around yawning
and half-asleep when he's supposed to be wide awake? Or the
wretch who for the last three hours has been sneezing fit to split
his skull and spill his brains out on the floor? What'll you say to
them?

FIGARO. What will I say?

BARTHOLO. Yes, what?

FIGARO. I'll say... er... Lord, yes! I'll say 'God bless you' to the
one who's sneezing and 'Go to bed' to the one who's yawning.
Don't worry, sir, it won't appear on the bill.

BARTHOLO. I should think not. But the bleeding and the medicine
will—over my dead body! And I suppose it was with the same

dedication that you bandaged up the eyes of my mule? Will your poultice make it see again?

FIGARO. If it doesn't bring its sight back, that won't be why it can't see—the blindfold will take care of that.

BARTHOLO. Just you try putting that on the bill. I'm not the sort who likes throwing money away.

FIGARO. The way I see it, sir, a man can only choose between being stupid or mad. So when I can't see a profit, I go for pleasure. Enjoy life, that's what I say! Who knows if we'll still be here three weeks from now?

BARTHOLO. Instead of standing there philosophizing you'd be better advised to pay me my hundred crowns, with interest, and stop all this nonsense. I'm warning you.

FIGARO. You're not casting aspersions on my honesty, sir? Your hundred crowns! I'd rather go on owing you the money for the rest of my life than refuse for one single moment to pay it back.

BARTHOLO. All right, then tell me this. How did your little girl like the sweets you took her?

FIGARO. Sweets? What do you mean?

BARTHOLO. I mean sweets. This morning. The ones in a bag made from a sheet of notepaper.

FIGARO. I'm damned if I know...

ROSINE [intervening]. I hope at least you remembered to give them to her and say they were from me, Monsieur Figaro. I did ask you to.

FIGARO. Oh, *those* sweets! This morning! What am I thinking of? Went clean out of my head... They were excellent, Madame, splendid.

BARTHOLO. Excellent! Splendid! That's right, barber, paper over your mistakes! You dabble in a murky business, sir.

FIGARO. In what way murky, sir?

BARTHOLO. And it won't do your reputation any good, sir!

FIGARO. I shall live up to it, sir.

BARTHOLO. Say that you will try to live it down, sir.

FIGARO. Your wish is my command, sir.

BARTHOLO. I don't like your tone, sir! Remember this: when I get into an argument with an overbearing ninny, I never back down.

FIGARO. That's where we differ. I always give in.

BARTHOLO. Eh? What's he getting at, Señor Alonzo?

FIGARO. You seem to think you're dealing with some village barber who's good for nothing but plying a razor. I'll have you know that when I was in Madrid I wielded a pen, and if it hadn't been for the resentment of...

BARTHOLO. So why didn't you stay there, instead of coming here and taking up another line of work?

FIGARO. We can only do our best. Put yourself in my shoes.

BARTHOLO. Put myself in your shoes? My God, if I did that, I'd talk complete rubbish.

FIGARO. I'd say you've made a pretty good start already. Perhaps I could ask your colleague here, who's got his head in the clouds, to adjudicate.

COUNT [*with a start*]. I... er... I'm not Doctor Bartholo's colleague.

FIGARO. Really? I just thought, seeing you in the middle of a diagnosis, that you were in the same business.

BARTHOLO [*furiously*]. Look, what have you come for? You don't have yet another letter to deliver to Mademoiselle Rosine tonight, do you? Well? Would you like me to leave?

FIGARO. Are you always so rude to people? Look, Doctor, I've come to shave you, that's all. Today is your day, isn't it?

BARTHOLO. Come back later.

FIGARO. Later? Can't be done. I've got to purge the entire garrison for worms in the morning. I landed the job through my contacts.

So I haven't got time to waste. If you would like to step into your consulting room, sir...

BARTHOLO. No, I would not like to step into my consulting room! What's stopping you shaving me here?

ROSINE [*scornfully*]. Where are your manners? Why not in my bedroom?

BARTHOLO. You're angry. I'm sorry, my dear, you shall finish your lesson. It's just that I don't want to miss a single moment of the pleasure it gives me to hear you sing.

FIGARO [*aside to the* COUNT]. There's no way of getting him out of here. [*Calling*] Wakeful! Old Youthful! Basin, hot water, bring all the gentleman's shaving things.

BARTHOLO. Go ahead, call them! They were so shattered, jiggered, and ground-down after you'd finished with them that they had to be put to bed.

FIGARO. No problem. I'll go and fetch it all myself. It's in your room, isn't it? [*Aside to the* COUNT] I'll try to lure him away.

BARTHOLO [*takes out his bunch of keys and then changes his mind*]. On second thoughts, I'll go myself. [*Aside to the* COUNT *as he leaves*] Keep an eye on these two for me, would you?

SCENE 6

FIGARO, *the* COUNT, ROSINE

FIGARO. Damn, and we were nearly there. He was about to hand over the whole bunch. The shutter key's on it, I assume?

ROSINE. It's the shiny new one.

SCENE 7

BARTHOLO, FIGARO, *the* COUNT, ROSINE

BARTHOLO [*to himself as he returns*]. Where are your brains, leaving that crafty barber here? [*Handing* FIGARO *the keys*] Here you are.

In my consulting room, desk, bottom drawer—and don't touch anything.

FIGARO. Oh for goodness sake! Anyway, there wouldn't be much point, you're not likely to leave anything lying about. [*To himself as he goes*] Thank you, Lord, for looking after your own!

SCENE 8

BARTHOLO, *the* COUNT, ROSINE

BARTHOLO [*whispers to the* COUNT]. That's the buffoon who brought the letter from the Count.

COUNT [*whispers back*]. He looks like a nasty piece of work to me.

BARTHOLO. But he won't pull any more wool over my eyes.

COUNT. As far as that's concerned, I'd say the worst is over.

BARTHOLO. On balance, I thought it safer to send him off to my room rather than leave him here with her.

COUNT. They couldn't have said a word to each other without my hearing.

ROSINE. It's not polite to whisper. What about my lesson?

[*At this moment, we hear a noise of crockery breaking*

BARTHOLO [*shouting*]. What the devil's that noise? That damned barber's dropped the lot down the stairs, all the finest china in my shaving kit!.

[*He rushes out*

SCENE 9

The COUNT, ROSINE

COUNT. Figaro is brilliant! But let's make the most of the opportunity he's given us. Please, you must agree to talk to me later tonight. It's vital that we speak if you are to be saved from a life of slavery: you are on the brink!

ROSINE. Oh, Lindor!

COUNT. I can climb up to your balcony. One other thing. The letter I received from you this morning, well, I was forced to...

SCENE 10

ROSINE, BARTHOLO, FIGARO, *the* COUNT

BARTHOLO. I was right. The whole set is broken, smashed to pieces.

FIGARO. That's what happens when people make a such a fuss about things. You can't see your hand in front of your face on those stairs. [*He shows the* COUNT *the key*] As I was going up, I was trying to find the right key and tripped.

BARTHOLO. You should pay more attention to what you're doing. Trying to find the key and tripped! And you think you're so smart!

FIGARO. You'd have your work cut out to find anyone smarter!

SCENE 11

ROSINE, BARTHOLO, FIGARO, *the* COUNT, *and* BAZILE

ROSINE [*alarmed*]. Don Bazile!

COUNT [*aside*]. Oh my God!

FIGARO [*aside*]. It's the old devil himself!

BARTHOLO [*goes towards* BAZILE]. Bazile, old friend! It's so good to see you up and about. Are you quite over your little upset? I don't mind telling you, I was rather anxious when Señor Alonzo told me you were ill. Ask him—I was about to come and see you, and if he hadn't stopped me...

BAZILE [*bewildered*]. Who's Señor Alonzo?

FIGARO [*stamping his foot*]. I don't believe this! Not more delay! How can it take two hours to give a man a shave?... It's no way to earn a living!

BAZILE [*eyeing them*]. Would you gentlemen be kind enough to tell me...

FIGARO. You can tell him all about it when I've gone.

BAZILE. But I really must...

COUNT. Shut up, that's what you really must do, Bazile. You don't seriously think you can tell Doctor Bartholo anything he doesn't know already? I've already explained that you asked me to come here and give the singing lesson instead of you.

BAZILE [*even more bewildered*]. Singing lesson? Alonzo?

ROSINE [*aside to* BAZILE]. Oh just be quiet!

BAZILE. Now she's at it too!

COUNT [*whispers to* BARTHOLO]. Look, you must tell him that we're agreed. And whisper!

BARTHOLO [*whispering*]. Look here, Bazile, you'll give the show away if you say he isn't your pupil. You'll ruin everything.

BAZILE. Eh?

BARTHOLO [*aloud*]. I'll say this much, Bazile: that's an extremely talented pupil you've got there.

BAZILE [*stupefied*]. Pupil?... [*Whispers*] I came to tell you the Count has moved out of his rooms.

BARTHOLO [*whispers*]. I know. Now shut up.

BAZILE [*whispers*]. Who told you?

BARTHOLO [*whispers*]. He did, of course.

COUNT [*whispers*]. I did. Who else? Don't say anything: just listen.

ROSINE [*whispers to* BAZILE]. Why is it so difficult for you to keep quiet?

FIGARO [*whispers to* BAZILE]. Moron! Are you deaf?

BAZILE [*to himself*]. I'm damned if I know who's deceiving who here. They're all in it together.

BARTHOLO [*aloud*]. Now, Bazile, what did your lawyer have to say?

FIGARO. You've got all night to tell us about the lawyer.

BARTHOLO [*to* BAZILE]. One word will do. Just tell me if you're happy with the lawyer.

BAZILE [*bewildered*]. Lawyer?

COUNT [*smiling*]. Didn't you see the lawyer?

BAZILE [*impatiently*]. No. I didn't see any lawyer.

COUNT [*whispers to* BARTHOLO]. You're not going to allow him to let the cat out of the bag in front of Rosine? Make him go away.

BARTHOLO [*whispers to the* COUNT]. You're right. [*To* BAZILE] Look, what's got into you?

BAZILE [*angry*]. What are you talking about?

COUNT [*furtively slipping a purse into his hand*]. Doctor Bartholo is only asking why you came here at all when you're obviously a sick man.

FIGARO. He looks like death warmed up.

BAZILE. Ah, now I'm with you!

COUNT. Bed's the place for you, Bazile. You're not well. We're all extremely concerned. Go home to bed.

FIGARO. I don't like the look of your face. Go home to bed.

BARTHOLO. Honestly, anyone can see you've got a temperature a mile off. Go home to bed.

ROSINE. Why did you come here? You're probably contagious. Go home to bed.

BAZILE [*completely flummoxed*]. You want me to go home to bed?

ALL. Yes!!

BAZILE [*looking at them*]. Now that you mention it, I think it best if I did go. I'm not feeling my usual self.

BARTHOLO. I'll see you tomorrow, as arranged. Provided you're better.

COUNT. Bazile, I'll be at your house first thing in the morning.

FIGARO. Take my advice. Stay in bed and keep warm.

ROSINE. Goodnight, Monsieur Bazile.

BAZILE [*aside*]. I'm damned if I understand any of this, and if it weren't for the money...

ALL. Goodnight, Bazile, goodnight.

BAZILE [*as he goes*]. All right, all right! Goodnight, then, goodnight all.

[*They see him out, laughing*

SCENE 12

BARTHOLO, ROSINE, *the* COUNT, FIGARO

BARTHOLO [*pompously*]. There's a man who's not at all well.

ROSINE. He had such a strange look in his eyes.

COUNT. I expect he caught a chill.

FIGARO. Did you notice the way he kept talking to himself? Still, it's the sort of thing that could happen to any of us... [*To* BARTHOLO] Well now, have you finally made up your mind?

[*He pushes the chair well away from the* COUNT *and holds the protective towel up for him*

COUNT. Before we finish, Madame, there are one or two important comments I'd like to make about your progress in the art which I have the honour of teaching you.

[*He steps close to her and whispers in her ear*

BARTHOLO [*to* FIGARO]. Just a moment! I have this feeling that you're deliberately standing so close in front of me to prevent me from seeing...

COUNT [*whispers to* ROSINE]. We've got the key to the shutter. We'll be here at midnight.

FIGARO [*tucks the towel under* BARTHOLO'*s chin*]. Seeing what? If it was a dancing lesson, I wouldn't wonder if you wanted to look. But this is singing... Oh! Ow!

BARTHOLO. What's the matter?

FIGARO. I've got something in my eye.

> [*He puts his head in* BARTHOLO'*s face*

BARTHOLO. Don't rub it.

FIGARO. It's the left one. Would you do me a favour and blow on it, hard?

BARTHOLO *takes* FIGARO'*s head in his hands, looks over the top of it, pushes him away roughly, creeps up behind the lovers and listens to their conversation*

COUNT. About your letter. A little earlier, I was having problems looking for some excuse to avoid leaving and...

FIGARO [*warning them from a distance*]. Ahem! Ahem!

COUNT. I was mortified to see that my new disguise wasn't working any better than the first...

BARTHOLO [*steps between them*]. Your disguise not working?

ROSINE [*startled*]. Oh!

BARTHOLO. That's right, Miss, don't mind me. What! How dare you carry on in this outrageous manner in front of me, before my very eyes?

COUNT. Whatever is the matter, Doctor Bartholo?

BARTHOLO. You've got a nerve, Alonzo.

COUNT. My dear Doctor, if you are in the habit of having delusions such as the one I am now, by chance, observing, then I'm not the least surprised that Mademoiselle Rosine should be so reluctant to become your wife.

ROSINE. His what! His wife? And spend the rest of my days with a jealous old man who thinks he can make a girl happy by offering her the hideous prospect of being sentenced to slavery for life?

BARTHOLO. What did you say?

ROSINE. I'll say it again, and I don't care who hears! I will give my heart and my hand to the first man who rescues me from this terrible prison, where I and everything I own are kept under lock and key, although it's against the law.

> [*She walks out*

SCENE 13

BARTHOLO, FIGARO, *the* COUNT

BARTHOLO. I'm so angry I could choke!

COUNT. Still, Doctor, it must be very difficult for a girl to...

FIGARO. That's right. A young woman and old age, it's enough to ruin any elderly husband's peace of mind.

BARTHOLO. What? But I caught them red-handed! Damn you, barber, just let me get my hands on you...

FIGARO. I'd better go. He's mad.

COUNT. I'll come with you. You're right, he *is* mad.

FIGARO. He's mad! Mad as a hatter!

[*They leave*

SCENE 14

BARTHOLO. *He runs after them, then stops*

BARTHOLO. Mad am I? Interfering, scheming weasels, sent by the devil to do his work! I hope he gets you in the end!... Mad am I? I saw them as clearly as I can see this table... and the way they tried to brazen it out... Wait a moment, Bazile is the only one who can explain what's been going on... Yes, I'll send for him... Hello! Look alive there!... Damn, I was forgetting, there's no one about... A neighbour, a passer-by, it doesn't matter who. Enough to drive anyone mad, it is! It's enough to drive anyone mad!

During the interval, the stage lights dim. There is the sound of a storm and the orchestra plays piece No. 5 in the printed score to The Barber

ACT IV

SCENE 1

The stage is in darkness. BARTHOLO, BAZILE

BARTHOLO. What do you mean, Bazile, you never saw him before? How can you possibly say that?

BAZILE [*he is carrying a paper lantern*]. You can ask me as many times as you like, and you'd still get the same answer. If he showed you the letter from Rosine, he'd obviously been sent by the Count. But judging by the size of the purse he gave me, he could easily be the Count himself.

BARTHOLO. Is that likely? But now you mention the money, why did you take it?

BAZILE. I had this impression you wanted me to. I hadn't a clue what was going on. And whenever a situation is hard to work out, I always think a purse full of money is a pretty conclusive argument. Besides, you know the proverb: a bird in the hand...

BARTHOLO. I know: is worth two in the bush.

BAZILE. ... lays golden eggs.

BARTHOLO [*taken aback*]. Oh!

BAZILE. Yes, I've modernized a number of those old sayings, with variations. But let's get on with it. What's your plan?

BARTHOLO. If you were me, Bazile, wouldn't you do your damnedest to make her your own?

BAZILE. Heavens no, Doctor! With property of any sort, ownership isn't important: it's the enjoyment you get out of what you own that gives the satisfaction. In my view, marrying a woman who doesn't love you leaves you exposed to...

BARTHOLO. You'd be afraid things might go wrong?

BAZILE. Look around, you. There's a lot of that sort of thing about these days. I wouldn't try to force her, not against her will.

BARTHOLO. I don't agree, Bazile. I'd rather see her cry because she had me than die myself because I couldn't have her.

BAZILE. If it's a matter of life and death, marry the girl, Doctor, marry her.

BARTHOLO. I intend to—I'll do it this very night.

BAZILE. I'll say goodbye, then. And remember: when you speak about them to your ward, make them sound blacker than the devil himself.

BARTHOLO. You're right.

BAZILE. Slander, Doctor, slander. It always comes down to that in the end.

BARTHOLO. Here's the letter from Rosine, the one Alonzo gave me. And though he didn't realize it, he showed me how I could use it against her.

BAZILE. Goodbye. We'll all meet here at four.

BARTHOLO. Why not earlier?

BAZILE. Can't be done. The notary has a previous appointment.

BARTHOLO. Another wedding?

BAZILE. Yes. At that barber Figaro's house. His niece is getting married.

BARTHOLO. His niece? He doesn't have a niece.

BAZILE. That's what he told the notary.

BARTHOLO. The villain's in the plot! Damn!

BAZILE. So what do you think?

BARTHOLO. By God, these people don't let the grass grow under their feet! Listen, old friend, I'm not too happy about this. Go to the notary and get him to come back here with you at once.

BAZILE. It's raining. I wouldn't send a dog out in it myself, but nothing will stop me if I can be of service to us. What are you doing?

BARTHOLO. I'm going to see you to the door—with Figaro's help, they've put all the servants out of action. I'm on my own in the house.

BAZILE. I've got my lantern.

BARTHOLO. Here, take my master-key, Bazile. I'll be watching out for you. I'll wait up. They can all come, but except for the notary and you, nobody's going to get through my front door tonight.

BAZILE. With all these precautions, you should be quite safe.

[*They both leave*

SCENE 2

ROSINE, *emerging from her room*

ROSINE. I thought I heard voices. It's after midnight and Lindor hasn't come. Even this awful weather was on his side. He'd be unlikely to meet anyone... Oh Lindor!... If you've deceived me!... What's that noise?... Oh no, it's my guardian! Quick, back to my room!

SCENE 3

ROSINE, BARTHOLO

BARTHOLO [*returns carrying a light*]. Ah Rosine. Since you haven't gone to bed yet...

ROSINE. I was just about to.

BARTHOLO. On a wild might like this you won't get much sleep, and I have something important to say to you.

ROSINE. What do you want with me now, Doctor? Am I not harassed and hounded all day long—isn't that enough for you?

BARTHOLO. Rosine, listen...

ROSINE. I'll listen in the morning.

BARTHOLO. Just give me a moment. Please.

ROSINE [*aside*]. What if he were to come now?

BARTHOLO [*showing her letter to her*]. Have you seen this letter before?

ROSINE [*recognizing it*]. Great heavens!

BARTHOLO. I won't hold it against you, Rosine. At your age, we all make mistakes. But I'm on your side, so listen.

ROSINE. I can't bear it.

BARTHOLO. This letter, which you wrote to Count Almaviva...

ROSINE [*astounded*]. Count Almaviva?

BARTHOLO. Listen and you'll see what an odious man this Count is. The moment he got it, he showed it off as though it were some kind of trophy. I got it from a woman he had given it to, to prove he loved her.

ROSINE. Count Almaviva!

BARTHOLO. You find it hard to believe anyone could behave so abominably, don't you? It's lack of experience, Rosine, that makes you young ladies so trusting and gullible. But let me tell you about the trap they set and how you were to be lured into it. This other woman made sure I was told the whole story, probably because she thought you were a dangerous rival and she wanted you out of the way. I shudder to think of it! This abominable plot was hatched by Almaviva, Figaro, and young Alonzo, who they passed off as Bazile's pupil. It's not his real name. The villain is the Count's right-hand man. They were about to drag you down into depths from which you would never have escaped.

ROSINE. It's horrible!... I can't believe that Lindor... you can't mean the young man...

BARTHOLO [*aside*]. So it's Lindor, is it!

ROSINE. ... could have been acting for Count Almaviva... for another man!

BARTHOLO. That's what I was told when I was given the letter.

ROSINE [*outraged*]. It's so degrading! He'll pay for this. Sir, you said you wished to marry me?

BARTHOLO. You know how I feel about you.

ROSINE. Well, if you still feel the same way, I am yours.

BARTHOLO. Splendid! The notary will be here later tonight.

ROSINE. But that's not all. Oh God, haven't I been humiliated enough already? Listen, at any moment now the lying hypocrite will climb through that window. They found a way of stealing the key to the shutter.

BARTHOLO [*examining his bunch of keys*]. Of all the cunning rogues! My dear, I won't leave you alone.

ROSINE [*frightened*]. What if they're armed?

BARTHOLO. You're right. And if they are, I won't get my revenge. Go to Marceline's room and double-lock yourself in. I'll go and summon the watch and wait for him outside. Having him arrested for burglary will kill two birds with one stone: we'll be safe and have our revenge! My love will make all this up to you, you can count on it.

ROSINE [*in despair*]. Can you forgive me for making such a terrible mistake? [*Aside*] God knows I'm paying a high enough price for it.

BARTHOLO [*as he goes*]. I'll go and set up the ambush. She's mine at last!

SCENE 4

ROSINE, *alone*

ROSINE. His love will make up for it! I'm so miserable! [*She takes her handkerchief and bursts into tears*] What am I to do? He'll be here any minute. I shall stay put and play him along so that for a moment I shall see him in his true colours, which are all black. The hateful way he has behaved will protect me against... And I shall need protection. That handsome face! His gentle manner! And such a tender voice!... and he is nothing more than the right-hand man of a wicked seducer! I'm so miserable, so very miserable. Heavens! Someone's opening the shutter!

[*She runs off*

SCENE 5

The COUNT, *outside, and* FIGARO, *wrapped in a cloak, who appears at the window*

FIGARO [*to the* COUNT, *off*]. Somebody just ran away. Shall I go in?

COUNT [*off*]. A man?

FIGARO. No.

COUNT. It must have been Rosine. She'll have been frightened out of her wits by the sight of your ugly face.

FIGARO [*clambering into the room*]. You're probably right. We're in, despite rain, thunder, and lightning!

COUNT [*he is wearing a long cloak*]. Give me a hand. [*He clambers into the room*] There's nothing to stop us now!

FIGARO [*removing his cloak*]. We're both soaked to the skin. Lovely weather for an elopement, I don't think. How does a night like this suit your Lordship?

COUNT. It's superb for a man in love.

FIGARO. Perhaps, but not for his valet. What if someone comes and catches us here?

COUNT. You're with me, aren't you? There's something else that's much more worrying: how am I going to talk her into walking out of her guardian's house tonight for ever?

FIGARO. You've got three cards in your hand that women can never trump: love, hate, and fear.

COUNT [*peering into the darkness*]. There's no way I can break the news gently that there's a notary waiting for her at your house to marry us. She'll think I'm moving too fast. She'll say I'm presumptuous.

FIGARO. If she says you are presumptuous, you tell her she's cruel. Women always like to be told that they're cruel. Besides, if she loves you as much as you hope she does, just say who you are and she won't have any more doubts about the way you feel.

SCENE 6

The COUNT, ROSINE, *and* FIGARO, *who lights all the candles on the table*

COUNT. Here she is. Rosine, you are so beautiful!

ROSINE [*coolly*]. I was beginning to think, Monsieur, that you weren't coming.

COUNT. How wonderful of you to worry! It is not my intention, Mademoiselle, to take advantage of the situation to ask you to share the life of a man who can offer you so little. But wherever you decide to seek refuge, I swear on my honour...

ROSINE. Sir, if I had not decided to give you my hand the moment I gave you my love, you would not be here. But you must understand that our meeting in secret like this can be justified only by the circumstances.

COUNT. Is it true, Rosine? Do you really consent to be the wife of a poor unfortunate who has neither money nor family?...

ROSINE. Leave money and family aside, for they are accidents of birth. But if you tell me your intentions are honest...

COUNT [*kneeling*]. Oh Rosine! I adore you!...

ROSINE. Stop it! You are beneath contempt! How dare you take the name of love in vain! Adore me, do you? You are no longer a threat to me, for I was only waiting to hear you say that word to know that I hate you. But before I leave you to face your conscience, as you surely must, [*she begins to cry*] I will confess that I loved you and believed that I could be happy only if I could share your life of hardship. You are despicable, Lindor! I was ready to give up everything for you. But the cynical way you abused my trust, and the ignoble conduct of that hateful Count Almaviva to whom I was to be sold, have come down to this: I have in my hand the evidence of my folly. Do you recognize this letter?

COUNT [*quickly*]. Your guardian gave it to you?

ROSINE [*proudly*]. He did, and I thank him for doing so.

COUNT. God, I'm so relieved! He got it from me. Yesterday, I was in a tight corner. I used it as a way of gaining his confidence and I never found an opportunity of telling you. Oh Rosine! It's true, then—you really do love me!

FIGARO. Your Lordship did say that you were looking for a woman who loved you for what you are, not who you are.

ROSINE. Your Lordship? What does he mean?

COUNT [removes his cloak and reveals a gorgeous suit beneath]. Rosine, you are the only woman I can ever love! The moment has come to end this charade. The happy man you see at your feet is not Lindor. I am Count Almaviva. I love you to distraction and have been looking for you everywhere for the last six months.

ROSINE [falling into the COUNT's arms]. Ah!

COUNT [alarmed]. Figaro!

FIGARO. No need to be alarmed, sir. Joy is a sweet sorrow and it has no harmful effects. There, she's coming to already. By God, she's beautiful!

ROSINE. Oh! Lindor! Ah, what have I done! I was going to marry my guardian this very night!

COUNT. You what, Rosine?

ROSINE. It was just my way of punishing myself. I should have spent the rest of my life hating you. Ah Lindor, is there any punishment more horrible than to be reduced to hating when you know you were born to love?

FIGARO [looking out of the window]. Sir, our escape route has been cut. Someone's taken the ladder away.

COUNT. The ladder's gone?

ROSINE [embarrassed]. It's my fault... The Doctor did it... That's what comes of being so trusting. He tricked me. I confessed, told him everything. He knows you're here and intends to come back with armed reinforcements.

FIGARO [looking out of the window again]. Sir, someone's coming in through the front door!

ROSINE [*running to the* COUNT *and into his arms in terror*]. Oh Lindor!

COUNT [*confidently*]. Rosine, you love me. I'm not afraid of anyone, and you shall be my wife. I look forward to the pleasure of finding a suitable punishment for that odious old man.

ROSINE. No, please be kind, Lindor! My heart is overflowing and there's no room in it for revenge.

SCENE 7

Enter NOTARY, BAZILE

FIGARO. Sir, it's the notary.

COUNT. And friend Bazile is with him.

BAZILE. Oh! What's all this?

FIGARO. Well now, what happy chance...

BAZILE. Ah, what ill wind...

NOTARY. Is this the happy couple-to-be?

COUNT. Yes, sir. You were supposed to marry Señora Rosine and me tonight at the home of the barber Figaro. But we decided to hold the ceremony in this house, for reasons I shall explain later. Have you brought the contract?

NOTARY. So I have the honour of addressing his Excellency Count Almaviva?

FIGARO. Quite right.

BAZILE [*aside*]. I don't think he gave me his master-key to have things turn out like this.

NOTARY. I seem to have two marriage contracts, my Lord, and I don't want to mix them up. This one is yours and this one is for the union of Doctor Bartholo with a Señora... also called Rosine. Do I take it that these two ladies are sisters, both with the same name?

COUNT. Let's just get on and sign. Don Bazile will be only too
pleased to stand as our second witness

[*They sign*

BAZILE. But, your Excellency, I don't quite follow...

COUNT. Dear Bazile, you are confused by details and amazed by
everything.

BAZILE. Yes, my Lord... But if Doctor Bartholo...

COUNT [*tossing him a purse*]. Stop being childish! Just sign, and
quick about it.

BAZILE [*amazed*]. Ah!

FIGARO. Do you have a problem signing?

BAZILE [*weighing the purse in his hand*]. Not any more. But that's
how I am. Once I've given my word, it takes weighty arguments
for me to break it.

[*He signs*

SCENE 8

Cast as before, plus BARTHOLO, *a* MAGISTRATE, CONSTABLES, *and*
SERVANTS *carrying torches*

BARTHOLO [*sees the* COUNT *kissing* ROSINE's *hand and* FIGARO
locked in a grotesque embrace with BAZILE: *he seizes the* NOTARY *by
the throat and shouts*]. What's Rosine doing here, with these burglars? Arrest the lot of them. I've collared this one.

NOTARY. I'm the notary.

BAZILE. He's the notary. What do you think you're playing at?

BARTHOLO. Bazile! Why are you here?

BAZILE. That's hardly the point. Why weren't you?

MAGISTRATE [*pointing to* FIGARO]. One moment. I know this man.
What are you doing in this house so late at night?

FIGARO. Night? Surely your worship can see it's nearer morning than night. Actually, I'm here in my capacity as valet to his Excellency Count Almaviva.

BARTHOLO. Almaviva!

MAGISTRATE. So these men are not burglars?

BARTHOLO. Let's not go into that now. Anywhere else, your Lordship, I would be your humble servant. But you must understand that titles count for nothing under my roof. I would be obliged, therefore, if you would be good enough to leave my house.

COUNT. You're right. Titles are irrelevant in this matter. What is relevant, however, is the fact that Mademoiselle Rosine has ranked me above you by consenting, of her own free will, to be my wife.

BARTHOLO. What's he talking about, Rosine?

ROSINE. It's true. I don't see why you should be so surprised. After all, wasn't I to be avenged tonight against a man who was telling me a pack of lies? Well, I am.

BAZILE. Didn't I tell you, Doctor, that the man was the Count himself?

BARTHOLO. I don't give a damn! This marriage is a farce. Where are the witnesses?

NOTARY. It's all perfectly in order. I was assisted by these two gentlemen.

BARTHOLO. Bazile! Did you sign?

BAZILE. What do you think? The Count's a devil of a man, with pockets stuffed with irresistible arguments.

BARTHOLO. I don't care a fig for his arguments! I shall use my authority as Rosine's guardian...

COUNT. Which you have abused and no longer have any right to invoke.

BARTHOLO. She's still a minor.

FIGARO. She's a big girl now.

BARTHOLO. Who asked you, you interfering busybody?

COUNT. The lady is nobly born and beautiful. I am a gentleman, young and rich. She is my wife, a title which does honour to us both. Do you intend to fight me for her?

BARTHOLO. You'll never force me to let her go!

COUNT. You no longer have any power over her. I hereby place her under the protection of the law. This gentleman, [*pointing to the* MAGISTRATE] who you brought here yourself, will see to it that she is safe from any violation of her freedom you might attempt. An upright magistrate is the defender of all who are oppressed.

MAGISTRATE. Quite right. And this futile opposition to an entirely honourable marriage is doubtless a clear indication of his misgivings about the maladministration of his ward's finances, of which we shall expect a full account.

COUNT. Provided he gives his consent, I shall ask nothing more of him.

FIGARO. Except that he forgets all about the hundred crowns I owe him. No need to lose touch entirely with reality.

BARTHOLO [*indignant*]. They were all against me. I walked straight into a hornet's nest.

BAZILE. I wouldn't call it a hornet's nest. You may not have got the girl, but don't forget, Doctor, you've ended up with the money...

BARTHOLO. Leave me alone, Bazile. Money is all you think about. I'm not interested in the money. Oh I'm not saying I won't get to keep all of it. But you don't seriously think that was what has made up my mind for me...

[*He signs*

FIGARO [*laughing*]. Ha ha ha! There, your Lordship! One's as bad as the other!

NOTARY. Listen, gentlemen, I am completely confused. Would I be right in thinking that there aren't two young ladies with the same name?

FIGARO. You would. They're one and the same.

BARTHOLO [*lamenting*]. And it was me that took their ladder away, so that my marriage would go ahead undisturbed. I lost. And all because I didn't take more care.

FIGARO. Didn't have any sense, more like. Let's face it, Doctor. When love and youth get together to outwit an old man, everything he does to stop them can only be described as a POINTLESS PRECAUTION.

The Follies of a Day

or,

THE MARRIAGE OF FIGARO

A Prose Comedy in Five Acts

*First performed by the Comédie Française
on Tuesday, 27 April 1784*

... folly must have its season
To give a human face to reason.

(*Couplet from the play*)

CHARACTERS

COUNT ALMAVIVA, *Lieutenant-Governor of Andalusia*
THE COUNTESS, *his wife*
FIGARO, *valet to the Count, and his steward*
SUZANNE, *personal maid to the Countess, engaged to Figaro*
MARCELINE, *keeper of the Count's household*
ANTONIO, *head-gardener at the chateau, uncle to Suzanne and father of Fanchette*
FANCHETTE, *daughter of Antonio*
CHERUBIN, *page to the Count*
BARTHOLO, *a Seville doctor*
BAZILE, *harpsichord-teacher to the Countess*
DON GUSMAN BRID'OISON, *a district justice*
DOUBLE-MAIN, *a clerk, secretary to Don Gusman*
A COURT USHER
GRIPPE-SOLEIL, *a young goatherd*
A SHEPHERDESS
PEDRILLO, *master of the Count's hunt*
SERVANTS, PEASANT MEN *and* WOMEN

*The Characters and Costumes of the Play**

COUNT ALMAVIVA should be played to express the nobility of rank, but also his grace and great ease of manner. The dastardly nature of his intentions should not detract from the sophistication of his manners. According to the custom of those days, gentlemen took a less than serious view of any attempt on a woman's virtue. The part is made more difficult to play by the fact that the character is consistently the least sympathetic. But in the hands of an excellent actor (Monsieur Molé), it raised the profile of all the other roles and ensured that the play was a success.

In Acts I and II he wears hunting clothes and half-length boots in the old Spanish fashion and, from Act III to the end, a sumptuous suit in the same style.

THE COUNTESS, torn between two conflicting emotions, should keep a tight rein on her feelings and show only muted anger, and above all there should be nothing to damage the audience's perception of her sweet, virtuous character. This part, one of the more difficult in the play, offered a challenge which was triumphantly met by the great talents of the younger Mademoiselle Saint-Val.

For Acts I, II, and IV she wears a loose indoor gown and nothing on her head or in her hair: she is in her own apartments and is supposed to be unwell. In the last Act she wears Suzanne's clothes and her headdress crowned with flowers.

FIGARO. The actor who plays this role cannot be urged too strongly to enter into the character's mind and feelings, as Monsieur Dazincourt did. If he construes the part as anything other than intelligence seasoned with high spirits and flashes of wit, and especially if he adds the smallest whiff of earnestness, he would reduce the impact of a role which, in the view of Monsieur Préville, the theatre's leading comic actor, should bring out the talent of any performer capable of capturing its many nuances and able to rise fully to the occasion.

His costume is the same as that worn in *The Barber of Seville*.

SUZANNE. A shrewd, sharp-witted young woman, fond of laughter but with none of the almost brassy high spirits of the scheming maids of theatrical tradition. Her character is sketched in the preface,* which actresses who did not see Mademoiselle Contat in the part should study if they are to play the role properly.

In the first four Acts she wears a very elegant white bodice with basques and skirt to match, and the toque subsequently dubbed *à la Suzanne* by milliners. During the festivities of Act IV the Count places on her head a headdress adorned with a long veil, long feathers, and white ribbons. In Act V she wears her mistress's loose gown, and her hair is unornamented.

MARCELINE is an intelligent woman, outspoken by nature, whose character has been modified by her past mistakes and experience. If the actress who plays her can invest the role with the dignity consistent with the high moral tone which follows the recognition scene in Act III, she will add considerably to the overall effect of the play.

Her costume is that of a Spanish *duenna*, subdued in colour. She wears a black hat.

ANTONIO should appear in only a partly drunken state which wears off by degrees, so that by Act V it is scarcely noticeable.

He is dressed like a Spanish peasant, with the sleeves of his jacket hanging at his back. White hat and white shoes.

FANCHETTE is a girl of 12, very innocent. Her costume consists of a brown bodice with silver buttons and braid, skirt of a contrasting colour, and a black toque with feathers. The same dress is worn by the other peasant girls at the wedding.

CHERUBIN. This part can only be played, as it was, by a pretty young woman. The stage currently boats no young male actor mature enough to grasp all its subtleties. Excessively timid in the presence of the Countess, he is at other times an engaging scamp. The basis of his character is a restless, vague longing. He has reached puberty but knows nothing, not even what he wants, and is completely vulnerable to every passing event. He is perhaps what every mother in her heart of hearts would like her own son to be, though he would be a source of great anxiety to her.

The splendid costume he wears in Acts I and II is the standard dress of a page in the Spanish court: white, with silver embroidery; short blue cloak worn over one shoulder; toque with feathers. In Act IV he appears in the same bodice, skirt, and small hat of the peasant girls who bring him to the castle, and in Act V in an officer's uniform, with cockade and sword.

BARTHOLO. Character and costume as in *The Barber of Seville*. The role is of secondary importance only.

BAZILE. Character and costume as in *The Barber of Seville*. The role is of secondary importance only.

BRID'OISON should display the uncomplicated, candid, trusting nature of an animal which has lost its shyness. His stammer is but one character-istic among others and should barely be perceptible. The actor who plays him would be quite wrong and would misconceive the role entirely if he sought only the humour of the part. The nub is the contradiction between the dignity of his occupation and the foolishness of the character, and the less the actor brings to the part, the better he will display his talents.

His costume is the robe of a Spanish judge, which is not as full as that of our advocates, and is more like a cassock; a full wig, a *golilla* or Spanish magistrate's collar round his neck, and a long white staff in his hand.

DOUBLE-MAIN. Costume as for the judge, but his white staff is shorter.

THE USHER or ALGUAZIL. A suit and cloak plus the long rapier of the valet in Italian comedy, except that it is worn at his side and is not held by a leather shoulder-belt. Black shoes instead of boots, a long white curl wig, and a short white staff.

GRIPPE-SOLEIL. Peasant costume, with sleeves hanging loose at the back; a coat of contrasting colour and a white hat.

YOUNG SHEPHERDESS. Costume like that of Fanchette.

PEDRILLO. Coat, waistcoat, waistband, horse-whip, and riding-boots, a *redecilla* for his hair and a dispatch-rider's hat.

NON-SPEAKING ROLES. Some are dressed as judges, others in peasant costume, and the rest in livery.

The Nominal Ranking of the Players

To make the mechanics of the action clear, special care has been taken to note the names of the characters at the beginning of each scene in order of their appearance. If they bring a dramatic charge to a scene, this is indicated by a new ordering of the names, as noted in the margin* at the exact point where they make their impact. It is important that these sound theatrical conventions be maintained. Any relaxation of the traditions created by the earliest actors quickly leads to chaos in the way plays are performed, and brings undisciplined companies of actors down to the level of the much less experienced players who indulge in amateur theatricals.

The action takes place in the chateau of Aguas-Frescas, three leagues from Seville.

ACT I

A room from which most of the furniture has been removed. A large invalid chair occupies the centre of the stage. FIGARO *is measuring the floor with a six-foot ruler.* SUZANNE *stands in front of a mirror fixing a bridal garland of orange blossom in her hair*

SCENE 1

FIGARO, SUZANNE

FIGARO. Nineteen foot by twenty-six.

SUZANNE. Look, Figaro, my wedding bonnet. Do you reckon it looks better like this?

FIGARO [*holding both her hands*]. My pet, it's perfect. Ah! what sight could be better calculated to enslave a doting bridegroom than a dainty, virginal garland on the head of his pretty wife-to-be on the morning they are to be married?

SUZANNE [*shrugs him off*]. What are you measuring, my sweet?

FIGARO. I'm trying to work out, Suzanne, dear girl, if the grand bed his Lordship's given us will fit snugly in here.

SUZANNE. Here? In this room?

FIGARO. In this very room. He's letting us have it.

SUZANNE. I don't want it.

FIGARO. Why not?

SUZANNE. I just don't want it.

FIGARO. But why ever not?

SUZANNE. I don't like it.

FIGARO. People usually give a reason...

SUZANNE. What if I don't want to?

FIGARO. The minute women get you in their pocket...

SUZANNE. Having to prove I'm right means admitting that I could be wrong. Are you or aren't you my slave?

FIGARO. But you just can't take against the most convenient room in the whole castle. It's between the two apartments. If her Ladyship doesn't feel well in the night, she'll ring from that side and, tipperty-flip, you're there in two ticks. If his Lordship wants something, all he has to do is ring on this side and, hoppity-skip, I'm there in two shakes.

SUZANNE. Exactly! But when he rings in the morning and sends you off on some long wild-goose chase, tipperty-flip, he'll be here in two ticks, and then, hoppity-skip, in two shakes...

FIGARO. What exactly do you mean by that?

SUZANNE. I want you listen quietly to what I'm going to say.

FIGARO. Good God, what are you getting at?

SUZANNE. This, my sweet. Count Almaviva is tired of chasing all the pretty women in the locality. Now he's got something closer to home in mind. Not his wife—it's yours he has his eye on, are you with me? And he thinks that putting us in this room won't exactly hinder his plans. That's what the ever-faithful Bazile, ignoble purveyor of pleasures to his Lordship and my esteemed singing-teacher, tells me every day when he gives me my lesson.

FIGARO. Bazile! The spineless wonder! What he needs is a damned good thrashing with a stick to beat the obsequious bend out of his backbone and make him stand up straight.

SUZANNE. Don't tell me you actually believed the dowry the Count's giving me was meant as a public recognition of your sterling qualities?

FIGARO. I've done more than enough to think so.

SUZANNE. Clever people aren't very bright, are they?

FIGARO. So they say.

SUZANNE. They say it but they don't believe it.

FIGARO. Obviously a mistake.

SUZANNE. Well you can believe this. He means to use the money to persuade me to give him a few moments in private for exercising the old *droit du seigneur** he thinks he's entitled to... You know what a disgusting business that was.

FIGARO. I do indeed. And if his Lordship hadn't renounced his nauseating right when he got married, I'd never have considered holding our wedding anywhere near his estate.

SUZANNE. Well, if he really gave it up he now wishes he hadn't. And it's with your bride that he's going to reinstate it. Today.

FIGARO [*scratching his head*]. The shock's softened my brains. I can feel cuckold's horns sprouting...

SUZANNE. Stop scratching, then.

FIGARO. I'm in no danger, am I?

SUZANNE [*laughing*]. Rub the spot red and superstitious people will start to think...

FIGARO. You're teasing me, you little minx! But if only there was some way of turning the tables on his cheating Lordship, we could set a trap for him to fall into and then walk off with his money.

SUZANNE. Plotting and money, you're in your element.

FIGARO. It's nothing to be ashamed of. Anyway, it's not shame that makes me hesitate.

SUZANNE. Is it fear?

FIGARO. Taking on a dangerous business is nothing. But bringing it off without putting yourself at risk, that's something else! Look, you can break into a man's house in the middle of the night, seduce his wife, and get a damned good hiding for your trouble: there's nothing to it. There are bungling oafs who do it all the time. But...

[*A bell rings*

SUZANNE. That's her Ladyship awake. She said I was to be sure to be the first person to speak to her on my wedding day.

FIGARO. Is there more funny business behind that too?

SUZANNE. The shepherd says it brings good luck to neglected

wives. I must go. Figure it out, Figaro. Put your mind to work on our little problem.

FIGARO. Give me a kiss to get me started.

SUZANNE. Kiss my lover today? Not likely! What would my husband have to say about that tomorrow?

[FIGARO *kisses her*

All right, that's enough.

FIGARO. You have no idea how much I love you.

SUZANNE [*patting her clothes*]. When are you going to stop bothering me by going on about it from morning to night?

FIGARO [*winking*]. When I can prove it to you from night until morning.

[*The bell rings again*

SUZANNE [*as she goes, she puts both fingers to her lips*]. You can have your kiss back, kind sir. I don't want anything else of yours.

FIGARO [*runs after her*]. That's not what you said when you took it from me...

SCENE 2

FIGARO, *alone*

FIGARO. She's wonderful—always laughing, fresher than springtime, sunny, funny, loving, and delightful in every conceivable way! But such a wise head too! [*He walks up and down rubbing his hands vigorously*] So, your Lordship and honoured sir, you thought you could put one over on me. It did cross my mind to wonder why, after making me steward of his chateau, he decided I should accompany him on his tours of duty and act as his official courier. Now I get it, Excellency: three promotions at a stroke! You, rising ambassador; me, diplomatic dogsbody; and Suzanne, circulating lady and undeclared ambassadress. Right you are, courier, away you go. And while I'm galloping this way, you're leading my Suzanne up the garden path that way. I splash through mud and give my all for the honour of your family, while you're kindly doing your bit to increase the size of mine! You reckon that's a fair exchange? But your Lordship's overdoing it. There you are in London, attending to your master's business and at the same time looking after your valet's interests! Deputizing for both the king and me in a foreign court is simply too much for one person. As for you, Bazile, you miserable squirt, I'll show you not to teach your grandmother to suck eggs. I'll—no, let's pretend to go along with them and then play one off against the other. Best foot forward, Figaro, this is the big day! Start by bringing the wedding forward one hour, to be sure the ceremony goes off as planned; fend off Marceline, who's taken a fancy to you; collect the dowry and the wedding presents; foil the Count's naughty little game; give Bazile a good hiding and then...

SCENE 3

MARCELINE, BARTHOLO, FIGARO

FIGARO [*breaks off*]. Why, if it isn't the fat physician! Now the gang's all here. [*Aloud*] Top of the morning to you, my dear, dear Doctor. Could it be my imminent marriage with Suzanne that directs your steps to the chateau?

BARTHOLO [*disdainfully*]. Certainly not, my good man.

FIGARO. It would show you in a forgiving light.

BARTHOLO. True, but it would be too absurd for words.

FIGARO. And all because I was the unfortunate impediment to your own nuptials?

BARTHOLO. Is that all you've got to say to me?

FIGARO. I don't suppose any one's looking after your mule?*

BARTHOLO [*furious*]. You talk too much! Go away!

FIGARO. You're not cross, Doctor? People in your line of work can be very hard. Really, you have no more sympathy for poor dumb animals than if they were human beings! Goodbye, Marceline. Still thinking of taking me to court?

'Though no love's lost between us
Let not black hate demean us'*

I'll leave the Doctor to adjudicate.

BARTHOLO. Adjudicate what?

FIGARO. She'll tell you all about it.

[*He leaves*

SCENE 4

MARCELINE, BARTHOLO

BARTHOLO [*watches him go*]. The clown! He never changes. If he doesn't get flayed alive first, I predict that he'll die the thickest-skinned, the most arrogant and insolent...

MARCELINE [*turns him to face her*]. And here you are too, the same old Doctor, still so grave and solemn that patients might die waiting for your help, just as once upon a time all your precautions failed to prevent a certain person being married.

BARTHOLO. And you are still as bitter and irritating. So why is my presence so urgently required at the chateau? Has something happened to the Count?

MARCELINE. No, Doctor.

BARTHOLO. Perhaps Rosine, his two-faced Countess, is, God willing, indisposed?

MARCELINE. She's depressed.

BARTHOLO. About what?

MARCELINE. The Count neglects her.

BARTHOLO [*exults*]. A fine upstanding husband and my avenger!

MARCELINE. It's hard to describe his Lordship. He's a rake and he's jealous.

BARTHOLO. He's a rake because he's bored and he's jealous because he's vain. It's all very straightforward.

MARCELINE. Take today, for example. He's arranged for our Suzanne to marry his man Figaro, who is being handsomely rewarded for going through with the wedding...

BARTHOLO. Which his Excellency has made necessary?

MARCELINE. Not exactly. But his Lordship intends to add a little spice to the occasion with the bride...

BARTHOLO. Figaro's bride? He'll go along with it if the terms are right.

MARCELINE. Apparently not, according to Bazile.

BARTHOLO. Is that oaf living here? It's a den of thieves! And what does he do?

MARCELINE. As much mischief as he can. But from my point of view the worst thing about him is the tedious way he harps on about always having been in love with me.

BARTHOLO. If it was me he was running after, I'd have stopped him a score of times.

MARCELINE. How?

BARTHOLO. By marrying him.

MARCELINE. A tasteless remark from an unfeeling man! Why don't you use the same solution to stop me bothering you? Don't you owe it to me? Have you forgotten your promises? Have you no memory of our little Emmanuel, fruit of a long-dead love that should have led to marriage?

BARTHOLO [removes his hat]. Did you bring me here all the way from Seville to make me listen to this rubbish? This attack of the matrimonials which you have in an acute form...

MARCELINE. Very well, let's drop the subject. But since it seems that nothing will persuade you to do the right thing and marry me, help me at least to marry someone else.

BARTHOLO. Of course! Consider the subject raised again! But what mortal man abandoned by gods and women...

MARCELINE. But who else could it be, doctor, but handsome, like-able, lovable Figaro?

BARTHOLO. That nasty piece of work?

MARCELINE. Never angry, always cheerful, living happily for the present, and worrying as little about the future as about the past, jaunty, generous, as giving...

BARTHOLO. As a burglar?

MARCELINE. As a lord. He is a charmer. Yet he's an unfeeling monster.

BARTHOLO. And Suzanne?

MARCELINE. She's a sly one. But she won't get him, provided, Doctor, you help me force him to keep a promise he has given me.

BARTHOLO. But he's getting married today!

MARCELINE. Weddings have been stopped at the last moment before now. And if it didn't mean giving away a feminine secret...

BARTHOLO. Do women have secrets from their doctor?

MARCELINE. You know I have none from you. We women are passionate but timid. We may well be charmed and attracted by pleasure, but the boldest of us is aware of a voice within her which says: be fair if you can and wise if you will, but be wary, you must. Now since being careful is so crucial, as every woman knows, let's start by giving Suzanne a fright by disclosing details of the other offers she's had.

BARTHOLO. What would that achieve?

MARCELINE. She'll choke on the shame of it. She will continue to say no to the Count. The Count will want his revenge and will back my objections to her marriage—leaving mine to go ahead unopposed.

BARTHOLO. You're right! By God, it's neat: my old housekeeper hitched to the swine who stopped me marrying my ward!

MARCELINE [quickly]. And thinks he can add to his enjoyment by disappointing my hopes.

BARTHOLO [quickly]. And once stole a hundred crowns from me which I haven't forgotten.*

MARCELINE. Oh, how deeply satisfying it would be...

BARTHOLO. To punish a rogue?

MARCELINE. To marry him, Doctor, to marry him!

SCENE 5

MARCELINE, BARTHOLO, SUZANNE

SUZANNE [*a woman's nightcap with a wide ribbon in her hand and a dress over her arm*]. 'To marry him! To marry him!' Marry who? My Figaro?

MARCELINE [*sharply*]. Why not? You're planning to, aren't you?

BARTHOLO [*laughing*]. A fine example of an angry woman's logic! We were just saying, Suzanne, what a lucky man he'll be to have a girl like you.

MARCELINE. Likewise his Lordship, but we won't go into that.

SUZANNE [*curtseys*]. Your humble servant, Madame. There's always something deeply unpleasant in everything you say.

MARCELINE [*curtseys*]. And I am yours, Madame. But where's the unpleasantness? Is it not meet and right that a generous Lord should share the happiness he procures for his servants?

SUZANNE. Procures?

MARCELINE. Procures, Madame.

SUZANNE. Fortunately, Madame, your jealousy is as much common knowledge as your claims on Figaro are slim.

MARCELINE. Those claims would have been more binding had I chosen to strengthen them by adopting the methods you have used.

SUZANNE. Oh, my methods, Madame, are those which any lady of your advanced years and intelligence would use.

MARCELINE. And what would a slip of a girl know about intelligence? As much as an old judge knows about innocence!

BARTHOLO [*pulling* MARCELINE *away*]. Goodbye, Figaro's pretty bride-to-be!

MARCELINE [*curtseys*]. And his Lordship's secret paramour.

SUZANNE [*curtseys*]. Who holds Madame in great esteem.

MARCELINE [*curtseys*]. And will Madame grant me the honour of favouring me with a little of her affection?

SUZANNE [*curtseys*]. In that respect, Madame has nothing further to desire.

MARCELINE [*curtseys*]. Madame is such a pretty young person.

SUZANNE [*curtseys*]. Pretty enough to give Madame bad dreams.

MARCELINE [*curtseys*]. Such a blameless reputation!

SUZANNE [*curtseys*]. Blameless reputations are for elderly housekeepers.

MARCELINE [*in a rage*]. Elderly housekeepers! Elderly house-keepers!

BARTHOLO. Marceline!

MARCELINE. We're going, Doctor, or I shan't be responsible for my actions. Good day to you, Madame.

[*She curtseys*

SCENE 6

SUZANNE, *alone*

SUZANNE. Yes, go! Go away! Pompous old fusspot! I'm not afraid of what you might do and I despise your insults. The old bat! Just because she went to school for a while and made her Ladyship's life a misery when she was young,* she thinks she rules the roost in the chateau. [*She throws the dress she is holding over the back of a chair*] Now what did I come in here for?

SCENE 7

SUZANNE, CHERUBIN

CHERUBIN [*running in*]. Ah, Suzette! I've spent two hours waiting for a chance of getting you all to myself. It's awful! You're going to be married and I'm going away.

SUZANNE. What's my marriage got to do with his Lordship's favourite page leaving the chateau?

CHERUBIN [*snivels*]. He's given me my marching orders.

SUZANNE [*imitating him*]. Cherubin, what have you been up to?

CHERUBIN. Last night he caught me with your cousin Fanchette. I was helping her with her lines: she's got a small part as a shepherdess in the revels tonight. He went mad when he saw me. 'Get out!', he said, 'you little...' I can't say the word he used when there's a lady present because it's rude. 'Get out! This is the last night you'll ever spend in this house!' If her Ladyship, my wonderful, beautiful godmother, can't talk him round, then it's all over with me, Suzette, and I'll be forever denied the happiness of seeing you.

SUZANNE. Seeing me? Oh, it's me now, is it, not the Mistress, that you secretly idolize?

CHERUBIN. Oh Suzette, she is as noble as she is fair. But she's a bit forbidding.

SUZANNE. And I'm not, I suppose, and you feel free to take liberties with me, but...

CHERUBIN. Don't be horrid. You know very well I never feel free enough to take a liberty. You're so lucky! You can see her any time, talk to her, dress her in the morning and undress her at night, pin by pin... Oh Suzette, I'd give... What's that you've got there?

SUZANNE [*teasing*]. This? Oh it's only the thrice-blessed cap and fortune-favoured ribbon that ties up the hair of someone's beautiful godmother every night...

CHERUBIN [*eagerly*]. The ribbon that goes round her hair at night! Give it to me, my precious!

SUZANNE [*holding it out of reach*]. Oh no you don't! 'My precious' indeed! You're getting above yourself! If you weren't such an insignificant, snivelling weevil... [CHERUBIN *snatches the ribbon from her*] Ah! the ribbon!

CHERUBIN [*runs round the chair*]. You can say it's been mislaid, lost, anything you like.

SUZANNE [*pursuing him*]. Oh, I give you three or four years and you'll be the biggest little villain that ever... Will you give me back that ribbon!

[*She makes a grab for it*

CHERUBIN [*taking a sheet of paper from his pocket*]. Let go! Oh Suzette, let me keep it! Look, I'll give you the words to this song I've written instead. And though the memory of your beautiful mistress will cast a pall of gloom over my every waking hour, thinking of you will be the one gleam of happiness that will light my aching heart!

SUZANNE [*seizes the paper*]. Light your aching heart! The cheek of it! You're not talking to your Fanchette now. You get caught with her, you drool over her Ladyship, and if that wasn't enough, you have the cheek to try it on with me!

CHERUBIN [*exalted*]. I know. You're right. I have no idea what's come over me. These last few days, I've felt my heart pound every time I see a woman. The words 'love' and 'tender' make it race. The need to tell someone 'I love you' has become so strong that when I'm by myself, running through the grounds, I shout it out loud to her Ladyship, to you, to the trees, the clouds, to the wind that blows the clouds away and my words with them. Yesterday, I met Marceline...

SUZANNE [*laughing*]. Ha ha ha!

CHERUBIN. Why not? She's a woman. She's not married. Not married! Woman! Oh, aren't they wonderful words! So exciting!

SUZANNE. You're mad!

CHERUBIN. Fanchette's so sweet. At least she listens to me. You're not sweet at all!

SUZANNE. Isn't that a crying shame? Now listen you me, young man.

[She tries to get the ribbon

CHERUBIN [*avoids her and runs off*]. Oh no you don't! If you want it back, it'll be over my dead body. And if you think that's too small a price to pay, I'll throw in a million kisses.

[Now he starts to chase her

SUZANNE [*turns and runs away*]. It'll be a million clips over the ear if you come any closer. I'm going to complain to her Ladyship. And instead of speaking up for you to his Lordship, I'll tell him straight: 'You're quite right, sir. Kick him out. He steals things. Send him back to his mother and father. He's a bad lot. He makes out he's in love with the Mistress and has made do trying to kiss me instead.'

CHERUBIN [*sees the* COUNT *enter, is terrified, and ducks behind the chair*]. That's torn it!

SUZANNE. What are you scared of?

SCENE 8

SUZANNE, *the* COUNT *and* CHERUBIN, *who is hiding*

SUZANNE [*seeing the* COUNT]. Oh!

[She moves closer to the chair to hide CHERUBIN

COUNT [*strides towards her*]. Something upset you, Suzanne? Alone, talking to yourself, and your little heart no doubt in a whirl... but all very understandable, really, on a day like today.

SUZANNE [*nervously*]. Was there something you wanted, sir? If I was seen alone with you...

COUNT. It would be most inconvenient if I were to be found here. But I think you are aware of my feelings. I assume Bazile has told you I love you. I've only got a moment to tell you my plan, so listen.

[*He sits down in the chair*

SUZANNE. I won't listen.

COUNT [*taking her hand*]. It won't take a moment. You've heard that the king has appointed me as his ambassador to London. I'm taking Figaro with me. It's a very good opportunity I'm offering him. And since it's a wife's duty to follow her husband...

SUZANNE. If I could only speak my mind!

COUNT [*pulls her a little closer*]. Go ahead, speak, my dear. Speaking freely is a right you have acquired over me for life, so you might as well make a start now.

SUZANNE [*fearfully*]. It's not a right I want. I don't want anything to do with it. Just leave me alone, please!

COUNT. But first say what you were going to say.

SUZANNE [*angry*]. I don't remember what it was.

COUNT. About a wife's duty.

SUZANNE. Very well. When your Lordship stole your wife away from under the Doctor's nose and married her for love and on her account abolished a certain horrible custom...

COUNT [*laughing*]. The one the girls all hated! But Suzette, it is a charming old custom! Come and talk to me in the garden later, when it's getting dark, and I'll make it worth your while—it's only a tiny favour...

BAZILE [*offstage*]. His Lordship's not in his room.

COUNT [*gets up*]. Whose voice is that?

SUZANNE. I can't bear this!

COUNT. Go and see what it's about. We don't want anyone coming in here.

SUZANNE [*hesitates*]. And leave you here?

BAZILE [*offstage*]. His Lordship went up to see the Mistress but he's not there now. I'll try in here...

COUNT. There's nowhere to hide. Ah! Behind this chair... It's only just big enough. Get rid of him as quickly as you can.

SUZANNE *stands in his way. He pushes her gently. She takes a step back and thus positions herself between him and the page. But as the* COUNT *crouches to take his place,* CHERUBIN *runs round to the front of the chair and, tucking his legs under him, jumps onto the seat where he cringes in terror.* SUZANNE *reaches for the dress she's been carrying, throws it over the page, and stands in front of the chair.*

SCENE 9

The COUNT *and* CHERUBIN, *hiding,* SUZANNE, BAZILE

BAZILE. I don't suppose you've seen the Count, Mademoiselle?

SUZANNE [*sharply*]. Why should I have seen him? Go away.

BAZILE [*advancing*]. If you weren't so prickly, you'd know it is a perfectly straightforward question. It's not me who's looking for him, it's Figaro.

SUZANNE. Then he's looking for someone who wants to do him more harm than anyone else on earth, except you.

COUNT [*aside*]. Let's see how well he serves me.

BAZILE. Is wanting to do a wife a good turn the same as wanting to do harm to her husband?

SUZANNE. Not by the appalling standards of a troublemaker like you.

BAZILE. What are you being asked to do that you aren't ready to do very willingly with another man? You go through a simple ceremony, and then what you were forbidden to do yesterday you will be required to do tomorrow.

SUZANNE. Don't be disgusting!

BAZILE. Of all the serious things in life, marriage is the most absurd. So I was thinking...

SUZANNE [*furious*]. Horrible thoughts, I imagine. Who said you could come in here?

BAZILE. Now, now! What a firebrand! May God give you patience. What will happen will only happen if you want it to. And don't you go thinking that I regard Figaro as the real obstacle in his Lordship's way. If that little page wasn't around...

SUZANNE [*apprehensively*]. You mean Cherubin?

BAZILE [*mimics her*]. *Cherubino di amore*, who's forever hanging around you, like this morning, when he was on the prowl outside waiting to come in as I was leaving. Just say if it's not true.

SUZANNE. That's a fabrication! Get out, you horrible man!

BAZILE. So I'm a horrible man, am I, because I can see beyond the end of my nose? And that poem he was keeping so quiet about, I suppose that was for you too?

SUZANNE [*angry*]. Yes! It was for me!

BAZILE. Unless, that is, he wrote it for her Ladyship. Now I think of it, they do say that when he's serving at table he stares at her with eyes like saucers... But by God he'd better watch his step. His Lordship is utterly *pitiless* where that sort of thing is concerned!

SUZANNE [*furious*]. And you are utterly unscrupulous, going around spreading slanderous rumours so you can ruin the chances of a vulnerable adolescent who's already got on the wrong side of the Count.

BAZILE. You think I made it up? I only mentioned it because it's all the talk.

COUNT [*standing up*]. What's all the talk?

SUZANNE. Oh mercy!

BAZILE. Ah!

COUNT. Bazile, go and have him thrown out of the house at once.

BAZILE. I wish I'd never set foot in this room.

SUZANNE [*alarmed*]. Oh my God!

COUNT [*to Bazile*]. She's going to faint. Sit her down in this chair.

SUZANNE [*pushing him away*]. I don't want to sit down! Bursting in here without so much as a by your leave, it's disgraceful!

COUNT. There are two of us here with you, my dear. You're in no danger now.

BAZILE. I apologize for having a little joke at the page's expense when you could overhear me. I only did it to find out what she really thought, for the fact is...

COUNT. Give him fifty pistoles and a horse and send him back to his parents.

BAZILE. Surely not on account of my little jest, your Lordship?

COUNT. He's a precocious little devil. Only yesterday I caught him at it with the gardener's daughter.

BAZILE. Fanchette?

COUNT. In her bedroom.

SUZANNE [*indignantly*]. Where no doubt your Lordship also had some business to see to.

COUNT [*laughing*]. That's what I like to hear!

BAZILE. At least she's thinking on the right lines.

COUNT [*good-humouredly*]. No, I was there trying to find your uncle Antonio, my drunken sot of a gardener. I had some instructions for him. I knock. It's a while before the door opens. Your cousin looks flushed. I get suspicious, I say something to her, and as we chat I take a good look round. Behind the door was a curtain or some such, hanging in front of a recess for keeping clothes in perhaps, I'm not sure. Casually, I reach out my hand and gently, very gently I lift the curtain [*to demonstrate, he lifts the dress from the chair*] and who do I see? [*He sees the page*] Good God!

BAZILE. Aha!

COUNT. As appearing acts go, this is as good as the last one.

BAZILE. Better!

COUNT (*to* SUZANNE). What's this then, young lady? You've only been engaged five minutes and this is the sort of thing you get up to! So that's why you wanted to be alone—so you could be with my page. As for you, my lad, your behaviour gets no better, you show little respect for your godmother, and you couldn't wait to start chasing her maid who is about to become the wife of your friend! But I won't let Figaro, a man I like and respect, be the victim of your duplicity. Was he with you, Bazile?

SUZANNE [*outraged*].   There was no duplicity and no victim. He was there all the time you were talking to me.

COUNT [*furious*].   I hope you don't mean that. Not even his own worst enemy would want to wish such a fate on him.

SUZANNE.   He was pleading with me to persuade her Ladyship to speak to you on his behalf. When you arrived he was so panic-stricken that he hid behind the chair.

COUNT [*enraged*].   That's a damned lie! When I came in, I sat in it myself.

CHERUBIN.   It's true sir, I was there, behind the chair, quaking like a jelly.

COUNT.   Another lie! That's where I was, not two moments ago.

CHERUBIN.   Excuse me, sir, but it was at that point that I got on to the seat and hid.

COUNT [*even more furious*].   You're as slippery as an eel, you damned... serpent! You were listening!

CHERUBIN.   Not at all, your Lordship. I tried ever so hard not to overhear anything.

COUNT.   The snake in the grass! [*To* SUZANNE] You'll not be marrying Figaro after this.

BAZILE.   Get a grip on yourself, someone's coming.

COUNT [*pulls* CHERUBIN *out of the chair and hauls him to his feet*].   You stand there where everyone can see you!

SCENE 10

CHERUBIN, SUZANNE, FIGARO, *the* COUNTESS, *the* COUNT,
FANCHETTE, BAZILE, *together with numerous servants and peasants all
dressed for the revels*

FIGARO [*bearing a woman's bridal bonnet decorated with white feathers and ribbons, addresses the* COUNTESS]. Madame, only you can persuade him to grant us this favour...

COUNTESS. You see how they are, my Lord—they credit me with an influence which I do not have. But since what they ask is not unreasonable...

COUNT [*embarrassed*]. It would have to be very unreasonable for me not to...

FIGARO [*aside to* SUZANNE]. Back me up to the hilt!

SUZANNE [*aside to* FIGARO]. It won't get you anywhere.

FIGARO [*aside*]. Try anyway.

COUNT [*to* FIGARO]. What is it you want?

FIGARO. My Lord, your loyal vassals, in appreciation of your having abolished a certain unseemly custom which, for love of her Ladyship...

COUNT. Yes, yes, the custom has ceased to exist. What are you trying to say?

FIGARO [*deviously*]. That it is high time the goodness of such a considerate master received some form of public acknowledgement. I myself am today a beneficiary of that goodness, and it is my wish to be the first to celebrate it at my wedding.

COUNT [*even more discomfited*]. No need for that, old friend. Banning a degrading custom is enough in itself to indicate the high regard I have for decency. Any full-blooded Spaniard is entitled to try to win a lady's love by paying his court to her. But demanding the first and sweetest use of her heart as though it were some servile due is uncivilized, barbarous behaviour, not a right which any true-born Castilian nobleman would ever wish to claim.

FIGARO [*taking* SUZANNE*'s hand*]. Then, by your leave, grant that this innocent young woman, whose virtue has been preserved intact through your goodness, might receive from your hand and before the people here assembled, this bridal bonnet trimmed with white feathers and ribbons as a symbol of the purity of your intentions. Adopt this practice for all wedding ceremonies hereafter, and may a few simple verses sung by all preserve the memory of this moment forever...

COUNT. If I didn't know that being a lover, poet, and musician gives you a triple licence for behaving in all sorts of tomfool ways...

FIGARO. All together, friends!

ALL. Long live his Lordship!

SUZANNE [*to the* COUNT]. Why do you shy away from praise which you fully deserve?

COUNT [*aside*]. Devious little minx!

FIGARO. Just look at her, sir. You couldn't have wished for a prettier face to demonstrate the magnitude of the sacrifice you made.

SUZANNE. Leave my looks out of it and concentrate on his Lordship's kindness.

COUNT [*aside*]. This was all set up in advance.

COUNTESS. I add my voice to theirs, my Lord. This ceremony will always have a special place in my heart, because it began in the tender love you once felt for me.

COUNT. And still feel, Madame. And it is in the name of that love that I now yield.

ALL. Long live his Lordship!

COUNT [*aside*]. They've got me in a corner! [*Aloud*] I would merely suggest that to make the ceremony a more illustrious occasion it should be put off until a little later today. [*Aside*] I must send for Marceline at once.

FIGARO [*to* CHERUBIN]. What's this, you little pest? You aren't clapping.

SUZANNE. He's feeling sorry for himself. His Lordship has told him to go away.

COUNTESS. Oh sir, won't you change your mind?

COUNT. He doesn't deserve it.

COUNTESS. But he's so young!

COUNT. He's not as young as you think!

CHERUBIN [*quaking*]. When you married Madame, the feudal privilege you renounced wasn't the right to pardon.

COUNTESS. He gave up only the right you all thought was a wrong.

SUZANNE. If his Lordship had really given up the right to pardon, I'm sure that in his heart it would the first he'd want to reinstate.

COUNT [*embarrassed*]. Naturally.

COUNTESS. Then there's no need to reinstate it.

CHERUBIN [*to the* COUNT]. I've behaved very badly, your Lordship, but I've never been indiscreet in anything I've said...

COUNT [*embarrassed*]. All right, that's enough.

FIGARO. What does he mean?

COUNT [*sharply*]. I said that's enough! Everyone wants him pardoned. Very well, I pardon him, and I'll even go one better: I shall give him a company in my regiment.

ALL. Three cheers for his Lordship!

COUNT. But only on condition that he leaves immediately for Catalonia to take up his command.

FIGARO. Oh sir, couldn't you make that tomorrow?

COUNT [*insistent*]. My decision is final.

CHERUBIN. I shall obey.

COUNT. Say goodbye to your godmother and ask her to pray for you.

[CHERUBIN *drops on one knee to the* COUNTESS *but is unable to speak*

COUNTESS [*emotionally*]. Since we cannot keep you for even one more day, go you must. A new career awaits you, make the most of the opportunity. Be a credit to his Lordship. Remember this house, where as a boy you were treated with great kindness. Be loyal, honourable, and brave, and we shall all share your success.

[CHERUBIN *gets to his feet and returns to his place*

COUNT. You seem very moved, Madame!

COUNTESS. I won't deny it. Who can say what might happen to a boy pushed into such a dangerous career? He is related to my family and he's also my godson.

COUNT [*aside*]. So Bazile was right. [*Aloud*] Come, young man. Kiss Suzanne... for the last time.

FIGARO. Why the last time, sir? He'll be back to spend his winter leaves here. Come, Captain, kiss me too! [*He embraces him*] Goodbye Cherubin, my boy. Your life is about to be turned upside down, laddie. From now on, there'll be no more prowling about outside ladies' rooms all day for you! No more cakes and cream teas, no more hunt the slipper and blind man's buff. Just tough old soldiers, by God! Weather-beaten, ragged, carrying long, heavy muskets. Right turn, left turn, forward march, onwards to glory—and no faltering on the way, unless a musket-shot...

SUZANNE. Stop that at once, it's horrible!

COUNTESS. What a picture!

COUNT. But where's Marceline? It's very odd that she isn't here with the rest of you.

FANCHETTE. Please sir, she's gone to town, along the lane that goes past the farm.

COUNT. When's she coming back?

BAZILE. When the good Lord decides.

FIGARO. Let's hope he never decides.

FANCHETTE. I saw her walking back on the Doctor's arm.

COUNT [*abruptly*]. Is the Doctor here?

BAZILE. She commandeered him the minute he arrived.

COUNT [*aside*]. He couldn't have come at a better time.

FANCHETTE. She looked very put out. She was talking in a great loud voice as she walked along, and then she'd stop and go like this, with her arms stretched out wide, and the Doctor went like this with his hand to calm her down. She was ever so cross! And she kept saying the name of my cousin Figaro.

COUNT [*takes her chin*]. Not quite yet. Cousin-to-be.

FANCHETTE [*gesturing to* CHERUBIN]. Your Lordship, have you for-given us for yesterday?

COUNT [*interrupting her*]. That'll be all for now, my dear.

FIGARO. Marceline's in love, it's all she thinks about. She'd have ruined our wedding.

COUNT [*aside*]. And she'll ruin it yet, that I guarantee. [*To the* COUNTESS] Come, Madame, let us go in. Bazile, I want to see you in my study.

SUZANNE [*to* FIGARO]. Will you drop by to see me later, my sweet?

FIGARO [*whispers to* SUZANNE]. Have we pulled the wool over his eyes?

SUZANNE [*whispers back*]. What a silly boy you are!

All leave. As they go, FIGARO *stops* CHERUBIN *and* BAZILE *and brings them back*

SCENE 11

CHERUBIN, FIGARO, BAZILE

FIGARO. Just a minute, you two. Part One—getting the ceremonial adopted—has been achieved. The celebration of my wedding later on is Part Two. But we need to run through the arrangements carefully. Let's not be like actors who never perform so badly as when the critics are in the theatre. Unlike them, we don't have a second night to make up for ruining the first. We've got to be word perfect tonight.

BAZILE [*foxily*]. My part is a lot harder than you think

FIGARO [*taking care not to be seen, pretends to give him a good thrashing*]. And you have no idea of what a startling success you're going to be in it.

CHERUBIN. But aren't you forgetting I'm going away?

FIGARO. But you'd prefer to stay?

CHERUBIN. If only I could!

FIGARO. We'll have to resort to low cunning. So no weeping and wailing when you leave. Hang your travel cloak over your shoulder, sling your bags over your saddle in full view, and make sure your horse is visible at the gate. Gallop as far as the farm and then return on foot the back way. His Lordship will think you've gone. Just keep out of his sight and leave me to smooth his feathers once the wedding is over.

CHERUBIN. But Fanchette hasn't learned her part.

BAZILE. Then what on earth have you been teaching her this past week? She's not been out of your sight!

FIGARO. You don't have anything to do today, so you might as well give her an extra lesson.

BAZILE. Have a care, young man, be on your guard! The girl's father is not best pleased. She's already had one good hiding from him. Learning her lines is the last thing she's been doing with you. Oh Cherubin, Cherubin, you'll land her in deep trouble. You can lead a horse to water...

FIGARO. Damn, he's off again, the old fool and his venerable proverbs. All right, professor, what has wisdom of the ages to say on the matter? You can lead a horse to water... and?...

BAZILE. And he'll drink if he's thirsty.

FIGARO [as he leaves]. That's not bad! Really not bad at all!

ACT II

A sumptuously appointed bedchamber. In a recess at the back of the stage is a large bed raised on a dais. The main door in and out is upstage right, another door to a dressing-room is downstage left, and a third, at the back of the stage, leads to the maids' quarters. Opposite this door is a window

SCENE 1

SUZANNE *and the* COUNTESS *enter through the door on the right*

COUNTESS [*throws herself into an armchair*]. Close the door, Suzanne, tell me the whole story down to the very last detail.

SUZANNE. I haven't held anything back, Madame.

COUNTESS. You mean, Suzanne, that he seriously intended to seduce you?

SUZANNE. Oh no! His Lordship wouldn't go to all that bother for a servant. He tried to buy me.

COUNTESS. And the page was there all the time?

SUZANNE. In the sense that he was hiding behind the large armchair, yes. He came to ask me to ask you to intervene on his behalf.

COUNTESS. But why didn't he just come straight to me? Do you imagine I would have said no, Suzanne?

SUZANNE. That's what I said. But he was so upset at the thought of going away and especially of leaving you, Madame! 'Oh Suzette, she is as noble as she is fair. But she's a bit forbidding.'

COUNTESS. Is that how I really seem, Suzanne? I've always tried to be kind to him.

SUZANNE. Then he saw your ribbon which I had in my hand and he grabbed it...

COUNTESS [*smiling*]. My ribbon? How like a child!

SUZANNE. I tried to get it back from him but, Madame, he fought like a lion. His eyes blazed. 'If you want it back, it'll be over my dead body', he said as loud as he could in that melting, piping voice of his.

COUNTESS [*dreamily*]. And then, Suzanne?

SUZANNE. Well, Madame, how does anyone stop a little devil like him? One minute it was respect for 'My godmother', the next 'If only I dared', and because he didn't even dare kiss the hem of your dress, he tried to kiss me instead!

COUNTESS [*dreamily*]. Let's... let's say no more of this foolishness... So, Suzanne my dear, what did my husband say to you?

SUZANNE. That if I wouldn't co-operate, he'd give Marceline his full backing.

COUNTESS [*gets up and walks about, fanning herself*]. He doesn't love me any more.

SUZANNE. Why is he so jealous, then?

COUNTESS. He's like all husbands, my dear! Simple pride! Ah, I loved him too much. I've bored him with my affection, wearied him with my love. Those are the only wrongs I have done him. But I won't allow your honesty in telling me this to harm your future. You shall marry Figaro. Only he can help us ensure that you do. Is he coming?

SUZANNE. As soon as he sees the hunt off.

COUNTESS [*fanning herself*]. Open the garden window a little. It's so hot in here...

SUZANNE. That's because your Ladyship has grown heated talking and walking like that.

[*She crosses to the window*

COUNTESS [*meditatively*]. If he weren't so determined to avoid me... Men have a great deal to answer for!

SUZANNE [*at the window*]. There goes his Lordship, riding out through the far garden with Pedrillo and two, three, four hounds.

COUNTESS. We've got plenty of time. [*She sits down*] Was that a knock at the door, Suzanne?

SUZANNE [*runs to open the door, and sings*]. My Figaro! It's my Figaro!

SCENE 2

FIGARO, SUZANNE, *the* COUNTESS *seated*

SUZANNE. Do come in, my sweet. Madame is desperate to talk to you.

FIGARO. And you aren't, Suzanne, my pet? There's no reason to despair, your Ladyship. Look, what's the problem? It's nothing. His Lordship takes a fancy to this young woman here present and wants her as his mistress. It's perfectly natural.

SUZANNE. Natural?

FIGARO. So he gives me the job of carrying his dispatches and adds Suzette to his embassy staff. Now that's a smart move.

COUNTESS. Have you finished?

FIGARO. And because Suzanne, my fiancée, won't accept the honour, he decides to take Marceline's side. Again, what could be simpler? You get even with those who upset your plans by spoiling theirs. Everybody does it—and we're going to do it too. There, I think that sums it up.

COUNTESS. Oh Figaro, how can you be so offhand about his intentions which threaten the happiness of all of us?

FIGARO. Who says I'm offhand?

SUZANNE. Instead of taking our fears seriously...

FIGARO. I'm serious enough to be doing something about them. Now, if we are to proceed as methodically as his Lordship, first we reduce his enthusiasm for acquiring what belongs to us by making him unsure of his grip on what belongs to him.

SUZANNE. Good idea. But how?

FIGARO. It's already done, your Ladyship. A wicked rumour has been spread about you...

COUNTESS. About me! Are you mad?

FIGARO. No, but he will be.

COUNTESS. A man as jealous as he is...

FIGARO. But that's all to the good. If you want to get the better of people like him, you only have to needle them lightly, as you ladies know only too well. Then, when you've made them suitably furious, it only takes some light steering and you can point them in any direction you choose—straight into the Guadalquivir if that's what you want. I've arranged for an unsigned letter to be delivered to Bazile. It warns his Lordship that tonight, during the celebrations, a man will try to approach you.

COUNTESS. But you can't play with the truth like this when a woman's good name is involved!

FIGARO. There are few women, Madame, with whom I would have been so bold, for fear my story turned out to be the truth.

COUNTESS. You mean I should be grateful!

FIGARO. But wouldn't you agree that it's rather amusing to think that we're filling up his day for him, so that he spends time prowling around, thinking the worst of his wife, which he would otherwise have passed agreeably with mine? Already he's in two minds. Should he run after this woman or keep an eye on that one? He doesn't know which way to turn. Look, there he goes, across the fields, chasing an exhausted hare! The time for our wedding is approaching fast. He'll have done nothing to prevent it and he won't have the nerve to object if your Ladyship's there.

SUZANNE. True, but Marceline, who's nobody's fool, will.

FIGARO. Pish! I'm not worried about her. You send word to his Lordship that you will be in the garden just as it's getting dark.

SUZANNE. You think it'll work?

FIGARO. Damn it all, listen! People who won't try to make something out of nothing, achieve nothing and are good for nothing. That's my motto.

SUZANNE. Sounds too clever by half.

COUNTESS. Just like this plan. You're not seriously intending to let her go?

FIGARO. Of course not. I shall dress someone else in Suzanne's clothes. Then we catch the Count red-handed and he won't be able to talk his way out of it.

SUZANNE. Who'll wear my clothes?

FIGARO. Cherubin.

COUNTESS. But he's gone.

FIGARO. Not as far as I'm concerned. Will you allow me to get on with it?

SUZANNE. You can always count on Figaro when there's a plot afoot.

FIGARO. Two plots, three, four at a time, as involved and tangled as you like. I should have been a politician.

SUZANNE. They say it's not an easy thing to be.

FIGARO. Take, grab, demand: that's the secret of it in three words.

COUNTESS. He exudes such confidence that some of it is wearing off on me.

FIGARO. That's what I was hoping for.

SUZANNE. You were saying?

FIGARO. That while his Lordship is out I will send Cherubin here. Do his hair and dress him up. I'll keep him out of harm's way and tell him what he has to do. Then his Lordship will have to dance to our tune!

[*He goes out*

SCENE 3

SUZANNE, *the* COUNTESS *seated*

COUNTESS [*reaching for her patch box**]. Heavens, Suzanne, I look a fright! And with that young man due at any moment...

SUZANNE. Your Ladyship's not intending to go easy on him?

COUNTESS [*staring dreamily into her mirror*]. Go easy?... I shall give him a good scolding. You'll see.

SUZANNE. Let's make him sing that song he wrote.

[*She puts it in the* COUNTESS*'s lap*

COUNTESS. No, but really, my hair is such a mess...

SUZANNE. All it needs is for me to put these two curls back where they belong, then you can scold away.

COUNTESS [*herself again*]. What were you saying, Suzanne?

SCENE 4

CHERUBIN, *looking sheepish*, SUZANNE, *the* COUNTESS *seated*

SUZANNE. Do come in, Captain. Madame is at home.

CHERUBIN. I hate being called Captain—it reminds me that I have to leave this house... and a godmother who is so... so kind.

SUZANNE. And so beautiful!

CHERUBIN [*sighing*]. Oh yes!

SUZANNE [*mimicking him*]. 'Oh yes!' Such a nice young man! Oh, those long, cheating eyelashes! Come on, my fine-feathered blue-bird,* sing the song for her Ladyship...

COUNTESS [*unfolds the paper*]. And who did you say it was by?

SUZANNE. Aha, the guilty party blushes! It's written all over his face!

CHERUBIN. Am I not allowed to... admire...

SUZANNE [*brandishing her fist in his face*]. I'll tell everything, you little worm!

COUNTESS. All right, all right... Can you sing?

CHERUBIN. Oh your Ladyship, I'm so nervous I'm shaking.

SUZANNE [*laughing*]. Get away with you! The minute Madame wants to hear your song, you come over all modest, like a real author. Come along, I'll accompany you.

COUNTESS. Take my guitar.

The COUNTESS, *who is seated, holds the paper and follows the*
words. Positioned behind her chair, SUZANNE *plays the introduction,*
reading the music over the COUNTESS's *shoulder.* CHERUBIN
stands facing them, head lowered. This composition is an exact
replica of the print after Vanloo entitled: The Spanish
Conversation*[1]

ROMANCE

(Sung to the tune of 'Marlbroug* s'en va-t-en guerre')

My careering steed was breathless
(Oh how my heart doth ache with sadness)
As, through a terrain featureless,
I rode where'er my charger led me.

I rode where'er my charger led me,
Without squire or lackey to attend me;
Until beside a fountain's freshness[2]
(Oh how my heart doth ache with sadness)
Mem'ries of my godmother surface
And I feel my tears flow free.

And I felt my tears flow free
Filling me with despondency;
I carved upon a cypress
(Oh how my heart doth ache with sadness)
Her name, but I remained anonymous.
The king passed by for all to see

The king passed by and all did see
His barons, knights, and splendid panoply;
Then up spake her Highness:
(Oh how my heart doth ache with sadness)
'Page, wherefore this distress?
Why do you weep so grievously?

Why do you weep so grievously?
Fear not, but speak and tell me.'

---

[1] CHERUBIN. The COUNTESS. SUZANNE.*
[2] In performance, the song began here: 'Once beside a fountain's freshness'...

The Spanish Conversation, engraving after Vanloo

'I mourn the loss, your Graciousness,
(Oh how my heart doth ache with sadness)
Of a godmother's gentleness
A lady I loved most tenderly.[1]

A lady I loved most tenderly
Whose loss will bring dark death to me.'
'Sir Page,' then quoth her Majesty,
(Oh how my heart doth ache with sadness)
'If now you are godmotherless
Her role henceforth shall fall to me.

Her role henceforth shall fall to me.
My very own page you shall be
And to Helen of the golden tress,
(Oh how my heart doth ache with sadness)
Who is daughter to a captain, no less,
One day you shall married be.

One day you shall married be.'
'I beg you, lady, stay this kind decree!
I would rather be bereft of gladness
(Oh how my heart doth ache with sadness)
And die of this sweet wretchedness
Than of its sweetness solaced be.'

COUNTESS. Very simple, very charming... and in fact rather touching.

SUZANNE [*moves and puts her guitar down on a chair*]. He's a young man who can be very touching... Now then, Captain, I suppose you've been informed that to add zest to this evening's jollity, we need to know in advance if one of my dresses will fit you?

COUNTESS. I'm afraid it won't.

SUZANNE [*measuring herself against him*]. He's the same height as me. Let's start by having that cloak off.

[*She removes his cloak*

COUNTESS. What if someone comes in?

---

[1] At this point the Countess stops the page by folding the paper. The rest is not sung in performance

SUZANNE. We're not doing anything wrong, are we? I'll lock the
door. [*She runs and locks the door*]. But first I want to see what can
be done about his hair.

COUNTESS. On my dressing-table. The bonnet with the turned-
down brim.

[SUZANNE *goes into the dressing-room, downstage left*

SCENE 5

CHERUBIN, *the* COUNTESS *seated*

COUNTESS. The Count won't know you're still in the castle until
just before the start of the ball. Afterwards we'll explain that we
had the idea because of the time it would take to get your commission signed and sealed...

CHERUBIN [*producing it*]. That's no good. I've got it here. His Lordship gave it to Bazile to give to me.

COUNTESS. That was quick. He doesn't let the grass grow under his
feet. [*She reads it*] He was in so much of a hurry he's forgotten to
put his seal on it.

[*She hands it back*

SCENE 6

CHERUBIN, *the* COUNTESS, SUZANNE

SUZANNE [*returning with a large bonnet*]. Seal? On what?

COUNTESS. His commission.

SUZANNE. It's already come?

COUNTESS. Exactly what I said. Is that my hat?

SUZANNE [*sits down next to the* COUNTESS]. Yes, and the pick of the
collection.

[*Sings through the pins in her mouth*

Come a little closer, don't be coy,
Johnny my lad, my blue-eyed boy.

[CHERUBIN *gets down on his knees and she arranges his hair*

There, Madame, he looks so sweet!

COUNTESS. Arrange his collar so that it looks a little more feminine.

SUZANNE [*arranges the collar*]. There. Would you believe it? The snotty-nosed brat makes a very pretty girl! I'm consumed with jealousy! [*She takes him by the chin*] If you don't mind, stop being so pretty!

COUNTESS. Don't be silly, Suzanne. That sleeve needs to be turned up so the cuff fits snugly. [*She turns the sleeve up*] What's this you've got round your arm? A ribbon!

SUZANNE. One of yours. I'm glad your Ladyship's seen it. I told him before that I'd tell you. If his Lordship hadn't come in, I'd have got the ribbon back from him. I'm nearly as strong as he is.

COUNTESS. What's this on it? Blood?

[*She removes the ribbon*

CHERUBIN. This morning, assuming I was going away, I was fixing my horse's curb when he tossed his head and the boss on the end of the bit caught my arm.

COUNTESS. No one ever used a ribbon to bandage...

SUZANNE. Especially a stolen ribbon. Anyway, bits and bosses, bits and bobs, all those horsey words don't mean a thing to me. Ooh, his arm's so white! It's like a woman's! Whiter than mine! Look, Madame!

[*She compares them*

COUNTESS [*frostily*]. You'd be more usefully occupied fetching the sticking-plaster from my dressing table.

[SUZANNE *laughs and pushes* CHERUBIN's *head away, with the result that he falls on all fours. She goes back into the dressing-room*

SCENE 7

CHERUBIN, *on hands and knees, the* COUNTESS *seated*

COUNTESS [*remains as she is for a moment without speaking, staring at her ribbon.* CHERUBIN *devours her with his eyes*]. This ribbon, sir...

it's a shade that suits me particularly and I was very cross to have lost it...

SCENE 8

CHERUBIN *on hands and knees, the* COUNTESS *seated,* SUZANNE

SUZANNE [*returning*]. What are you going to use to tie the plaster round his arm with?

> [*She gives the* COUNTESS *the plaster and a pair of scissors*

COUNTESS. When you fetch your dress for him, take the ribbon off another hat.

> [SUZANNE *leaves through the door at the back of the stage, taking the page's cloak with her*

SCENE 9

CHERUBIN, *on hands and knees, the* COUNTESS *seated*

CHERUBIN [*eyes lowered*]. The one you took off would have made it better in no time.

COUNTESS. Why? What's so special about it? [*Holds up the plaster*] This will do more good.

CHERUBIN [*haltingly*]. When a ribbon... has been tied round the hair... has touched the skin of... a person...

COUNTESS [*stopping him in mid-sentence*]. ... or persons unknown, it acquires healing properties? I never knew that. I'll have to keep the one you had round your arm, to test the theory. The next time I... one of the maids cuts herself, I'll try it out.

CHERUBIN [*glumly*]. It will stay here with you. But I have to go away.

COUNTESS. Not for always.

CHERUBIN. I'm so unhappy!

COUNTESS [*moved*]. Now he's crying. It's all that thoughtless Figaro's fault, with his talk of musket-shots.

CHERUBIN [*exalted*]. I long for the moment he predicted! If I knew for sure I was about to die, perhaps my voice would find the courage to...

COUNTESS [*interrupts and wipes his eyes with her handkerchief*]. Hush, child, not another word. You're not making any sense. [*A loud knocking; she raises her voice*] Who can be knocking on my door like that?

SCENE 10

CHERUBIN, *the* COUNTESS, *the* COUNT, *outside*

COUNT [*outside*]. Why have you locked this door?

COUNTESS [*alarmed, she rises*]. Merciful heavens, my husband! [*To* CHERUBIN, *who has also got to his feet*] And you with no cloak, collar undone and arms bare, alone here with me! It looks very bad. He'll have got the letter! He'll be so jealous!...

COUNT [*outside*]. Are you going to open this door?

COUNTESS. It's just that... I'm alone.

COUNT [*outside*]. Alone? Then who's that you're talking to?

COUNTESS [*desperate*]. Er... you, obviously.

CHERUBIN [*aside*]. After what happened yesterday and again this morning, he'll kill me!

[*He runs into the dressing-room and closes the door behind him*

SCENE 11

The COUNTESS *removes the key and hurries to let the* COUNT *in*

COUNTESS. How could I have let this happen?

SCENE 12

The COUNT, *the* COUNTESS

COUNT [*grimly*]. You don't usually lock your door

COUNTESS [*awkwardly*]. We... I was sorting some old clothes... that is, I was sorting clothes with Suzanne. She's just gone to her room for a minute.

COUNT [*suspiciously*]. You look and sound flustered.

COUNTESS. It's hardly surprising. Not surprising at all. I do assure you... we were talking about you... as I said, she's gone...

COUNT. Talking about me, were you? I came back because I was worried. I was just getting on my horse when I was given a note... I don't believe a word of it... but it's upset me all the same.

COUNTESS. What do you mean? What note?

COUNT. I'll say this, Madame: you and I are surrounded by some very unsavoury people. I've been warned that some time today, someone I thought was no longer here will attempt to approach you secretly.

COUNTESS. Whoever this bold person is, he'll have to come here, for I am not planning to leave this room all day.

COUNT. Not even for Suzanne's wedding tonight?

COUNTESS. Not for anything. I am not feeling at all well.

COUNT. It's a good thing the Doctor's here. [*The page in the dressing-room knocks over a chair*] What's that noise?

COUNTESS [*anxiously*]. What noise?

COUNT. Someone knocked a chair over.

COUNTESS. I didn't hear anything.

COUNT. Then you must have your mind on something else.

COUNTESS. Something else? What?

COUNT. There's someone in that room, Madame.

COUNTESS. Ah!... Who do you suppose could be there?

COUNT. That's what I asked you. I only got here a moment ago.

COUNTESS. Oh. Well, it's... Suzanne. Probably putting things away.

COUNT. But you said she'd gone to her room.

COUNTESS. Gone to her room, gone into that room, I really couldn't say.

COUNT. If it really is Suzanne, why are you looking so perturbed?

COUNTESS. Perturbed? About my maid?

COUNT. I have no idea if it's about your maid. But perturbed you certainly are.

COUNTESS. And you, sir, are most certainly perturbed by that girl. You're far more perturbed about her than I am.

COUNT [*angry*]. I'm so perturbed about her, Madame, that I insist on seeing her at once.

COUNTESS. I believe that's something you often insist on. But there is absolutely no foundation for your suspicions...

SCENE 13

The COUNT, *the* COUNTESS, *and* SUZANNE, *who pushes the upstage door open and comes in carrying clothes*

COUNT. Then they will be easily disposed of. [*He talks towards the door of the dressing-room*] Come out, Suzette. I order you to come out of there.

[SUZANNE *pauses at the recess upstage*

COUNTESS. But she's practically naked! You don't just come and invade a woman's privacy in her own rooms! She's been trying on some dresses I've given her as a wedding present. She ran away when she heard you arrive.

COUNT. If she's too afraid to show her face, at least she can speak.

[*Turning to the dressing-room*] Answer me, Suzanne. Are you in there?

        [*Upstage,* SUZANNE *dodges into the recess and takes cover*

COUNTESS [*indignantly, to the dressing-room*]. Suzanne, I forbid you to answer. [*To the* COUNT] Was there ever such an example of overbearing behaviour?

COUNT [*advancing on the dressing-room*]. Very well. Since she's not answering, I intend to see her—dressed or undressed!

COUNTESS [*standing in front of him*]. Anywhere else, I couldn't stop you. But I hope that here, within my own four walls...

COUNT. And I hope to find out in very short order who this mysterious Suzanne is. I can see it's no good asking you for the key. But there's one sure way of breaking down a feeble door like this. [*Calls*] Ho! Is there anyone there?

COUNTESS. You surely don't intend to call the servants and turn a suspicion into a public scandal which would make us the talk of the chateau?

COUNT. You're right, Madame. Very well, I'll manage all by myself. I'll go to straight to my room and get what I need. [*He begins to leave, then comes back*] But so that everything remains exactly as it is now, I would be obliged if you would come with me, without making a noise or causing a fuss, since you don't care much for either. It's a simple enough thing to ask, so I can't think you'll refuse.

COUNTESS [*dismayed*]. Ah! Who would ever dream of going against your wishes?

COUNT. Oh! I was forgetting the door to your maids' rooms. I must lock that one too, so that you are exonerated on all counts.

[*He walks to the back of the stage, locks the door, and removes the key*

COUNTESS [*aside*]. Oh Lord! How could I have been so careless as to let this happen?

COUNT [*returns*]. Now that this room is secure, take my arm, would you? [*Louder*] And as for Suzanne in the dressing-room, I ask her to be so kind as to wait there. When I return, the least that she can expect to happen to her is...

COUNTESS. Really, this is the most odious proceeding...

[*The* COUNT *escorts her out and locks the door behind them*

SCENE 14

SUZANNE, CHERUBIN

SUZANNE [*emerges from the recess, runs to the dressing-room, and speaks through the keyhole*]. Open up, Cherubin, open the door at once. It's Suzanne. Open the door and come out.

CHERUBIN [*emerges*].[1] Oh Suzette! What an awful scene!

SUZANNE. Now be off with you. There's not a moment to lose.

CHERUBIN [*panicking*]. How do I get out?

SUZANNE. I've no idea, but you must go.

CHERUBIN. What if there's no way out?

SUZANNE. Given what happened at your last meeting with him, you'd be massacred and the Mistress and I would be finished. Run and find Figaro, and tell him...

CHERUBIN. Perhaps the window overlooking the garden isn't all that high.

[*He runs and checks*

SUZANNE [*alarmed*]. But we're one floor up! It's not possible! Oh my poor mistress! And my wedding! Oh my Lord!

CHERUBIN [*rejoins her*]. The melon patch is directly underneath. Apart from squashing a row or two...

SUZANNE [*tries to stop him, shouting*]. You'll kill yourself!

CHERUBIN [*exalted*]. I'd jump into a burning pit, Suzette, I would, I'd throw myself in, before I'd let any harm come to her... But first a kiss to bring me luck!

[*He kisses her, runs to the window, and jumps out*

[1] CHERUBIN, SUZANNE.

SCENE 15

SUZANNE, *alone*

SUZANNE [*gives a cry of fright then collapses briefly into a chair. She crosses fearfully to the window and comes back*]. He's far away already. Oh, the little scamp! As nimble as he's pretty! He'll never be short of women hanging round him... Quickly, take his place. [*She goes into the dressing-room*] And now, your Lordship, you can smash the door down if that's what amuses you. And you can think again if you imagine I'm going to say a word!

[*She closes the door behind her*

SCENE 16

The COUNT *and the* COUNTESS *return*

COUNT [*carrying a crowbar, which he tosses on to a chair*]. Everything is exactly as I left it. Now Madame, before you force me to break that door down, give a thought to the consequences. I ask you again: will you unlock it?

COUNTESS. What possible motive could you have for riding rough-shod like this over the ties that bind husband and wife? If it were your love for me that was the cause of your rage, then however unreasonably you behaved, I could forgive you. If love were really the reason, I might even forget how offensive I find your way of expressing it. But surely vanity alone cannot be enough to drive a gentleman to such unbecoming conduct?

COUNT. Call it love, call it vanity, but you will open this door, or else I'll...

COUNTESS [*stands in front of him*]. Stop, sir! I beg you! Do you think me so lacking in principles?

COUNT. Whatever you say, Madame. But I intend to see who is in your dressing-room!

COUNTESS [*terrified*]. Very well, sir, you shall see. Listen to me... calmly.

COUNT. So it's not Suzanne!

COUNTESS. Nor is it a person... from whom you have anything to fear... We were planning a practical joke for this evening... all very innocent I assure you... and I swear... I swear...

COUNT. What do you swear?

COUNTESS. That neither of us had any intention whatsoever of upsetting you.

COUNT. Neither of us? Is this person a man?

COUNTESS. A boy.

COUNT. What boy?

COUNTESS. I hardly dare say his name!

COUNT [*furious*]. I'll kill him!

COUNTESS. Merciful heavens!

COUNT. Tell me!

COUNTESS. It's young... Cherubin.

COUNT. Cherubin! The insolent puppy! This confirms my suspicions and explains the note!

COUNTESS [*clasping both hands*]. Oh, you mustn't think...

COUNT [*stamping his foot, to himself*]. Wherever I look, I find that damned page! [*Aloud*] Come, Madame, open the door. It's all clear to me now. You wouldn't have been so upset when you said goodbye to him this morning, he'd have gone when I told him to, you wouldn't have concocted that cock-and-bull story about Suzanne, and he wouldn't have taken such good care to stay hidden, if there wasn't something underhand going on!

COUNTESS. He was afraid he'd make you angry if he showed himself.

COUNT [*beside himself, shouting at the dressing-room*]. Will you come out, you wretched boy!

COUNTESS [*throws her arms around him and drags him away*]. Oh sir, you are so angry I fear for his life! I beg you, do not be misled by unfounded suspicions or the fact that he's half-undressed...

COUNT. Undressed?

COUNTESS. Regrettably, yes. He was getting ready to be disguised as a woman—a wig of mine on his head, just his shirt, no coat, collar open, bare arms. He was about to try on...

COUNT. And you were intending to stay in your room! As befits a good wife? Oh, you shall stay in your room... a good long stay. But first I must make sure he's kicked out so I don't keep coming across him any more.

COUNTESS [*falls to her knees, arms raised in supplication*]. My Lord! Spare him, he's only a boy. I should never forgive myself for being the cause...

COUNT. Your fears increase his guilt.

COUNTESS. He's not guilty. He was leaving. It was I who had him called back.

COUNT [*furious*]. Stand up! Get out of my way... How dare you presume to plead for another man!

COUNTESS. Very well, I shall get out of your way, I shall stand up, I will even give you the key to my dressing-room. But for the sake of your love...

COUNT. My love! For a faithless wife?

COUNTESS [*gets up and offers him the key*]. Promise me you'll let the boy go without harming him. And then you may take your anger out on me if I can't convince you...

COUNT [*takes the key*]. I'll not listen to another word.

COUNTESS [*collapses into a chair, dabbing her eyes with a handkerchief*]. Oh my God! He'll be killed!

COUNT [*opens the door and recoils*]. It's Suzanne!

SCENE 17

The COUNTESS, *the* COUNT, SUZANNE

SUZANNE [*comes out laughing*]. 'I'll kill him, I'll kill him.' Go on, then, kill the dratted page!

COUNT [*aside*]. This is a disaster! [*Looking at the* COUNTESS *who is rigid with astonishment*] And I suppose you're play-acting too, pretending to be amazed? But perhaps she wasn't in there by herself.

[*He enters the dressing-room*

SCENE 18

The COUNTESS *seated,* SUZANNE

SUZANNE [*runs to her mistress*]. Don't take on so, Madame, he's miles away—he jumped for it.

COUNTESS. Suzanne, I think I'm going to die.

SCENE 19

The COUNTESS *seated,* SUZANNE, *the* COUNT

COUNT [*emerges looking embarrassed, and pauses briefly*]. There's no one there. As it turns out, I was wrong. Madame, you are a most talented actress.

SUZANNE [*chirpily*]. And I suppose I'm not, sir?

[*The* COUNTESS *does not reply but holds her handkerchief to her mouth while she settles her nerves*[1]

COUNT. So, Madame, it was all just a joke?

COUNTESS [*recovering her composure*]. And why not, sir?

COUNT. It was in abominable taste. May I ask why you did it?

COUNTESS. Does your outrageous behaviour deserve to be treated otherwise?

COUNT. What you call 'outrageous behaviour' is a matter of honour.

COUNTESS [*steadily becoming more confident*]. Did I marry you so that I could be the eternal victim of your neglect and jealousy, which only you would dare try to justify?

[1] SUZANNE, *the* COUNTESS *seated, the* COUNT.

COUNT. Oh Madame, it was never deliberate.

SUZANNE. Her Ladyship could easily have let you go ahead and call the servants.

COUNT. You're right, and I am the one who should apologize... I'm sorry, I feel very ashamed of myself...

SUZANNE. Why not admit, sir, that you deserve to be?

COUNT. Why didn't you come out when I called, you wicked girl!

SUZANNE. I was trying to get dressed as best I could, I had pins sticking in me everywhere, Madame was telling me not to, and I assumed she had her reasons for doing so.

COUNT. Instead of going on and on about how wrong I was, why don't you help me put things right with her?

COUNTESS. No, sir. The affront is too grave to be forgiven. I shall withdraw to a convent. I see it is high time I went.

COUNT. Could you go with no regrets?

SUZANNE. I'm quite sure there'd be tears ever after.

COUNTESS. And what if there were, Suzette? I'd prefer regrets to the thought that I'd stooped so low as to forgive him. He has wounded me too deeply for that.

COUNT. Rosine!

COUNTESS. I have ceased to be the Rosine you once pursued so passionately! I am poor Countess Almaviva, the sad, deserted wife you do not love any more.

SUZANNE. Your Ladyship!

COUNT [*beseechingly*]. For pity's sake!

COUNTESS. Pity? You showed me no pity.

COUNT. But there was the note... it made my blood boil.

COUNTESS. I never agreed it should be written:

COUNT. You knew about it?

COUNTESS. It was that hare-brained Figaro...

COUNT. He had a hand in this?

COUNTESS. ...who gave it to Bazile.

COUNT. Who told me he'd got it from some yokel. Oh, I'll make him change his double-dealing tune!... of all the two-faced... I'll see he pays for the whole lot of them!

COUNTESS. You want to be forgiven yourself but won't forgive others. Just like a man! If I ever felt I could forgive you because you were misled by the note, I'd insist that everyone involved was forgiven too!

COUNT. And so they shall, with all my heart, Countess. But how can I atone for making such a shameful mistake?

COUNTESS [*rising*]. We should both be ashamed.

COUNT. No, no, say it was all my fault. It's still beyond me how quick women are to adopt exactly the right gestures and tone of voice to suit the situation. You blushed, you wept, your face was tragic... Upon my word, it still is!

COUNTESS [*with a forced smile*]. I blushed... because I resented your insinuations. But does a man have the sensitivity to distinguish the honest indignation of a woman wronged from the agitation of those who are justly accused?

COUNT [*smiling*]. And the page, half-dressed, in his shirt, more or less naked?

COUNTESS [*pointing to* SUZANNE]. Here he is, before your very eyes. Aren't you glad it was this one, not the other? You don't normally recoil from her company!

COUNT [*laughing louder*]. And all that pleading and pretending to cry?

COUNTESS. You're making me laugh, but I really don't feel like laughing.

COUNT. We men think we're rather good at politics but really we're only children who play at it. You're the one, Madame, the king should send as his ambassador to London! Have all women put themselves through an advanced course of self-control to be as good at it you are?

COUNTESS. Men leave us no alternative.

SUZANNE. If you'd only treat women like prisoners on parole, you'd soon see if we can be left to do the decent thing.

COUNTESS. Let's leave matters there, Count. Perhaps I did go too far. But since I have been so understanding, despite the gravity of the provocation, then surely you will respond in kind?

COUNT. But I want to hear you say once more that you forgive me.

COUNTESS. Did I say I forgave him, Suzanne?

SUZANNE. I didn't hear you, Madame.

COUNT. All right, but won't you say it now?

COUNTESS. Do you think you deserve it, unfeeling man?

COUNT. Yes, because I'm genuinely sorry.

SUZANNE. Suspecting that there was a man in Madame's dressing-room!

COUNT. She has punished me harshly!

SUZANNE. Refusing to take her word when she said it was her maid!

COUNT. Rosine, are you really immovable?

COUNTESS. Oh Suzette, I'm so weak! What an example I am to you. [*Holding out her hand to the* COUNT] After this, no one will ever believe in a woman's fury again.

SUZANNE. Can't be helped, Madame. With men, doesn't it always come down to this in the end?

[*The* COUNT *kisses his wife's hand passionately*

SCENE 20

SUZANNE, FIGARO, *the* COUNTESS, *the* COUNT

FIGARO [*enters breathless*]. They said her Ladyship wasn't well. I came at the double... I'm delighted to see there's nothing wrong.

COUNT [*sharply*]. You seem very attentive.

FIGARO. All part of the service. But since everything seems as it should be, my Lord, all the young men and women on the estate have assembled downstairs with fiddles and pipes, ready to accompany me whenever you give the word and I lead my bride...

COUNTESS. Who'll stay here and keep an eye on her Ladyship at the castle?

FIGARO. Keep an eye?... But she's not ill.

COUNT. No, but what about this man who isn't here but will try to approach her?

FIGARO. What man who isn't here?

COUNT. The one in the note you gave to Bazile.

FIGARO. Who said I did?

COUNT. If I hadn't already been reliably informed that you did, wretch, the guilt written all over your face would prove that you're lying.

FIGARO. If that's so, it's not me that's lying but my face.

SUZANNE. Poor Figaro, the game's up. Don't waste your breath trying to come up with complicated excuses. We've told him everything.

FIGARO. Told him what? You're not talking to Bazile, you know!

SUZANNE. That you wrote that note this morning, so that when his Lordship came he would think that the page was in the dressing-room where I was, with the door locked.

COUNT. Well, what have you got to say to that?

COUNTESS. It's no good trying to hide anything, Figaro, the charade's over.

FIGARO [*struggling to get his bearings*]. The charade... is over?

COUNT. Over. Finished. Now what do you say?

FIGARO. I say... that I wished as much could be said about my wedding. So if you'll give the order...

COUNT. So you admit knowing all about the letter!

FIGARO. Since her Ladyship says I do, Suzanne says I do, and you yourself say I do, then I'd better say I do too—though if I were you, I honestly wouldn't believe a word of what we're saying.

COUNT. You've not got a leg to stand on and still you go on lying! I tell you, I'm beginning to lose my temper.

COUNTESS [*laughing*]. Oh, poor Figaro! Do you really expect him to tell the truth for once in his life?

FIGARO [*whispers to* SUZANNE]. I warned him of the danger—I honestly couldn't have done more.

SUZANNE [*whispers*]. Did you see the page?

FIGARO [*whispers*]. Still a bit shaken.

SUZANNE [*whispers*]. Poor boy!

COUNTESS. Come, sir, they can't wait to be married. It's only natural they should be impatient. Let us go down for the ceremony.

COUNT [*aside*]. Where's Marceline? Why isn't she here? [*Aloud*] I should... like to be dressed for the occasion at least.

COUNTESS. For the servants? I won't be.

SCENE 21

FIGARO, SUZANNE, *the* COUNTESS, *the* COUNT, ANTONIO

ANTONIO [*half-drunk, carrying a pot of wallflowers*]. Sir! Your Lordship!

COUNT. What do you want, Antonio?

ANTONIO. Get some proper bars put on them windows once and for all, the ones my flowerbeds is under. All sorts of things get throwed out of them windows. Somebody just throwed a man out.

COUNT. Out of this window?

SUZANNE [*aside to* FIGARO]. On your toes, Figaro. Stay awake!

FIGARO. He's always drunk before breakfast, sir.

ANTONIO. You're way off the mark. Bit of a hangover from yesterday, that's all. Jumping to conclusions like that, it's... unethicalacious.

COUNT [*furiously*]. What about the man? Where is he now?

ANTONIO. Where's he at?

COUNT. Yes.

ANTONIO. That's exackly what I'm saying. He's gotter be found. I'm your gardener. There's only me that looks after your garden. So when a man falls on it, you can see it's my good name wot gets trampled on, not just my flowers.

SUZANNE [*whispers to* FIGARO]. Get him off the subject!

FIGARO. Still on the bottle, then?

ANTONIO. If I didn't take a drink, I'd go mad.

COUNTESS. But drinking like this when there's no need...

ANTONIO. Drinking when we're not thirsty and making love all year round, your Ladyship, them's the only things that make us different from the beasts of the field.

COUNT [*sharply*]. Answer the question, or I'll send you packing!

ANTONIO. Maybe I wouldn't go.

COUNT. What do you mean?

ANTONIO [*tapping his temple*]. If you've not got enough upstairs to keep hold of a good gardener, I ain't so daft as to let go of a good employer such as yourself.

COUNT [*shakes him furiously*]. You said somebody threw a man out of that window?

ANTONIO. Yes, Excellency. Just now. Had a white shirt on. Ran away, by jingo, went off like a scared rabbit.

COUNT [*impatient*]. And then?

ANTONIO. I would have gone after him. But I fetched up against the gate and gave myself such a knock on the hand that I still can't move head nor tail of this finger.

[*He holds it up*

COUNT. But at least you'd recognize this man?

ANTONIO. I would indeed... if only I'd got a proper look at him.

SUZANNE [*aside to* FIGARO]. He didn't see who it was.

FIGARO. You're making a great fuss over a flowerpot! How many flowerpots make one fusspot? Whinging about wallflowers! There's no need to look any further, my Lord, it was me who jumped.

COUNT. What! It was you?

ANTONIO. 'How many flowerpots make one fusspot?' You've growed a lot since then. I thought you was a good bit shorter and more spindly.

FIGARO. Of course you did. When you jump, you bunch up.

ANTONIO. I reckon it was rather... how shall I say, more like that skinny page.

COUNT. You mean Cherubin?

FIGARO. Yes, with his horse too, rushed back for that very purpose from the gates of Seville which is where he probably is now.

ANTONIO. No, I never said that, I never! I didn't see no horse jump out. I'd have said so.

COUNT. God give me patience!

FIGARO. I was in the maids' room, in a white shirt—it was so hot! I was waiting there for Suzanne when suddenly I heard his Lordship's voice and this great hullabaloo. I don't know why but I panicked because of the note. And I must say I behaved very foolishly. Without thinking, I jumped into the flowerbed and landed awkwardly on my right foot.

[*He massages his foot*

ANTONIO. Since it was you, I better give you back this scrap of paper that fell out of your shirt when you was falling.

COUNT [*pouncing on it*]. Give that to me!

[*He opens the paper then refolds it*

FIGARO [*aside*]. He's got me!

COUNT [*to* FIGARO]. I can't imagine you were so frightened that you've forgotten what's written on this paper, or how it came to be in your pocket

FIGARO [*flustered, he runs through his pockets and produces various papers*]. Absolutely not... But the fact is I've got lots of bits of paper and they're all to be dealt with... [*Looks at one*] What's this one? oh, a letter from Marceline, four pages of it, wonderful stuff!... It wouldn't be the appeal sent by that wretched poacher who's in jail?... No, I've got that here... I did have the inventory of the furniture in the dower house in my other pocket...

[*The* COUNT *reopens the paper he is holding*

COUNTESS [*aside to* SUZANNE]. Oh Lord, Suzanne! It's Cherubin's commission!

SUZANNE [*aside to* FIGARO]. It's hopeless. It's Cherubin's commission!

COUNT [*recloses the paper*]. Well? You're a man who's never at a loss for words: can't you guess?

ANTONIO [*coming right up to* FIGARO].[1] His Lordship says can't you guess?

FIGARO [*pushes him away*]. Phew, you disgusting oaf. Do you have to stand so close when you're talking to me?

COUNT. So you can't remember what it is?

FIGARO. Got it! How stupid can I get. It'll be the poor lad's commission. He gave it to me and I forgot to return it. I'm such a fool! What'll he do without his commission? I'd better hurry...

COUNT. Why would he give it to you?

FIGARO [*flustered*]. He... wanted me to do something to it.

COUNT [*examines the paper*]. Everything's as it should be.

COUNTESS [*aside to* SUZANNE]. The seal.

SUZANNE [*aside to* FIGARO]. The seal's missing.

[1] ANTONIO, FIGARO, SUZANNE, *the* COUNT, *the* COUNTESS.

COUNT. You're not answering.

FIGARO. Actually, there is one small thing missing. He said it was usual...

COUNT. Usual? Usual? What's usual?

FIGARO. To add the seal with your coat of arms. Probably you didn't think it worth the bother.

COUNT [*reopens the paper and then tears it up angrily*]. So it seems fate has decided that I shall never get to the bottom of all this. [*Aside*] Figaro's the ringleader and it looks as if I'll never get my revenge.

[*He turns bad-temperedly to leave.* FIGARO *halts him.*

FIGARO. You're not going without giving the word for my wedding to proceed?

SCENE 22

BAZILE, BARTHOLO, MARCELINE, FIGARO, *the* COUNT, GRIPPE-SOLEIL, *the* COUNTESS, SUZANNE, ANTONIO, *plus servants and tenants of the* COUNT

MARCELINE [*to the* COUNT]. Do not give the word, my Lord! Before you grant his request, you owe us justice. He has obligations to me.

COUNT [*aside*]. My vengeance has come in person!

FIGARO. Obligations? What kind of obligations? Explain yourself!

MARCELINE. Oh I shall explain myself, you philanderer!

[*The* COUNTESS *sits in a chair and* SUZANNE *stands behind her*

COUNT. What's this all about, Marceline?

MARCELINE. A promise of marriage.

FIGARO. A receipt I signed, for some money she loaned me. That's all.

MARCELINE [*to the* COUNT]. A loan made on condition that he would marry me. You are a great lord and chief justice of the province...

COUNT. Present yourselves before the court and I shall do justice to all parties.

BAZILE [*pointing to* MARCELINE]. In that case, would your Excellency also allow me to set out the claim I have with respect to Marceline?

COUNT [*aside*]. Aha, it's the villain who gave me the note.

FIGARO. Another lunatic from the same stable!

COUNT [*angrily, to* BAZILE]. Claim! Your claim! You've got an infernal cheek standing there talking to me of claims, you great booby!

ANTONIO. By God, got him to a T straight off. Booby is right.

COUNT. Marceline, none of the planned arrangements will go ahead until we have looked into your claims. This will be done in open court, which will sit in the great council chamber. Honest Bazile, trusted and dependable bearer of messages, you will go into town and notify the members of the Bench.

BAZILE. To hear her case?

COUNT. And you will also bring back the yokel who gave you the note.

BAZILE. How would I know him again?

COUNT. Are you refusing?

BAZILE. I'm not here to act as the castle messenger boy.

COUNT. Why are you here?

BAZILE. As a distinguished village organist, I teach the harpsichord to her Ladyship, singing to her maids, and the mandoline to the pages. But my principal function is to entertain your Lordship's guests with my guitar, as and when it pleases you so to command.

GRIPPE-SOLEIL [*steps forward*]. I'll go if you like, your Honourship.

COUNT. What's your name and what do you do?

GRIPPE-SOLEIL. Grippe-Soleil, your Lordness, that looks after the goats. I was ordered along to help with the firey-works, so I gave the goats the day off. I knows where all them there fancy lawyers' houses are.

COUNT. You're keen, I like that. You can go—but you [*to* BAZILE] will escort this fine upstanding man and play your guitar and sing to entertain him on the way. He's a guest.

GRIPPE-SOLEIL [*delighted*]. Me? A guest!

[SUZANNE *calms him with a gesture of her hand and reminds him that the* COUNTESS *is present*

BAZILE [*astounded*]. I am to escort a goatherd and play my...

COUNT. That's what you're paid for. Now go, or I'll have you shown the door permanently.

[*He goes out*

SCENE 23

Cast as before, except the COUNT

BAZILE [*mutters*]. No use me trying to fight him. An iron fist in the bush is worth...

FIGARO. ...A dozen old birds like you!

BAZILE [*aside*]. I'll do nothing to help their wedding along. Instead, I'll make damned sure I marry Marceline. [*Aloud to* FIGARO] Take it from me, don't settle anything before I get back.

[*He picks up the guitar from the chair upstage*

FIGARO [*following him*]. Settle anything! Now don't you worry, I won't, even if you never come back... You don't look as if you feel much like singing. Do you want me to start you off?... Come on, look cheerful, chin up, and music, maestro! A song for the girl I shall marry.

[*He walks backwards, dancing and singing the seguidilla. He is accompanied by* BAZILE *and the procession follows him out*

SEGUIDILLA
Tune: as before

I'd swap all of your money
For the sweetness of honey
  That is my Suzanne
  Zanne, zanne, zanne,
  Zanne, zanne, zanne,
  Zanne, zanne, zanne.

She's so gentle and kind
I surrender my mind
  To my Suzanne
  Zanne, zanne, zanne,
  Zanne, zanne, zanne,
  Zanne, zanne, zanne.

[*The music recedes and we do not hear the rest*

SCENE 24

SUZANNE, *the* COUNTESS

COUNTESS [*seated*]. Suzanne, you saw what a dreadful scene your precious Figaro let me in for with that note of his?

SUZANNE. Oh Madame! when I came out of the dressing-room, you should have seen your face! It went all white, but that was just like a cloud passing over it and gradually it turned red, red as a beet-root all over!

COUNTESS. So he jumped out of the window?

SUZANNE. Without batting an eye. Such an attractive boy. And light as a butterfly.

COUNTESS. And then that horrible gardener! I was so shaken... I couldn't put two ideas together.

SUZANNE. But it was the very opposite, Madame! It made me real-ize what an advantage moving in high society gives a lady—it teaches her to lie convincingly.

COUNTESS. Do you think the Count was taken in? And what if he finds Cherubin here in the chateau?

SUZANNE. I'll go and make sure that he's hidden so well that...

COUNTESS. He must go away. After what's happened, you'll appreciate that I'm not happy about sending him to the garden instead of you.

SUZANNE. You can take it as read that I'm not going either. So once again my wedding...

COUNTESS [*stands*]. Wait a minute! Instead of sending him or you, what if I went myself?

SUZANNE. You, Madame?

COUNTESS. That way, no one would be running any risk... The Count couldn't deny the facts... And when I'd punished him for being jealous and proved he's being unfaithful, it would be... Look! We've come through one crisis: I'm tempted to try again. Send word to him at once that you'll meet him in the garden. But don't let anyone else...

SUZANNE. Not even Figaro?

COUNTESS. Certainly not. He'd only try to meddle. Fetch my velvet mask and my cane. I'll be on the terrace, mulling it all over.

[SUZANNE *goes into the dressing-room*

SCENE 25

The COUNTESS, *alone*

COUNTESS. This little scheme of mine is really quite bold. [*She turns*] Ah! the ribbon! My pretty ribbon. I'd almost forgotten all about you! [*She picks it up from the chair and rolls it up*] From now on, you'll stay with me... you remind me of the moment when that unfortunate boy... Ah, Count Almaviva, what have you done? And what do I think I'm doing now?

SCENE 26

The COUNTESS, *hiding the ribbon down the front of her dress*, SUZANNE

SUZANNE. Here are your cane and your mask.

COUNTESS. Remember: I've told you you're not to say a word about this to Figaro.

SUZANNE [*beaming*]. Your Ladyship, your plan is wonderful. I've just been thinking about it. It makes everything come together, brings it all to a conclusion and doesn't leave any loose ends. And whatever happens, I'm certain now that I shall be married after all.

[*She kisses the* COUNTESS*'s hand. Then they go out*

End of Act II

During the interval, SERVANTS *convert the set into the Great Council Chamber. Two benches with backs are brought in for the lawyers, one at each side of the stage, with sufficient space behind to allow free passage. A dais two steps high is placed in the middle of the stage and the* COUNT*'s chair is set on it. The table and stool of the clerk of the court are to one side downstage and seats for* BRID'OISON *and the other magistrates are provided on both sides of the* COUNT*'s dais.*

ACT III

A hall in the chateau, called the Throne Room, which now serves as a courtroom. On one wall a canopy hangs over a portrait of the king.

SCENE 1

The COUNT, PEDRILLO *in riding-coat and boots, a sealed packet in his hand*

COUNT. You're sure you've understood?

PEDRILLO. Yes, Excellency.

[*He goes out*

SCENE 2

The COUNT, *alone*

COUNT. Pedrillo!

SCENE 3

The COUNT, PEDRILLO

PEDRILLO [*returns*]. Excellency?

COUNT. Did any one see you?

PEDRILLO. Not a soul.

COUNT. Take the Arab.

PEDRILLO. He's tethered at the garden gate, all saddled and ready.

COUNT. Get moving, then, and don't stop till you get to Seville.

PEDRILLO. It's only three leagues, and the going's easy.

COUNT. The minute you arrive, find out if they've seen the page.

PEDRILLO. At the house?

COUNT. Yes, and ask how long he's been there.

PEDRILLO. Understood.

COUNT. Give him his commission. Then come straight back here.

PEDRILLO. And if he's not there?

COUNT. Come back even faster and report to me. Now, go!

SCENE 4

The COUNT *walks up and down, thinking*

COUNT. Sending Bazile away was a bad mistake... Losing your temper never helps. That note I got from him warning me that a man would try something on with the Countess... the maid in the dressing-room when I went back... her mistress quaking with terror, real or feigned... one man who jumps out of the window and then another man admits it was him... or claims it was him... I can't make any sense of it. There's something here that's not clear... Taking the odd liberty with your own servants is neither here nor there with people of that type. But the Countess! What if some determined swine thought he could... What am I saying? The fact is, when you start losing your temper, even the most tightly controlled imagination will run wild, just as it does in dreams. She was playing a game—all that suppressed laughter and barely disguised glee. She has her self-respect, and I have my honour... where the devil does my honour come in all this? Given all that, how do I stand? Has that minx Suzanne let my plans for her out of the bag? Maybe: nothing's happened yet, so there's nothing for her to keep quiet about. How did I get mixed up in this nightmare? I've tried many times to forget the whole thing. That's where being indecisive has got me! Now if it was all simple and uncomplicated, I wouldn't want her anywhere near as much. Figaro's a long time! I must probe him very carefully [FIGARO *appears upstage, then stops*] and try, in the course of the conversation, by subtle questioning, to find out whether or not he knows what my real feelings are for Suzanne.

SCENE 5

The COUNT, FIGARO

FIGARO [*aside*]. So that's it!

COUNT. ... and if she's as much as said one word to him about it...

FIGARO [*aside*]. I suspected as much.

COUNT. ... I shall force him to marry the old woman.

FIGARO [*aside*]. So much for Bazile's fond hopes.

COUNT. ... and then I'll see what's to be done with the girl.

FIGARO [*aside*]. My intended, if it's all the same to you.

COUNT [*turns*]. Eh? What? Who's that?

FIGARO [*steps forward*]. Only me. You rang, sir.

COUNT. Why did you say that?

FIGARO. I didn't say anything.

COUNT. 'My intended, if it's all the same to you.'

FIGARO. It was the end of a sentence. I was saying: 'And you can tell that to my intended, if it's all the same to you.'

COUNT [*pacing*]. 'Your intended'! Perhaps you'd be good enough to tell me, sir, what urgent matter kept you when I had sent for you?

FIGARO [*pretending to straighten his clothes*]. I got dirty when I fell into the flowerbed. I was getting changed.

COUNT. Does that take an hour?

FIGARO. It takes as long as it takes.

COUNT. The servants in this house take longer to dress than their masters.

FIGARO. That's because they haven't got servants to help them.

COUNT. I still can't understand what made you put yourself unnecessarily at risk by jumping...

FIGARO. Risk? Anybody would think I'd leaped into the abyss and been swallowed alive...

COUNT. You're avoiding the question by pretending to answer it. Don't be clever with me! You know very well that what concerns me is not the risk you took but why you took it.

FIGARO. You believe some tale that's not true and you burst in furiously, scattering all before you like some raging torrent in the Sierra Morena. You're hunting for a man. You've got to get him or you'll smash down doors and break through walls. I happen to be there by chance. How was I to know if, given the fact that you were incandescent...

COUNT [interrupts]. You could have got away down the stairs.

FIGARO. And you could have caught me in the corridor.

COUNT [furious]. In the corridor! [Aside] I mustn't lose my temper or I'll never find out what I want to know.

FIGARO [aside]. String him along, but play your cards close to your chest.

COUNT [more controlled]. That's not what I meant, so let's drop it. I was... yes, I was toying with the idea of taking you to London as my official courier, but on reflection...

FIGARO. Has your Lordship changed your mind?

COUNT. To start with, you can't speak English.

FIGARO. I can say 'God-damn'.*

COUNT. Sorry?

FIGARO. I said I can say 'God-damn'.

COUNT. So?

FIGARO. Devil take it, English is a marvellous language. A little of it will take you a long way. In England, if you've got God-damn, you can go anywhere and want for nothing. Fancy a nice plump chicken? You step into a tavern, you waggle your arm at the waiter like this [mimes turning a spit], you say God-damn! and they bring you a lump of salt beef and no bread! Marvellous! Feel like a glass of good burgundy or claret? Just do this [mimes opening a bottle] and God-damn!, they serve you foaming beer in a handsome pewter pot. Very satisfying! Say you happen to run across one of those pretty fillies who go tripping along all dainty, eyes on the ground, elbows back, hips gently swaying. All you do is give her a great big come-on of a wink and God-damn!, she fetches you one so hard you see stars. Which proves she understands exactly what you mean. I won't deny the English themselves do put in a few extra words here and there when they're talking to each other. But it's quite obvious that God-damn! is the key to the language. Now, if that's the only reason your Lordship has for leaving me here in Spain...

COUNT [*aside*]. He wants to go to London. So she hasn't talked.

FIGARO [*aside*]. He thinks I don't know a thing. Let's see how far we get by playing it his way.

COUNT. Tell me, what was the Countess's reason for playing her little game with me?

FIGARO. Really, sir, your Lordship knows far more about that than I do.

COUNT. I indulge her in every way. I shower her with gifts.

FIGARO. You give her presents, but you're unfaithful. Is a man without bread grateful for butter?

COUNT. There was a time when you told me everything.

FIGARO. I'm not hiding anything from you now.

COUNT. How much did the Countess pay you for your part in her little game?

FIGARO. How much did you pay me for extracting her from the Doctor's clutches? Look, sir, it's not very sensible to turn against a man who has proved his usefulness: you might make a bad valet of him.

COUNT. Why is it that there's always something louche about everything you do?

FIGARO. Because when you start looking for faults, you think everybody is louche.

COUNT. Your reputation is appalling.

FIGARO. Maybe I'm better than my reputation. Do you know many noble lords who could say that?

COUNT. How many times have I seen you set off on the road to fortune and never once stay on the straight and narrow?

FIGARO. That's hardly surprising—it's such a busy road: everyone fighting to get ahead, pushing, shoving, using their elbows and feet, every man for himself and anyone who gets in the way is trampled in the crush. That's what you have to do. Personally, I've given up on it.

COUNT. Given up on fame and fortune? [Aside] That's a novelty!

FIGARO [aside]. And now it's my turn. [Aloud] Your Lordship was good enough to appoint me steward to your household. It's a very nice life. As it happens, I won't ever rise to be an official messenger who carries the exciting dispatches. But on the other hand, I'm looking forward to living happily with my wife here in deepest Andalusia.

COUNT. What's to stop you taking her with you to London?

FIGARO. A man who was married and had to be away so much? I'd never hear the end of it.

COUNT. But with your qualities and brains you could climb the ladder and end up with an important government post one of these days.

FIGARO. Brains? Climb the ladder? Your Lordship must think I'm stupid. Second-rate and grovelling, that's the thing to be, and then the world's your oyster.

COUNT. All you'd have to do is take a few lessons in politics from me.

FIGARO. I know what politics is.

COUNT. Like you know the key to the English language?

FIGARO. Not that it's anything to boast about. It means pretending you don't know what you do know and knowing what you don't, listening to what you don't understand and not hearing what you do, and especially, claiming you can do more than you have the ability to deliver. More often that not, it means making a great secret of the fact that there are no secrets; locking yourself in your inner sanctum where you sharpen pens and give the impression of being profound and wise, whereas you are, as they say, hollow and shallow; playing a role well or badly; sending spies everywhere and rewarding the traitors; tampering with seals, intercepting letters, and trying to dignify your sordid means by stressing your glorious ends. That's all there is to politics, and you can have me shot if it's not.

COUNT. But what you've defined is intrigue.

FIGARO. Call it politics, intrigue, whatever you want. But since to me the two things are as alike as peas in a pod, I say good luck to whoever has anything to do with either. 'Truly, I love my sweetheart more', as old King Henry's song goes.*

COUNT [aside]. He intends to stay. I understand: Suzanne has told him.

FIGARO [aside]. I've led him up the garden path, which is what he wanted to do to me.

COUNT. So, you're hoping to win your case against Marceline?

FIGARO. Surely you don't think I'm wrong to say no to an old maid when your Excellency believes you're entitled to relieve us of all the young ones?

COUNT [laughing]. In court, a judge puts all personal feelings to one side and is concerned only with the law.

FIGARO. Which goes easy on the strong and hard on the weak.

COUNT. You think I'm joking?

FIGARO. Ah, who can tell, sir. *Tempo è galant'uomo*, as the Italians say, time is a gentleman, a gentleman who always tells the truth. And he will let me know who has my interests at heart and who has not.

COUNT [aside]. It's obvious he's been told everything. He'll marry the old baggage.

FIGARO [aside]. He was playing cat and mouse with me. How much does he really know?

SCENE 6

The COUNT, FOOTMAN, FIGARO

FOOTMAN. Don Gusman Brid'oison, sir.

COUNT. Brid'oison?

FIGARO. But of course. His worship, chairman of the Bench, your legal officer.

COUNT. Tell him to wait.

[*The* FOOTMAN *leaves*

SCENE 7

The COUNT, FIGARO

FIGARO [*stands for a moment watching the* COUNT, *whose mind is elsewhere*]. Is everything as you wanted it, sir?

COUNT [*with a start*]. What?... I gave orders that the room was to be set out for the public hearing.

FIGARO. Well, anything missing? The big chair for you, suitable seating for the magistrates, a stool for the clerk of the court, two benches for the lawyers, the floor area for the gentry, and then the rabble behind. I'll go and get rid of the men who've been polishing the floor.

SCENE 8

The COUNT, *alone*

COUNT. The jackanapes made me work hard there. Engage him in an argument and he takes the initiative, gets you by the throat, and then runs rings round you... Oh, he and she make a fine couple! So you've joined forces to get the better of me! Be friends, lovers, anything you want, and you have my blessing. But by God, husband and wife...!

SCENE 9

SUZANNE, *the* COUNT

SUZANNE [*out of breath*]. Your Lordship... Beg pardon, sir...

COUNT [*bad-temperedly*]. Well, what's the matter Suzanne?

SUZANNE. You're angry!

COUNT. I gather you want something.

SUZANNE [*shyly*]. The Mistress has the vapours again. I ran all the way here to ask if you'd lend us your smelling bottle. I'll bring it back straight away.

COUNT [*gives it to her*]. No, no, you can keep it. You'll be needing it soon yourself.

SUZANNE. Since when did girls of my sort have the vapours? Vapours is for ladies and you can only catch it in boudoirs...

COUNT. Still, a girl who's engaged and head over heels in love and about to lose the man she's going to marry...

SUZANNE. But what if I paid Marceline with the dowry money you promised me...

COUNT. Did I promise?

SUZANNE [*lowering her eyes*]. That was what I took you to say, your Lordship.

COUNT. Quite so, but only if you'd been willing to take my meaning.

SUZANNE [*eyes down*]. But isn't it my duty to obey, your Excellence?

COUNT. Why on earth didn't you say so sooner, you heartless girl?

SUZANNE. It's never too late to tell the truth.

COUNT. So you'll come to the garden, just when it's getting dark?

SUZANNE. I go there to take the air every evening, don't I?

COUNT. This morning you treated me very callously.

SUZANNE. This morning? With the page there hiding behind the chair?

COUNT. You're right, I'd forgotten about him. But why did you persist in saying no when Bazile kept telling you from me...

SUZANNE. Why do we need a Bazile?

COUNT. You're right every time. Still, there's a man by the name of Figaro, and I'm afraid you might have told him everything.

SUZANNE. Of course I tell him everything—except what he has no business knowing.

COUNT [*laughing*]. Delightful! So it's a promise? If you don't keep your word, let's be quite clear, my sweet: no meeting in the garden, no dowry, no wedding bells.

SUZANNE [*curtseying*]. But also no wedding bells means no old Spanish practices, sir.

COUNT. How does she do it? I tell you, I shall love you madly! But your mistress will be waiting for the smelling salts.

SUZANNE [*laughing and handing back the bottle*]. I had to have an excuse to talk to you, didn't I?

COUNT [*tries to kiss her*]. You delicious creature!

SUZANNE [*breaking free*]. Someone's coming!

COUNT [*aside*]. She's mine!

[*He hurries out*

SUZANNE. And now to report to her Ladyship.

SCENE 10

SUZANNE, FIGARO

FIGARO. Suzanne, Suzanne! Where do you think you're rushing like that? You were alone with his Lordship!

SUZANNE. You can go to court now if you want. You've just won your case.

[*She runs off*

FIGARO [*follows her*]. Hey, wait a minute...

SCENE 11

The COUNT *returns alone*

COUNT. 'You've just won your case!' I almost fell into a very cunning trap. Such lovely people—but so two-faced! I'll have you both for this! A good clean verdict should do it, all legal and above board... But what if he pays the old woman... but what with?... if he did pay... Aha! I can always fall back on Antonio, a man of the loftiest pride who thinks Figaro's a nobody and not good enough to marry his niece. If I encourage his snobbery... Why not? In the vast field of intrigue, you must know how to make use of everything, even the vanity of a fool. [*He begins to call*] Anton...

[*But, seeing* MARCELINE *and the others arrive, he leaves*

SCENE 12

BARTHOLO, MARCELINE, BRID'OISON

MARCELINE [*to* BRID'OISON]. Sir, may I put my side of the case?

BRID'OISON [*in judge's robes and speaking with a slight stammer*]. Very well. Let's talk about it oho-orally.

BARTHOLO. It's a breach of promise.

MARCELINE. Involving the loan of a sum of money.

BRID'OISON. I see, and then et cetera and so on and so fer-forth.

MARCELINE. No, sir, there was no et cetera.

BRID'OISON. I see. You have the money to per-pay?

MARCELINE. No, sir. I am the lender.

BRID'OISON. I see per-perfectly. You are asking for the money ber-back?

MARCELINE. No, sir. I want him to marry me.

BRID'OISON. Aha! I see, it's ker-crystal clear. And does he want to mer-marry you?

MARCELINE. No, sir. That's why we're going to trial.

BRID'OISON. Are you suggesting I don't understand this ker-case?

MARCELINE. No, sir. [To BARTHOLO] Is this getting us anywhere?
[To BRID'OISON] So will it be you who actually tries the case?

BRID'OISON. Why do you think I bought my jer-judgeship?

MARCELINE [sighs]. It's scandalous that public offices are sold.

BRID'OISON. Quite right. It would be far better if they gave them
out to us for ner-nothing. Who are you ser-suing?

SCENE 13

BARTHOLO, MARCELINE, BRID'OISON, and FIGARO, who enters
rubbing his hands

MARCELINE [points to FIGARO]. This worthless man, sir.

FIGARO [cheerfully to MARCELINE]. I trust I'm not getting in your
way? His Lordship will be back shortly, sir.

BRID'OISON. Haven't I seen you somewhere bee-before?

FIGARO. In Seville, your Worship, in your lady wife's service.

BRID'OISON. When was the-this?

FIGARO. A little under a year before the birth of your youngest son.
A very pretty boy. I'm very proud of him.

BRID'OISON. Yes, he's the best looking of all the tcher-children.
They tell me you've been up to your old ter-tricks again?

FIGARO. Your Worship is too kind. It's nothing, a minor matter.

BRID'OISON. A breach of promise? Aha, a poor, simple-mer-
minded...

FIGARO. Your Worship...

BRID'OISON. Have you seen my ser-secretary, young man?

FIGARO. You don't mean Double-Main, the clerk of the court?

BRID'OISON. Yes, he's got his snout in two ter-troughs.

FIGARO. Snout! I guarantee he's got both hands in as well! Yes of course I've seen him. About the abstract and the supplementary abstract, you know, the standard drill.

BRID'OISON. These fer-formalities have to be observed.

FIGARO. Absolutely, your Worship. The rights and wrongs of a case are the business of the parties involved, but we all know that procedure is the business that keeps the courts and the lawyers going so strong.

BRID'OISON. This young man is not as stupid as I fer-first thought. Well, my friend, since you know so much about these things, we shall take a special interest in your ker-case.

FIGARO. Sir, I shall trust to your innate sense of fairness, though I realize you are one of the judges.

BRID'OISON. Eh?... Yes, I'm one of the judges. But when you owe money and don't per-pay...

FIGARO. Then you do see, your Worship, that it's the same as if the money had never been owed in the first place.

BRID'OISON. Very possibly. Er!... What did he ser-say?

SCENE 14

BARTHOLO, MARCELINE, *the* COUNT, BRID'OISON, FIGARO, USHER

USHER [*preceding the* COUNT, *shouts*]. Gentlemen—his Lordship!

COUNT. Why the full robes, my dear Brid'oison? This is only a domestic matter. Town clothes would have been more than good enough.

BRID'OISON. It's your Lordship who is mer-more than good enough. I never sit without them, for fer-form's sake, you see, for the sake of fer-form. People will laugh at a judge in a short gown but they kwer-quake at the mere sight of a prosecuting counsel in full dress. Form, fer-form, fer-fer-form!

COUNT [*to the* USHER]. Open the doors!

USHER [*opens the doors, barking*]. Court's in session!

SCENE 15

Cast as before, plus ANTONIO, *men and women from the chateau and the estate in festive clothes. The* COUNT *sits in the large chair, with* BRID'OISON *at his side. The* CLERK OF THE COURT *goes to his stool behind his table. The* JUDGES *and* LAWYERS *fill the benches.* MARCELINE, *standing next to* BARTHOLO, *and* FIGARO *are on the bench opposite; the* SERVANTS *and* TENANTS *stand at the back*

BRID'OISON. Double-Main, call the list of parties and ser-suits.

DOUBLE-MAIN [*reads from a paper*]. The noble, right noble, and infinitely noble lord Don Pedro George, Hidalgo, Baron de los Altos, y Montes Fieros, y Otros Montes* *versus* Alonzo Calderon, a young playwright. The case concerns a comedy, stillborn, which each party disowns and seeks to have attributed to the other.

COUNT. Both are right. Case dismissed. If they collaborate on another play it is the ruling of this court that, with a view to ensuring that the said work achieves wide success, the noble shall contribute his name and the playwright his talent.

DOUBLE-MAIN [*reads from another paper*]. André Petrutchio, farmer, *versus* the district tax-collector. The case involves an appeal against liability to tax, alleged to be excessive.

COUNT. The case falls outside my jurisdiction. I can do my people far more good by protecting their interests through having the king's ear. Next!

DOUBLE-MAIN [*takes a third paper.* BARTHOLO *and* FIGARO *rise*]. Barbe-Agar-Raab-Madeleine-Nicole-Marceline de Verte-Allure, a spinster having attained the age of majority [MARCELINE *rises and curtseys*] *versus* Figaro... Christian name not given.

FIGARO. Anonymous.

BRID'OISON. Anonymous? Is there a Saint Aaa-Anonymous?

FIGARO. Yes. My patron saint.

DOUBLE-MAIN [*writing*]. *Versus* Anonymous Figaro. Rank?

FIGARO. Gentleman.

COUNT. A gentleman? You?

[*The* CLERK *writes*

FIGARO. If Heaven had so decreed, I'd have been the son of a prince.

COUNT [*to the* CLERK, *who has been writing it down*]. Carry on.

USHER [*bawls*]. Silence in court!

DOUBLE-MAIN [*reads*]. The case concerns an objection to the marriage of the said Figaro, which is opposed by the aforesaid Verte-Allure, Doctor Bartholo acting for the plaintiff and the aforementioned Figaro representing himself, if the court so permits, such a practice being contrary to the custom and usage of this Bench.

FIGARO. Usage, Mr Clerk, is often another name for abusage. Every client with a rudimentary education always has a better grasp of his own case than some floundering lawyer who loves the sound of his own voice, knows everything except the facts, and is no more concerned about ruining his client than about boring the court and putting their worships to sleep. And afterwards he is as pleased with himself as if he'd personally written the oration *Pro Murena*, Cicero's finest.* But I shall set out the facts in a few words. Your honours...

DOUBLE-MAIN. Those few words are too many: you're not the plaintiff. What you've got to do is defend yourself. Step forward, Doctor, and read out the promise of marriage.

FIGARO. Yes, the promise!

BARTHOLO [*putting on his glasses*]. It is clearly set out.

BRID'OISON. We shall ner-need to see it.

DOUBLE-MAIN. Quiet please, gentlemen.

USHER [*bawls*]. Silence in court!

BARTHOLO [*reads*]. 'I the undersigned acknowledge receipt from Mademoiselle... et cetera, et cetera... Marceline de Verte-Allure, residing at the chateau of Aguas-Frescas, the sum of two thousand milled piastres,* which sum I shall repay at her request at the chateau and I will marry her in consideration thereof, and so forth.' Signed: just Figaro. I shall argue for repayment of the moneys and enforcement of the promise, with costs. [*Begins his opening speech*] Your honours. A more fascinating case was never brought before a court of law. And since the time of Alexander the Great, who promised marriage to beautiful Thalestris*...

COUNT [*interrupting*]. Before you proceed further, counsel, are we agreed that the document is not in dispute?

BRID'OISON [*to* FIGARO]. Do you object to anything ker-Counsel has just read out?

FIGARO. Yes, your Honours, to wit, that there was malice, error, or carelessness in the reading of it. For the document does not say: 'which sum I shall repay *and* I will marry her' but 'which sum I shall repay *or* I will marry her', which is completely different.

COUNT. Does the document say 'and' or 'or'?

BARTHOLO. It says 'and'.

FIGARO. It says 'or'.

BRID'OISON. Mr Clerk, you read the der-document.

DOUBLE-MAIN [*taking the document*]. It's the safest way, for when the parties read out documents themselves, they often falsify... [*Reads*] Bla-bla-bla... Mademoiselle... bla bla bla... de Verte-Allure... bla bla... ah! 'which sum I shall repay at her request at the chateau of Aguas-Frescas... and... or... and... or'. The writing's very bad... there's a blot.

BRID'OISON. A blot? I know all about ber-blots.

BARTHOLO [*for the prosecution*]. I contend that the word is the copulative conjunction *and* which connects the two correlative elements of the sentence, thus: 'I shall repay at her request in the chateau of Aguas-Frescas *and* marry her.'

FIGARO [*for the defence*]. And I submit that it is the alternative conjunction *or* and that it separates the two aforesaid elements, thus: 'I shall repay the lady *or* I shall marry her.' I can be pedantic too.

He can rabbit on in Latin if he wants, I'll talk Greek. I'll slaughter him!

COUNT. How is this matter to be resolved?

BARTHOLO. To abridge the discussion and avoid further quibbling over a word, we concede that the document says *or*.

FIGARO. I want that written down.

BARTHOLO. And we will stand by it. It is a flimsy refuge and will afford no shelter for the guilty party. Let us look at the sentence again in the light of this. [*He reads*] 'Which sum I undertake to repay or I will marry her'—but both things 'at the chateau'! Now this *or*, your Honours, has the same sense as in: 'you can be bled here in the cold *or* have the leeches applied in your own warm bed', where the location is far from immaterial. Again: 'Always take rhubarb with wine *or* a pinch of tamarind': here the rhubarb is crucial and the 'wine *or* tamarind' are subordinate to it. It follows clearly that the marrying, like the repaying, is be done at the chateau.

FIGARO. Not at all. The sentence should be read according to this model: 'either the illness will kill you *or* the doctor will': *or alternatively* the doctor will—there's no getting round it. Another example: 'either you'll never write anything that's any good *or* fools will mock your success'—'*or else* fools...', the meaning's clear. For in this case, 'fools *or* rogues' is the subject, the nominative case. Does my learned friend think I have forgotten all my grammar? Therefore I shall repay her in this chateau, *comma*, or I will marry her...

BARTHOLO [*quickly*]. There's no comma.

FIGARO [*quickly*]. There is! Your honours, it's '*comma*, or else I'll marry her'.

BARTHOLO [*examines the paper and barks*]. There's no comma, your honours.

FIGARO [*quickly*]. It was there, your honours. In any case, can a man who marries be required to reimburse his wife?

BARTHOLO [*quickly*]. Yes. We will marry the defendant opting to keep accounts and possessions separate.

FIGARO. And we will marry the plaintiff opting to keep bodies separate, if marriage does not mean wiping the slate clean.

[*The* JUDGES *rise and confer in a whisper*

BARTHOLO. A strange way of balancing your accounts!

DOUBLE-MAIN. Quiet please, gentlemen.

USHER [*bawls*]. Silence in court!

BARTHOLO. And the unmitigated rogue calls that settling his debts!

FIGARO. Is it your own case, Counsel, that you're arguing?

BARTHOLO. I am defending this lady.

FIGARO. Carry on spouting nonsense by all means, but please, no more slurs. When courts first allowed litigants, whose feelings might otherwise run away with them, to be represented by so called third parties, they did not intend these neutral advocates to turn into licensed mud-slingers. They are an insult to a noble institution.

[*The* JUDGES *rise and continue to consult in a whisper*

ANTONIO [*to* MARCELINE, *pointing to the* JUDGES]. What they got to be chewing the fat about all this time?

MARCELINE. Someone's got at the chief judge, he's getting at the assistant judge, and I'm going to lose my case.

BARTHOLO [*grimly*]. I'm afraid so.

FIGARO [*cheerily*]. Chin up, Marceline!

DOUBLE-MAIN [*who has heard* MARCELINE'*s remark, rises and says to her*]. You go too far! I am reporting you. And to protect the good name of this court, I demand that, before the other matter is considered, this issue be settled first.

COUNT [*he sits*]. No, Mr Clerk, I shall not give a judgement on the slight against my person. A Spanish judge may safely disregard an outburst which belongs more properly to the courts of Asia. There are plenty of other abuses to deal with! I shall correct one such by setting out the reasons for my judgement: any judge who refuses to do likewise is no friend of the law. What is the plaintiff entitled to claim? Marriage, if payment is not forthcoming, for the one excludes the other.

DOUBLE-MAIN. Quiet please, gentlemen.

USHER [*bawls*]. Silence in court!

COUNT. What is the defendant's response? That he wishes to retain his unmarried status. This he is free to do.

FIGARO [*delighted*]. I've won.

COUNT. But since the document says, 'which sum I shall repay at her request at the chateau *or* I will marry her', the decision of this court is that the defendant will pay the plaintiff two thousand piastres, or marry her today.

[*He rises*

FIGARO [*flabbergasted*]. I've lost!

ANTONIO [*overjoyed*]. A grand verdict!

FIGARO. Why is it grand?

ANTONIO. 'Cos it means you ain't going to be my nephew, o' course. Thank you very much, your Lordship.

USHER [*bawls*]. The Court will rise.

[*The public files out*

ANTONIO. I'm going straight off and tell my niece all about this.

SCENE 16

The COUNT, *toing and froing*, MARCELINE, BARTHOLO, FIGARO, BRID'OISON

MARCELINE [*sits down*]. Ah! I can breathe again!

FIGARO. And I'm suffocating!

COUNT [*aside*]. I've got my revenge at least, which is something.

FIGARO [*aside*]. And where was Bazile who was going to object to the marriage? How come he's not back yet? [*To the* COUNT *as he leaves*] You're not going, sir?

COUNT. The court's delivered its verdict.

FIGARO [*to* BRID'OISON]. It was this fat legal windbag...

BRID'OISON. Me, a fat wer-windbag?

FIGARO. Yes. And I won't marry her. I'm a gentleman, let's be quite clear about that.

[*The* COUNT *stops*

BARTHOLO. You will marry her!

FIGARO. Without the blessing of my noble parents?

BARTHOLO. What's their name? Can you produce them?

FIGARO. Just give me a little time. I'm very close to finding them. Fifteen years I've been searching.

BARTHOLO. How pretentious! Found as a baby, I expect.

FIGARO. Lost as a baby, Doctor, or more accurately, stolen.

COUNT [*comes back*]. Stolen, lost, where's the proof? He must be allowed to provide the evidence, or he'll say he's been hard done by.

FIGARO. My Lord, if the lace baby-clothes, embroidered shawls, and gold-mounted gems found on me by the robbers are not enough to prove my high birth, then the care someone took to give me a distinctive mark should be sufficient evidence that I was a much-loved son. This strange symbol on my arm...

[*He begins to bare his right arm*

MARCELINE [*jumping to her feet*]. A spatula? On your right arm?

FIGARO. How do you know that?

MARCELINE. Merciful heaven! It's him!

FIGARO. Yes, it's me.

BARTHOLO [*to* MARCELINE]. Who? Who's this 'him'?

MARCELINE [*euphoric*]. Emmanuel!

BARTHOLO [*to* FIGARO]. Were you stolen by gypsies?

FIGARO [*excited*]. Near a chateau. Good Doctor Bartholo, restore me to my noble family and you can name your price. Ask a mountain of gold, and my illustrious parents would not quibble...

BARTHOLO [*pointing to* MARCELINE]. There's your mother.

FIGARO. You mean, my old nursemaid.

BARTHOLO. Your own mother.

FIGARO. Explain yourself.

MARCELINE [*pointing to* BARTHOLO]. He's your father.

FIGARO [*deflated*]. Oh no!

MARCELINE. Didn't your instinct tell you over and over...?

FIGARO. Never.

COUNT [*aside*]. His mother!

BRID'OISON. Well, it's quite clear—he can't mer-marry her now.

☞ BARTHOLO. Nor will I.[1]

MARCELINE. You won't? But what about your son. You swore to me that...

BARTHOLO. I didn't know what I was saying. If memories of that sort were legally binding, we'd all be obliged to marry everybody else.

BRID'OISON. And if you think about it, nobody would ever mer-marry anybody.

BARTHOLO. Such unbecoming conduct! Yours was a wayward youth!

MARCELINE [*gaining momentum*]. Yes, wayward! And much more so than you think! I don't propose to deny my faults, they are all too clear today! Yet it is hard to have to atone after leading an irreproachable life for thirty years. Nature intended me to be virtuous, which I indeed was once I was allowed to use my own judgement. But at that age of illusion, innocence, and hardship

---

[1] The following exchanges, between the two pointing fingers, were omitted by the actors of the Comédie Française during the Paris run.

when predatory men besiege us and we are most vulnerable to poverty, what can a girl do against so many concerted enemies? The man who judges us severely today may perhaps have ruined the lives of a dozen unfortunates!

FIGARO. The guiltiest have the hardest hearts. 'Twas ever thus.

MARCELINE [*with passion*]. Unfeeling men, who brand the play-things of your lust with the stigma of your contempt: we are your victims. It's you who should be punished for the mistakes we make in our youth—you and your magistrates, who preen themselves on their right to judge us and, through their culpable negligence, leave us with no honest way of earning a living. Is there any form of employment that's left for poor working girls? Once they had a natural right to the women's fashion trade but now men are being trained to do women's work.

FIGARO. They're even employing soldiers to do embroidery!

MARCELINE [*passionately*]. Even in the highest ranks of society, all that women get from men is condescension and contempt. Women are lured by a show of sham respect into very real slavery. If we have property, the law treats us like children; if we stray, it punishes us as responsible adults. Ah! in all your dealings with us, your attitudes deserve nothing but disgust or pity.

FIGARO. She's right.

COUNT [*aside*]. Absolutely right!

BRID'OISON. By God, she's rer-right!

MARCELINE. But what difference will it make, my son, if you and I are rejected by a man who is not just? Don't look back at where you came from, keep your eyes on the road ahead: that is all that matters to any of us. Then, a few months from now, your fiancée will be in charge of her own fate—she'll marry you, that I guarantee. Share your life with a loving wife and a devoted mother who will compete only to show how much they love you. Be kind to both of us, happy for yourself, my son, and cheerful, frank, and generous to every one you meet. That's all your mother will ever ask.

FIGARO. You speak words of wisdom, Mother, and I shall take them to heart. Really, we are such fools. The world's been going round and round for thousands and thousands of years, an ocean of time from which I've fished out thirty footling years that I'll never see again, and you think I'm going to worry about who I owe them to? Too bad if that bothers some people. Spending your life brooding is like having someone pulling on a collar round your neck all the time, like some wretched horse on the tow-path dragging a load upstream, that never rests even when it's halted but goes on straining though its legs have stopped moving. We'll just have to wait and see!*

COUNT. This silly business has wrecked my plan!

BRID'OISON. What happened to your noble birth and the sher-chateau? You can't play games with the ler-law!

FIGARO. The law was about to land me in a fine mess! How many times have I almost brained that man there over his damned hundred crowns, and now he turns out to be my father! But since the good Lord has seen fit to deliver me from that danger, please accept my apologies, father. And you, mother, embrace me... as maternally as you can manage.

[MARCELINE *throws her arms around his neck*

SCENE 17

BARTHOLO, FIGARO, MARCELINE, BRID'OISON, SUZANNE, ANTONIO, *the* COUNT

SUZANNE [*runs in holding a purse*]. My Lord, stop! Don't make them marry. I've come to pay Marceline with the dowry her Ladyship has given me!

COUNT [*aside*]. Damn her Ladyship! It looks as everything's conspiring against me!

[*He leaves*

SCENE 18

BARTHOLO, ANTONIO, SUZANNE, FIGARO, MARCELINE,
BRID'OISON

ANTONIO [*watches* FIGARO *embrace his mother then turns to* SUZANNE]. Did you ever! Still going to pay up?

SUZANNE [*turns*]. I've seen enough. Come, uncle, we're going.

FIGARO [*detaining her*]. No you're not, if you don't mind. What did you see?

SUZANNE. How stupid I am and what a rat you are.

FIGARO. You saw neither.

SUZANNE [*angry*]. Go ahead, marry her, since you like kissing her so much!

FIGARO [*teasingly*]. I kissed her but I'm not marrying her.

[SUZANNE *starts to leave,* FIGARO *holds her back and she slaps his face*

SUZANNE. You've got a nerve, trying to make me stay!

FIGARO [*to the company*]. Isn't this what they call love? [*To* SUZANNE] Before you go, please take a good look at this wonderful lady.

SUZANNE. I'm looking.

FIGARO. And what do you think of her?

SUZANNE. She's horrible.

FIGARO. Ah, jealousy! The green-eyed god does not mince its words!

MARCELINE [*opens her arms*]. Won't you kiss your mother-in-law, my pretty Suzy? That awful man who's teasing you is my son.

SUZANNE [*runs to her*]. You're his mother!

[*They remain locked in each other's arms*

ANTONIO. Happened just this minute, did it?

FIGARO. Seems like.

MARCELINE [*joyously*]. No. My heart was strangely drawn to him and misled me only because I did not guess the real reason why. The feeling was instinctive.

FIGARO. And with me, Mother, it was common sense, not instinct, that made me refuse to marry you. I never hated you, far from it. The money, for example...

MARCELINE [*handing him a paper*]. It's yours. Here, take the deed, it's your dowry.

SUZANNE [*throws him the purse*]. And take this too.

FIGARO. I thank you with all my heart.

MARCELINE [*joyously*]. I was very unhappy when I was a girl. I was on the way to becoming the most miserable of wives. And now I am blessed among mothers! Kiss me, my children. I vest all my affection in you both. Oh, I couldn't be more happy! Oh my dears, I shall love you so much!

FIGARO [*deeply moved and voluble*]. Stop it, mother, not another word! Do you want to see me reduced to tears, the first I ever shed? At least they are tears of happiness. Oh I'm such a fool—I was starting to feel ashamed of crying. I felt the tears running through my fingers, look, [*shows both hands, fingers splayed*] and stupidly tried to hold them back! I refuse to be ashamed! I want to laugh and cry at the same time. Feeling the way I do is something that happens only once in a lifetime.

[*He embraces his mother on one side and* SUZANNE *on the other*

MARCELINE. Oh my boy!

SUZANNE.[1] Oh my darling boy!

BRID'OISON [*wiping his eyes with a handkerchief*]. Dear me! I think I must be a fer-fool like that too!

FIGARO [*euphoric*]. Away, dull care! Now I defy you to do your worst! Come for me if you dare, but first you'll have to get past these two loving women!*

---

[1] BARTHOLO, ANTONIO, SUZANNE, FIGARO, MARCELINE, BRID'OISON.

ANTONIO [*to* FIGARO]. Not so much of the lovey-dovey, if you don't mind. Now, when it comes to marriages in families, the parents gotter be wed first. You take my meaning. How's about yours? Hands been offered and accepted?

BARTHOLO. Me, offer my hand! It will dry up and drop off before I give it to the mother of a clown like him!

ANTONIO [*to* BARTHOLO]. So you're just one of them unnatural fathers. [*To* FIGARO] Since that's how it is, Romeo, there's nothing more to say.

SUZANNE. But uncle!

ANTONIO. You don't think I'd give the child of my own sister to a man that's nobody's child?

BRID'OISON. That can't be right, oaf. Everybody is somebody's tcher-child.

ANTONIO. Bah! He'll not have her.

[*He leaves*

SCENE 19

BARTHOLO, SUZANNE, FIGARO, MARCELINE, BRID'OISON

BARTHOLO [*to* FIGARO]. You'd better start looking for someone who'll adopt you.

[*He makes as if to leave*

MARCELINE [*runs after him, grabs him, and drags him back*]. Stop, Doctor, don't go!

FIGARO [*aside*]. Aah! I think all the morons in Andalusia are lining up to stop my marriage.

SUZANNE [*to* BARTHOLO]. You're a dear and he's your son.[1]

MARCELINE [*to* BARTHOLO]. He's got brains, talent, looks...

FIGARO [*to* BARTHOLO]. ... and never cost you a penny.

---

[1] SUZANNE, BARTHOLO, MARCELINE, FIGARO, BRID'OISON.

BARTHOLO. What about the hundred crowns he got out of me?

MARCELINE [*stroking him*]. We'll take such good care of you, my dear.

SUZANNE [*stroking him*]. We'll love you so much, you dear man.

BARTHOLO [*weakening*]. Dear! My dear! You dear man! It looks like I'm an even bigger fool than this gentleman [*pointing to* BRID'OISON]. I'm letting myself be talked round like a child. [MARCELINE *and* SUZANNE *hug him*] Hold on, I haven't said yes. [*Turns away*] What's become of his Lordship?

FIGARO. We'd better run and catch him quick and force him to give the word. If he starts on some new plot, we'll have to start all over again from scratch.

ALL TOGETHER. Hurry! hurry!

[*They drag* BARTHOLO *outside*

SCENE 20

BRID'OISON, *alone*

BRID'OISON. A bigger fer-fool than this gentleman! People can ser-say that sort of thing to themselves, but... really, the per-people around here aren't very per-polite.

ACT IV

A gallery decorated with candelabras, lighted chandeliers, flowers, garlands, and, in short, made ready for the festivities. Downstage right is a table, with an inkstand, and behind it, an armchair

SCENE 1

FIGARO, SUZANNE

FIGARO [*his arm around* SUZANNE'*s waist*]. Well, my love, are you happy? My persuasive, golden-tongued mother has talked the Doctor into it. He's not all that keen but he's going to marry her, so your miserable uncle hasn't a leg to stand on. There's only his Lordship who's furious, because at long last our wedding is going to take place, immediately after theirs. So smile, it's all turned out fine in the end.

SUZANNE. Did you ever see anything so strange?

FIGARO. Or as cheering. All we wanted was to worm a dowry out of his Excellency and we've ended up getting our hands on two, neither of which is from him. You had to contend with a determined rival; I was tormented by a harpy. But now both have turned, to our benefit, into the best of mothers. Yesterday, I was what you would call an orphan. Now I have both parents, not as grand as I had convinced myself they would be, I grant you, but good enough for us, for we're not as choosy as rich people are.

SUZANNE. But none of the things you planned and we had such high hopes of has happened!

FIGARO. Chance performed better than the whole lot of us, my sweet. That's how things work. You strive and plan and propose on the one hand; and on the other, chance disposes. From the empty-bellied conqueror who sets out to gobble up the whole world to the harmless blind man who follows where his dog leads, we are all fortune's playthings. And the blind beggar is often better led and less frustrated in his plans than that other blind fool, for all his retinue of advisers. And that's reckoning without the obliging blind god we call Cupid...

[*He puts his arm back around* SUZANNE'*s waist*

SUZANNE. He's the only one I'm concerned about.

FIGARO. If—to continue in this foolish vein—if you let me be the dog that guides him to your pretty door, we'll move in and be happy ever after.

SUZANNE [*laughing*]. Cupid and you?

FIGARO. Me and Cupid.

SUZANNE. And you'll never look for alternative accommodation?

FIGARO. If you catch me trying, may a zillion lovers...

SUZANNE. Now you're exaggerating. Tell me the honest truth.

FIGARO. I'm telling you the most honest truth I know.

SUZANNE. Don't give me that. You mean there's more than one kind?

FIGARO. Of course. Ever since people started noticing that in time yesterday's inanity turns into today's wisdom, and that little old lies, planted haphazardly, grow into vast and mighty truths, there have been countless varieties! Truths you know but cannot reveal, for not every truth is suitable for telling. Truths you repeat but don't believe, for not every truth is worth believing. The vows of lovers, the threats of mothers, the pledges of drinkers, the promises of politicians, the businessman's handshake—there's no end to it. There's only one truth that's pure and unadulterated: my love for Suzette.

SUZANNE. I love to see you in such high spirits, because you say such crazy things and that tells me you're happy. But we've got to discuss this meeting with the Count.

FIGARO. Or preferably, let's never mention it again. It almost lost me my Suzanne.

SUZANNE. So now you'd rather it didn't happen?

FIGARO. If you love me, Suzette, give me your word that you won't go. Leave him to kick his heels by himself: that'll teach him.

SUZANNE. It was harder for me to say I'd go than to agree to stay away. That's settled then.

FIGARO. Is that your honest truth?

SUZANNE. I'm not like all you clever men. I know only one sort.

FIGARO. And you love me a little?

SUZANNE. A lot.

FIGARO. A lot's not much.

SUZANNE. How do you mean?

FIGARO. You see, where love's concerned, too much is never enough.

SUZANNE. All that's too subtle for me. But I shall love no one but my husband.

FIGARO. If you stay true to that, you'll be a glorious exception to the rule.

[*He tries to kiss her*

SCENE 2

FIGARO, SUZANNE, *the* COUNTESS

COUNTESS. Ah! I was right. I said wherever they are, they're sure to be together. Really, Figaro! Arranging cosy trysts like this is anticipating the future, and degrading to marriage and yourself. His Lordship's waiting for you and he's getting impatient.

FIGARO. You're right, Madame, I was forgetting myself. I'll take my excuse with me to show him.

[*He begins to lead* SUZANNE *off*

COUNTESS [*detains her*]. She'll be along presently.

SCENE 3

SUZANNE, *the* COUNTESS

COUNTESS. Have you got everything we need for the exchange of clothes?

SUZANNE. We won't need anything, Madame. The meeting's been cancelled.

COUNTESS. Oh? You've changed your mind?

SUZANNE. It was Figaro.

COUNTESS. You're deceiving me.

SUZANNE. Heaven forbid!

COUNTESS. Figaro's not the sort to let a dowry slip through his fingers.

SUZANNE. Your Ladyship! Whatever are you thinking!

COUNTESS. That you're in the Count's pocket and you're wishing you hadn't told me his plans. I can read you like a book. Leave me.

[*She starts to leave*

SUZANNE [*falls to her knees*]. In the name of God in whom we all hope, don't you realize how hurtful you're being, Madame? After all the kindness you've shown and the dowry you gave me...

COUNTESS [*helps her to her feet*]. Oh please! I don't know what got into me! If I take your place in the garden, you, sweet girl, won't have to go. You'll be keeping your word to your husband and you'll be helping me to get mine back.

SUZANNE. You made me feel awful!

COUNTESS. A foolish woman being stupid, that's all. [*Kisses her on the forehead*] Where are you supposed to meet him?

SUZANNE [*kisses her hand*]. The garden is all I remember.

COUNTESS [*points to the table*]. Take this pen and we'll decide on a place.

SUZANNE. Write to him?

COUNTESS. There's no other way.

SUZANNE. But Madame, at least you should be the one who...

COUNTESS. I'll take full responsibility. [SUZANNE *sits at the table while the* COUNTESS *dictates*] New lyric to the old tune: 'How sweet at eve the balmy breeze, Under the spreading chestnut trees.' How sweet at eve...

SUZANNE [*writing*]. 'Under the spreading chestnut trees.' Go on.

COUNTESS. You think he won't understand?

SUZANNE [*rereads*]. It's fine. [*She folds the note*] What shall we seal it with?

COUNTESS. A pin, and hurry. It will do for the reply. Write on the back: 'Please return pin.'

SUZANNE [*laughs as she writes*]. Ha ha! A pin! This is more amusing than that business with the commission!

COUNTESS [*a sad sigh*]. Ah!

SUZANNE [*looks through her pockets*]. I haven't a pin on me.

COUNTESS [*unpins the top of her robe*]. Use this one. [*The page's ribbon falls out of the top of her dress*] Oh, my ribbon!

SUZANNE [*picks it up*]. It's that little thief's! You weren't so cruel as to...

COUNTESS. I could hardly leave it round his arm. That wouldn't have done at all! Give it back!

SUZANNE. You shouldn't keep it on you, Madame, it's got the lad's blood on it.

COUNTESS [*takes it back*]. It will do fine for Fanchette. The next time she brings me flowers...

SCENE 4

A SHEPHERDESS, CHERUBIN *dressed as a girl*, FANCHETTE, *a number of girls dressed like her and also holding posies of flowers, the* COUNTESS, SUZANNE

FANCHETTE. Your Ladyship, these are girls from the town. They've come with flowers for you.

COUNTESS [*quickly hides the ribbon*]. They're quite lovely. I'm sorry, my dears, but I don't know all of you. [*Points to* CHERUBIN] Who is this lovely girl? She looks so shy.

SHEPHERDESS. She's my cousin, your Ladyship. She's come for the wedding.

COUNTESS. She's very pretty. Now I can't possibly hold twenty posies, so let the visitor do the honours. [*She takes the posy from* CHERUBIN *and kisses him on the forehead*] Why, she's blushing! [*To* SUZANNE] Suzanne, don't you think... she looks like someone?

SUZANNE. You're right, the spitting image.

CHERUBIN [*puts one hand on his heart*]. Oh! she kissed me!... In my wildest dreams I never thought...

SCENE 5

The girls, CHERUBIN *in their midst*, FANCHETTE, ANTONIO, *the* COUNT, *the* COUNTESS, SUZANNE

ANTONIO. I tell your Lordship, he's 'ere. They dressed him up at my daughter's. His own clothes is still there. Here's his officer's cap. I picked it out of the pile.

[*He goes towards the girls, peers at them, recognizes* CHERUBIN *and removes his bonnet, so that his long hair cascades down. He puts the officer's cap on his head and says*

Aha! By stars! There's your officer!

COUNTESS [*recoils*]. Oh my God!

SUZANNE. The ruffian!

ANTONIO. Didn't I say it were him when we was upstairs?

COUNT [*angry*]. Well, Madame?

COUNTESS. Well, sir! Can't you see that I'm even more surprised than you and at least as angry.

COUNT. Yes. But what about earlier this morning?

COUNTESS. I would be truly guilty if I continued the pretence. He'd come to my room. We were planning the charade which these girls have just acted out. You caught us while we were dressing him. Your first reaction was so furious that he ran away, I became flustered, and the rest flowed from the general panic.

COUNT [*resentfully, to* CHERUBIN] Why didn't you leave?

CHERUBIN [*quickly removing his cap*]. Your Lordship...

COUNT. I'm going to punish you for disobeying.

FANCHETTE [*without thinking*]. Oh listen to me, your Lordship. Every time you come looking for me wanting to kiss me, you know, you always say: 'Love me, my pretty Fanchette, and I'll give you anything you like!'

COUNT [*blushing*]. Me? Did I say that?

FANCHETTE. Yes, your Lordship. So instead of punishing Cherubin, give him to me for my husband and I'll love you till I burst!

COUNT [*aside*]. I'm jinxed by this page!

COUNTESS. Well, sir, now it's your turn. This child's admission, which is as innocent as my own, demonstrates two things: that if I give you cause to be uneasy I always do so unintentionally, while you go out of your way to multiply and give grounds for my anxieties.

ANTONIO. You an' all, your Lordship? By the stars, I'll tan her hide like what her late mother, who's departed, used to... It ain't for anything she's done. It's for what your Ladyship knows very well, that when little girls grow up to be big girls...

COUNT [*disconcerted, aside*]. There's some evil genius bent on turning everything against me.

SCENE 6

The girls, CHERUBIN, ANTONIO, FIGARO, *the* COUNT, *the* COUNTESS, SUZANNE

FIGARO. If your Lordship keeps these girls here, we won't be able to start either the celebrations or the dancing.

COUNT. You? Dancing? Have you forgotten? After your fall this morning and twisting your right ankle?

FIGARO [*tries out his leg*]. It still hurts a bit but it's nothing. [*To the girls*] Come on, my little beauties, let's be off.

COUNT [*spins him round*]. It was lucky for you that flowerbed was just soft earth.

FIGARO. Most fortunate, as you say, otherwise...

ANTONIO [*spins him round*]. And don't forget he bunched hisself up all the way down to the ground.

FIGARO. You mean somebody fitter would have stayed suspended in mid-air? [*To the girls*] Are you coming, young ladies?

ANTONIO [*spins him round*]. And for all that time, I s'pose that young page was galloping to Seville on his horse?

FIGARO. Galloping, or trotting...

COUNT [*spins him round*]. And you had his commission in your pocket?

FIGARO [*taken aback*]. Of course. But why the inquisition? [*To the girls*] Best foot forward, girls!

ANTONIO [*pulling* CHERUBIN's *arm*]. And here's a girl that says my future nephew is nothing more'n a liar.

FIGARO [*surprised*]. Cherubin!... [*Aside*] Blast the little weed!

ANTONIO. Tumbled yet?

FIGARO [*struggling*]. Of course I've tumbled. Now what yarn has he been telling?

COUNT [*dryly*]. It's no yarn. He says he's the one who jumped onto the wallflowers.

FIGARO [*thinking*]. Well, if he says so, perhaps he was. I can't argue about things I don't know.

COUNT. So the two of you...?

FIGARO. Why not? The urge to jump can be catching—remember Panurge's sheep?* And when you lose your temper, sir, there's no one who wouldn't prefer to risk...

COUNT. What! both together?

FIGARO. We'd have jumped if there'd been a couple of dozen of us. Anyway, what does it matter, your Lordship, since nobody got hurt? [*To the girls*] Look, are you coming or not?

COUNT [*outraged*]. Have we strayed into some kind of farce?

[*A fanfare is heard*

FIGARO. That's the cue for the procession. To your places, girls, to your places. Come, Suzanne, give me your arm.

[*All hurry out save the* COUNT, *the* COUNTESS, *and* CHERUBIN, *who has a hangdog air*

SCENE 7

CHERUBIN, *the* COUNT, *and the* COUNTESS

COUNT [*watching* FIGARO *leave*]. Did you ever see such brass-faced nerve? [*To the page*] And you, you little sneak, spare me the blushes and go and get dressed properly at once. And stay out of my sight for the rest of the evening.

COUNTESS. He'll be so bored.

CHERUBIN [*blurting the words*]. Me, bored? There's enough happiness here on my forehead to last me a hundred years in prison!

[*He puts on his cap and runs off*

SCENE 8

The COUNT, *the* COUNTESS, *who says nothing but fans herself vigorously*

COUNT. What happiness has he got on his forehead?

COUNTESS [*embarrassed*]. His... first officer's cap, I imagine. Boys love toys.

[*She prepares to leave*

COUNT. Aren't you staying, Madame?

COUNTESS. You know I'm not feeling well.

COUNT. Just stay long enough for a word about Suzanne. Otherwise I'll think you're angry with me.

COUNTESS. Both wedding groups are coming. We'd better sit down and welcome them.

COUNT [*aside*]. The wedding! Best grin and bear it. What can't be cured must be endured!

[*The* COUNT *and* COUNTESS *take their seats on one side of the gallery*

SCENE 9

The COUNT *and the* COUNTESS, *seated. 'The Spanish Follies', played in march tempo, accompanies the entrance of* GAMEKEEPERS, *with guns over their shoulders; the* CONSTABLE, *the* MAGISTRATES, BRID'OISON; FARMERS *from the estate and their wives in Sunday clothes; two* YOUNG GIRLS *carrying the bride's headdress of white feathers; two girls carrying her white veil; two girls carrying her gloves and bouquet.*

ANTONIO, *who is to give* SUZANNE *away, leads her by the arm. Other* GIRLS *carry a separate headdress, veil, and white bouquet in the same way for* MARCELINE.

FIGARO, *who is to give* MARCELINE *in marriage to* BARTHOLO, *leads her by the arm.* BARTHOLO *brings up the rear holding a large bouquet. As the girls file past the* COUNT, *they hand the wedding regalia of* SUZANNE *and* MARCELINE *to the servants.*

When the FARMERS *and their wives have formed into two columns at the sides of the stage, a fandango is danced, with castanets (tune as before). While the* ritournelle *is played,* ANTONIO *leads* SUZANNE *to the* COUNT. *She kneels before him.*

While the COUNT *places the circlet on her head, adjusts the veil, and gives her the bouquet, two girls sing (tune as before):*

> Proclaim now, young bride, the great bounty and fame
> Of a Lord who surrenders his rights in your name.
> Setting the just and the good above his own pleasure
> To your husband he gives you: a pure, chaste treasure.

During the last line of the song, SUZANNE, *still kneeling, pulls at the* COUNT's *coat and shows him a note she is holding. She raises the hand nearest the audience to her head. While the* COUNT *pretends to adjust her headdress she gives him the note, which he puts surreptitiously into his breast pocket.*

The song comes to an end. The bride stands and curtseys. FIGARO *steps forward to receive her from the* COUNT *and then withdraws with her to the opposite side of the room, where they take up a position next to* MARCELINE.

Meanwhile, another fandango is danced.

The COUNT, *impatient to read what he has been given, moves to the front of the stage and takes the note from his pocket. As he does so, he winces like a man who has pricked his finger badly. He shakes it, squeezes and sucks it, and, glaring at the note which is fastened by a pin, says:*

COUNT [*while he and then* FIGARO *speak, the orchestra plays very softly*]. Blast these women! They stick pins in everything!

[*He throws the pin on the floor, reads the note, and then kisses it*

FIGARO [*who has watched the* COUNT, *turns to his mother and* SUZANNE]. It's a love-letter. No doubt one of the girls slipped it to him as she filed past. It was fastened with a pin and it had the impertinence to prick him.

The dancing resumes. The COUNT, *who has read the note, turns it over and sees the request to return the pin. He looks for it on the ground until he finds it. He sticks it in his sleeve*

FIGARO [*to* SUZANNE *and* MARCELINE]. Anything touched by the one we love is precious. Look, he's picking up the pin! What a strange man he is!

Meanwhile, SUZANNE *communicates by signs with the* COUNTESS. *The dance ends and the music of the* ritournelle *is repeated.* FIGARO *leads* MARCELINE *to the* COUNT, *just as* SUZANNE *was led. At the moment when the* COUNT *takes the bride's headdress and the song is about to be repeated, the proceedings are interrupted*

USHER [*appears at the door*]. Stay where you are! You can't all come in... Guards! Lend a hand here!

[*The* GUARDS *rush to the door*

COUNT [*getting to his feet*]. What's happening?

USHER. It's Don Bazile, your Lordship, he's brought the whole village with him, they followed because he was singing as he walked back.

COUNT. Let him in. No one else.

COUNTESS. Will you allow me to withdraw?

COUNT. I shall not forget your compliance...

COUNTESS. Suzanne!... She will be back directly. [*To* SUZANNE] Come, we must go and exchange clothes.

[*She leaves with* SUZANNE

MARCELINE. Whenever he turns up he makes trouble.

FIGARO. Don't worry! I'll put a spoke in his wheel!

SCENE 10

Cast as before, except SUZANNE *and the* COUNTESS; BAZILE, *carrying his guitar enters with* GRIPPE-SOLEIL

BAZILE [*sings*].

> Hearts so tender, hearts so faint
> Who groan that love is callous,
> Cease now your fond complaint.
> It is no crime to be capricious.
> Cupid has wings, Cupid has darts
> Is it surprising he flits among hearts?
> Is it surprising he flits among hearts?
> Is it surprising he flits among hearts?

FIGARO [*advances to meet him*]. No. That's exactly why he has wings on his back. Now, friend, what's the meaning of all this hullabaloo?

BAZILE [*gesturing to* GRIPPE-SOLEIL]. Having demonstrated my obedience to his Lordship by entertaining this gentleman, who is a guest of his, I in turn can appeal to his justice.

GRIPPE-SOLEIL. Go on! Your Honourship, he din't entertain me one little bit with all them rubbish old songs.

COUNT. What exactly do you want, Bazile?

BAZILE. What is rightly mine, your Lordship, the hand of Marceline. I've come to object formally...

FIGARO [*steps forward*]. When was the last time, sir, you saw the face of a lunatic?

BAZILE. I'm looking at one now, sir.

FIGARO. Since my eyes give such a perfect reflection of yourself, look into them and heed my prediction. If you so much as attempt to go anywhere near the lady...

BARTHOLO [*laughing*]. Ha ha! Why shouldn't he? Let him speak.

BRID'OISON [*steps between them*]. Surely there's no reason for two fer-friends...

FIGARO. Friends!!

BAZILE. You must be joking!!

FIGARO. Because he composes boring church music?

BAZILE. Because he churns out poems for the newspapers?

FIGARO. Bar-room strummer!

BAZILE. Scribbling hack!

FIGARO. Pedant of the oratorio!

BAZILE. Jockey of the diplomatic bag!

COUNT [*seated*]. And impudent ruffians the pair of you.

BAZILE. He snipes at me but never hits the target.

FIGARO. That's as maybe. But you're one person I'd never miss.

BAZILE. Going round telling everybody I'm stupid.

FIGARO. I suppose that makes me an echo?

BAZILE. There isn't a singer who, on the strength of my talent, hasn't been cheered.

FIGARO. Jeered.

BAZILE. He's doing it again!

FIGARO. And why not, since it's true? Are you some royal prince who has to be fawned over? Since you can't afford to pay people to lie to you, you have to face the truth, you weevil. And if you're afraid of hearing the truth from me, why did you come here and disrupt my wedding?

BAZILE [*to* MARCELINE]. Did you, or did you not, promise me that if, within four years, you weren't spoken for, you would give me first refusal?

MARCELINE. On what condition did I promise that?

BAZILE. That if you ever found a son you said was lost, I would agree to adopt him.

ALL TOGETHER. He's been found.

BAZILE. That's no problem.

ALL TOGETHER [*pointing to* FIGARO]. And here he is!

BAZILE [*recoils in horror*]. This is a nightmare!

BRID'OISON. Does that mean you give up all claims to his loving mer-mother?

BAZILE. Can you think of anything worse than to have people believe you're the father of a bad lot, a good-for-nothing?

FIGARO. Yes, that people think you are the son of one! Don't make me laugh.

BAZILE [*pointing to* FIGARO]. If this... gentleman has some role in this business, then I declare I want no part of it.

[*He leaves*

SCENE 11

Cast as before, except BAZILE

BARTHOLO [*laughing*]. Ha ha ha!

FIGARO [*jumping for joy*]. So in the end I'm to have my bride after all!

COUNT [*aside*]. And I my mistress.

[*He stands*

BRID'OISON [*to* MARCELINE]. And so everyone's her-happy.

COUNT. Let both contracts be drawn up and I'll sign them.

ALL TOGETHER. Long live his Lordship!

[*The crowd leaves*

COUNT. I need an hour to myself.

[*He makes for the door with the rest*

SCENE 12

GRIPPE-SOLEIL, FIGARO, MARCELINE, *the* COUNT

GRIPPE-SOLEIL [*to* FIGARO]. And I gotter go and help with they firey-works we was told is to be put under the big chestnut trees.

COUNT [*returns quickly*]. What cretin ordered you to do that?

FIGARO. Why? Is there a problem?

COUNT [*angrily*]. Her Ladyship is not well. How can she see the display? The place for it is on the terrace, under her window.

GRIPPE-SOLEIL. Hear that, Grippe-Soleil? The terrace.

COUNT. Under the chestnuts, indeed! [*Aside, as he leaves*] They were about to send my plans up in flames!

SCENE 13

FIGARO, MARCELINE

FIGARO. He seemed unusually concerned about his wife.

[*He is about to leave*

MARCELINE [*detains him*]. I must have a word, my son. I'd like to clear the air between us. I misread my feelings for you and as a result I was unfair to your charming Suzanne. I assumed she was conniving with the Count, even though I'd heard from Bazile that she always kept him at arm's length.

FIGARO. You don't know much about your son if you think I can be put off my stride by female wiles. I defy the most designing woman to pull the wool over my eyes.

MARCELINE. It's always nice to think so. But jealousy, son...

FIGARO. ...is merely the foolish offspring of pride, or a madness of the brain. No, mother, on that subject I have a philosophy which is... unassailable. If some day Suzanne is unfaithful, I forgive her here and now. But she'll have had to work hard at it...

[*He turns and sees* FANCHETTE, *who is looking for somebody*

SCENE 14

FIGARO, FANCHETTE, MARCELINE

FIGARO. Hey! It's my little cousin. You were listening!

FANCHETTE. No I wasn't, I never did. People say it's not nice to listen.

FIGARO. Quite right. But since it can be useful, people don't always worry about that.

FANCHETTE. I was just looking to see if somebody was here.

FIGARO. Aha! already up to no good, are we? You know very well he can't possibly be here.

FANCHETTE. Who do you mean?

FIGARO. Cherubin.

FANCHETTE. I know where he is. It's not him I'm looking for, it's Suzanne, my cousin.

FIGARO. And what does my dear cousin want her for?

FANCHETTE. Since you're my dear cousin too, I'll tell you. It's... it's just a pin and I'm supposed to give it back to her.

FIGARO [quickly]. A pin! A pin!... Who told you to return it, you little pest? At your age, and already acting as go-bet... [He recovers himself and continues] You've already been a great help, Fanchette. I know you always do your best. My little cousin is very pretty and so kind.

FANCHETTE. Then why did you get so cross? I'm going.

FIGARO [detaining her]. No, no, I was just joking. Listen, that little pin of yours is the one his Lordship told you to give back to Suzanne. It was used to fasten a little letter he had. You see, I know all about it.

FANCHETTE. If you know, why did you ask?

FIGARO [trying to think]. Because it might be rather fun to know how his Lordship went about getting you to run his errand for him.

FANCHETTE [*innocently*]. He said it just like you did. 'Oh, Fanchette, give this pin to your pretty cousin. Just tell her that it's the
one that fastened the chestnuts.'

FIGARO. Chest...?

FANCHETTE. ... nuts. Oh, and he also said: 'Take care no one sees
you.'

FIGARO. And mind you do. Luckily, no one has seen you. So off you
go and run your errand like a good girl. And don't tell Suzanne
anything except what he told you to say.

FANCHETTE. Why would I do that? There's no need to treat me like
a child, cousin.

[*She leaves, skipping*

SCENE 15

FIGARO, MARCELINE

FIGARO. Well, mother?

MARCELINE. Well, son?

FIGARO [*as if choking*]. I don't believe it!... Really, of all things...

MARCELINE. Of all things... What things? What's wrong?

FIGARO [*both hands on heart*]. What I've just heard, mother, has
struck here, like a bullet.

MARCELINE [*laughing*]. So the heart that was brimming with confidence was in fact just an over-inflated balloon? A prick with a pin
and whoosh, all gone.

FIGARO [*furious*]. But that pin, mother, was the one he picked up!

MARCELINE [*repeating his words*]. 'Jealousy? On that score I have a
philosophy which is... unassailable. If some day Suzanne is
unfaithful, I forgive her here and now.'

FIGARO. Oh mother! The way we feel dictates the way we speak.
Get the steeliest judge to plead his own defence and what does he

do? He exploits points of law! I'm not surprised now why he got so worked up about the fireworks. As to our Lady of the Pins, she's not as smart as she thinks she is, mother, with her chestnuts. I'm enough of a husband to have a right to be angry. But on the other hand, I'm not sufficiently married yet to rule out the possibility that I might just drop her and marry someone else.

MARCELINE. You call that thinking? You'd throw it all away for a mere suspicion? Tell me, how do you know it's you she's deceiving and not the Count? Have you so revised your opinion of her character that you can convict her out of hand? How do you know if she'll go anywhere near the chestnuts? Or why she would go, or what she'd say or do? I credited you with more common sense.

FIGARO [*kisses her hand respectfully*]. You're right, mother, so right, always right! But let's make some allowance for human nature, we'll feel better for it afterwards. We'll make some enquiries before we start throwing accusations about and taking steps. I know where they've arranged to meet. Goodbye, mother.

[*He leaves*

SCENE 16

MARCELINE, *alone*

MARCELINE. Goodbye. I know too. Now that I've stopped him doing anything silly, let's find out what Suzanne has been getting up to. No, I'll warn her. She's such a pretty girl! Ah! Provided our own personal interest does not set us at each other's throats, we poor, oppressed women are more than prepared to rise up and defend ourselves against the whole of the proud, the fearsome, and [*laughing*] really rather simple-minded male sex!

[*She leaves*

ACT V

A grove of chestnut trees in a park. Two pavilions, gazebos or garden temples, one on either side of the stage. At the back of the stage is a clearing hung with decorations and at the front a garden seat. The stage is dark

SCENE 1

FANCHETTE, *alone. In one hand she has two biscuits and an orange, and in the other, a lighted paper lantern*

FANCHETTE. In the pavilion on the left, he said. This is it. What if he doesn't come? What about my little role in the pageant?...* Those horrible people in the kitchen wouldn't even let me have an orange and two measly biscuits. 'Who're they for?' 'They are for somebody, sir.' 'Oh yes, and we know who.' What if they do? Just because his Lordship doesn't want to see him about the place, does that mean he's got to starve to death? So I had to pay for them with a great big kiss on the cheek. Still, you never know, perhaps he'll pay me back in kind. [*She sees* FIGARO *watching her and gives a shriek*] Ah!

[*Then she runs off and enters the pavilion on her left*

SCENE 2

FIGARO, *wearing a long cloak and a wide-brimmed hat pulled down over his eyes, then* BAZILE, ANTONIO, BARTHOLO, BRID'OISON, GRIPPE-SOLEIL, *and* SERVANTS *and* WORKMEN

FIGARO [*briefly alone*]. That's Fanchette! [*He watches the others as they arrive, and greets them as if he means business*] Good evening, gentlemen, good evening. Is every one here?

BAZILE. All those you told to come.

FIGARO. What time is it, give or take?

ANTONIO [*looks at the sky*]. Moon must be up.

BARTHOLO. Well? What dark deeds are you plotting? You're dressed like a plotter.

FIGARO. Look, you came to the chateau for a wedding, didn't you?

BRID'OISON. Aaa-absolutely.

ANTONIO. We was heading over there, further down the park, to wait for the signal to start the shenanigans.

FIGARO. This is as far as you go, gentlemen. Here, under these chestnuts, is where we're all going to celebrate the virtues of the girl I'm marrying, and the generosity of his Lordship who had his own plans for her.

BAZILE [*recalling the events of the day*]. Ah! I see what all this is about. Believe me, we'd best make ourselves scarce. There's an assignation in the offing. I'll explain later.

BRID'OISON [*to* FIGARO]. We'll come back ler-later.

FIGARO. When you hear me shout, you must all come, at the double. And you can call Figaro all the names you can think of if he fails to show you a marvel.

BARTHOLO. Remember, a man with any sense does not tangle with great lords.

FIGARO. I'll remember.

BARTHOLO. They can always trump your ace because they will pull rank.

FIGARO. They've also got wide sleeves, don't forget. You should also bear in mind that if a man is known to be a doormat, every scoundrel will walk all over him.

BARTHOLO. That's true.

FIGARO. And also that I have a title, de Verte-Allure, inherited through my mother.

BARTHOLO. What's got into him?

BRID'OISON. Yes, wer-what?

BAZILE [*aside*]. Have the Count and Suzanne come to an understanding behind my back? I shan't be sorry to see the tables turned.

FIGARO [*to the* SERVANTS]. As for you rogues, I've told you what to do, I want this grove lit up. Otherwise, as surely as I wish I had death by the throat, if I catch one of you...

[*He shakes* GRIPPE-SOLEIL *by the arm*

GRIPPE-SOLEIL [*goes off bawling through his tears*]. Ow! Ouch! Ah! You're a brute!

BAZILE [*as he goes*]. And may heaven give the bridegroom joy of it!

[*All leave*

SCENE 3

FIGARO, *alone, pacing in the darkness, and in the gloomiest tones*

FIGARO. Ah woman, woman, woman! What a weak, deceitful creature you are! Nothing that lives and breathes in creation can deny its nature: is it yours to be unfaithful? After she swore, in front of her Ladyship, that she would not go... And then as she was pronouncing her vows... And even while the ceremony was going on... And the swine laughed when he read the note! With me standing there like an idiot! No Count, you won't have her, you shall not have her! You think that because you are a great lord you are a great genius! Nobility, wealth, rank, high position, such things make a man proud. But what did you ever do to earn them? Chose your parents carefully, that's all. Take that away and what have you got? A very average man. Whereas I, by God, was a face in the crowd. I've had to show more skill and brainpower just to stay alive than it's taken to rule all the provinces of Spain for the last hundred years. And you dare cross swords with me!... Someone's coming... It's her... it's nobody. It's as dark now as the devils' cauldron, and here I am behaving like some witless husband, though I'm not properly married yet! [*He sits on the garden seat*] Was there ever a man whose fate was stranger than mine? Son of God knows who, carried off by bandits, brought up in their ways. I could not stomach the life and decided to make my living honestly, only to find myself rejected at every turn. I take up chemistry, pharmacy, surgery, but even with the backing of an influential aristocrat I'm lucky to get a job lancing boils as a vet.* I weary of tormenting sick horses and, deciding to try my hand at something different, I plunge enthusiastically into the theatre. I might as well have tied a large rock around my neck! I cobble together a verse comedy about the customs of the harem, assuming that, as a Spanish writer, I can say what I like about Mohammed without drawing hostile fire. Next thing, some envoy from God knows where turns up and complains that in my play I have offended the Ottoman empire, Persia, a large slice of the Indian peninsula, the whole of Egypt, and the kingdoms of Barca,* Tripoli, Tunisia, Algeria, and Morocco. And so my play sinks without trace, and all to placate a bunch of Muslim princes, not one of whom, as far as I know, can read but who beat the living daylights out of us and say we are 'Christian dogs!' Since they can't stop a man thinking, they take it out on his hide instead. I grew hollow-cheeked, my prospects were nil. In the distance I could see the dreaded bailiff coming with his pen stuck in his wig. I quaked, but then I stiffened the sinews. A debate starts up about the nature of wealth. Since you don't need to know anything about a subject to be able to talk about it, I, who didn't have a penny to my name, compose a Treatise on the value of money and the theory of the net surplus.* The next moment, I'm whisked off in an official carriage and watch the drawbridge of a prison being lowered for me. As I'm driven in, I abandon all hope and lose my freedom. [*He gets up*] Oh, those powerful officials who are here today and gone tomorrow and never stop to think how much grief they cause! If I could get my hands on one of them when his pride has been crushed by some humiliating public disgrace, I'd tell him... I'd say that the nonsense that finds its way into print only matters to the people who would like to ban it; that without the freedom to criticize, praise is meaningless;* that only trivial minds are afraid of trifling books. [*He sits down again*] One day, when they'd got sick of feeding a prisoner who was no danger to anyone, they kicked me out. And since a man has to eat, even if he's no longer behind bars, I sharpen my pen and ask around for the latest topic of debate. I'm told that while I've been away, all expenses paid, a free-market principle* has taken over Madrid which even extends to the press, and that provided I refrain in my articles from mentioning the government, religion, politics, morality, public figures, influential bodies, opera or any other kind of theatre, and anyone who is somebody, I am free to publish whatever I like—once I've got permission from two or three censors! Taking advantage of this generous new freedom, I inform the public of my plans for a new paper which, confident that I'm not invading anyone else's patch, I call *The Unnecessary News*. And damn me if I don't get attacked by every miserable hack who's paid by the line. My paper is banned and I lose my livelihood. I'd come very near to losing hope and giving up, when someone thought of me for a government post. Unfortunately I was admirably qualified for it: they wanted someone who was good with figures, so they appointed a dancer. After that, my only option was stealing. So I became a banker at Faro.* And how did I do? I dined in town and people said to be 'top drawer' politely opened their doors to me on condition that they kept three-quarters of the takings for themselves. I could have been a success at something, for it began to dawn even on me that if you want to be rich, know-how is far more important than knowledge. But since all the people I knew were lining their pockets while at the same time expecting me to be honest, there was no way I could survive. So I turned my back on the world, and a hundred feet of water was about to separate me from it for good when my guardian angel recalled me to my original trade. I dust down my razors and my strop of stout English leather and then, leaving the delusions to the fools who live by them and my pride by the roadside as baggage too heavy for a man on foot, away I go, barbering from town to town and at last living without a care in the world. A noble lord arrives in Seville. He recognizes me. I find a way of getting him safely married. And to reward all I did to give him a wife, he now wants to walk off with mine! Intrigue! High winds, stormy weather! I'm about to step into a deep hole, I'm on the point of marrying my mother, when both my parents turn up, first one then the other. [*He stands up as the words come faster*] Then everybody starts arguing. It's you, it's him, it's me, no, it's not us, so who is it then? [*He sinks on to the seat again*] Such a fantastic chain of events! How did it all happen to me? Why those things and not others? Who pointed them in my direction? Having no choice but to travel a road I was not aware I was following, and which I will get off without wanting to, I have strewn it with as many flowers as my good humour has permitted. But when I say my good humour, how can I know if it is any more mine than all the other bits of me, nor what this 'me' is that I keep trying to understand: first, an unformed bundle of indefinable parts, then a puny, weak-brained runt, a dainty frisking animal, a young man with a taste for pleasure and appetites to match, turning his hand to all trades to survive—sometimes master, sometimes servant as chance dictated, ambitious from pride, hard-working from necessity, but always happy to be idle! An orator when it was safe to speak out, a poet in my leisure hours, a musician as the situation required, in love in crazy fits and bursts. I've seen it all, done it all, had it all. Then the bubble burst and I was too disillusioned... Disillusioned! Oh Suzanne, Suzanne, Suzanne, you put me through agony! I hear footsteps... Someone's coming... The moment of crisis has arrived.

[*He takes up a position downstage right*

SCENE 4

FIGARO, *the* COUNTESS, *dressed in* SUZANNE'*s clothes,* SUZANNE, *wearing the* COUNTESS'*s clothes,* MARCELINE

SUZANNE [*whispers to the* COUNTESS]. Yes, Marceline told me Figaro would be here.

MARCELINE. And so he is. Don't talk so loud.

SUZANNE. So one of them is listening to us and the other will come looking for me. Let's begin.

MARCELINE. I wouldn't miss a word of this for worlds. I'm going to hide in this pavilion.

[*She enters the pavilion where* FANCHETTE *is hiding*

SCENE 5

FIGARO, *the* COUNTESS, SUZANNE

SUZANNE. Your Ladyship is shivering. Are you cold?

COUNTESS. It's the evening damp. I think I'll go in.

SUZANNE. If Madame doesn't need me, I'd like stay here under the trees for a moment, and catch my breath.

COUNTESS. A cold is what you'll catch with this heavy dew.

SUZANNE. I'll be all right.

FIGARO [*aside*]. Oh yes, but there's not just dew to worry about!

[SUZANNE *walks into the wings, stage left, opposite* FIGARO

SCENE 6

FIGARO, CHERUBIN, *the* COUNT, *the* COUNTESS, SUZANNE, *with* FIGARO *and* SUZANNE *downstage, on opposite sides.*

CHERUBIN [*in officer's uniform, enters blithely singing the Romance from Act II, scene 4*]. La la la la la...

> Of a godmother's gentleness
> A lady I loved most tenderly.

COUNTESS [*to herself*]. It's the page!

CHERUBIN. I can hear footsteps. Quick, back to my hideout where Fanchette... It's a woman!

COUNTESS [*overhearing*]. Oh heavens!

CHERUBIN [*ducks down and peers into the dark*]. Are my eyes playing tricks? That headdress made of feathers I can just pick out in the gloom—I'd say it was Suzanne.

COUNTESS [*aside*]. What if the Count came...

[*The* COUNT *appears upstage*

CHERUBIN [*approaches and takes the hand of the* COUNTESS *who tries to take it back*].   Yes it is, it's that delightful girl they call Suzanne. There's no mistaking the softness of this hand, the way it trembles, but especially the beat of my heart!

[*He attempts to put the back of her hand against his heart; she takes her hand away*

COUNTESS [*whispers*].   Go away!

CHERUBIN.   If it was pity that made you come to this part of the park where I've been hiding since this afternoon...

COUNTESS.   Figaro will be here soon.

COUNT [*edging forward*].   Surely that's Suzanne?

CHERUBIN [*to the* COUNTESS].   I'm not afraid of Figaro. Anyway, it's not him you're waiting for.

COUNTESS.   Who is it, then?

COUNT [*aside*].   She's with someone.

CHERUBIN.   His Lordship, you slyboots. He asked you to meet him here this morning when I was hiding behind the chair.

COUNT [*aside, furious*].   It's that damned page again!

FIGARO [*aside*].   And they say you shouldn't listen to other people's conversations!

SUZANNE [*aside*].   Why can't he keep his mouth shut!

COUNTESS.   Please oblige me by going away.

CHERUBIN.   Not before I get my reward for obeying.

COUNTESS [*alarmed*].   You wouldn't... would you?

CHERUBIN [*passionately*].   Twenty kisses for you to start with and then a hundred for your beautiful mistress.

COUNTESS.   You wouldn't dare!

CHERUBIN.   Oh yes I would! You take her place with his Lordship and I'll take his with you. The only one who loses out is Figaro.

FIGARO [*aside*].   The swine!

SUZANNE [*aside*]. Bold as brass! Aha, the page has turned!

[CHERUBIN *tries to kiss the* COUNTESS. *The* COUNT *steps between him and receives the kiss*

COUNTESS [*stepping back*]. Merciful heavens!

FIGARO [*hearing the kiss*]. A nice girl! And I nearly married her!

[*He listens*

CHERUBIN [*aside, as he runs his hands over the* COUNT'*s clothes*]. It's his Lordship!

[*He rushes into the pavilion where* FANCHETTE *and* MARCELINE *are hiding*

SCENE 7

FIGARO, *the* COUNT, *the* COUNTESS, SUZANNE

FIGARO [*coming forward*]. I'll just...

COUNT [*convinced he is talking to the page*]. If you're not going to give me a second kiss... try this...

[*He takes aim at what he thinks is the page*

FIGARO [*standing close, he is struck*]. Ow!

COUNT. That was for the first one.

FIGARO [*mutters as he moves away, rubbing his jaw*]. There's not as much to be said for eavesdropping as I thought...

SUZANNE [*laughs loudly from the opposite side of the stage*]. Ha ha ha!

COUNT [*to the* COUNTESS, *whom he mistakes for* SUZANNE]. I'll never understand that boy. He takes a hefty punch and then runs away laughing!

FIGARO [*aside*]. He wouldn't be laughing if he'd been hit like that...

COUNT. Damn it all! Can't I go anywhere without... [*To the* COUNTESS] But let's not say any more about this nonsense. It would spoil my pleasure in finding you here in this grove.

COUNTESS [*imitating* SUZANNE's *way of talking*]. Were you expecting to?

COUNT. What, after your ingenious note? [*He takes her hand*] You're trembling.

COUNTESS. I got a fright.

COUNT. It wasn't to deny you a kiss that I intercepted the page's.

[*He kisses her on the forehead*

COUNTESS. That's a liberty!

FIGARO [*aside*]. Has she no shame?

SUZANNE [*aside*]. How charming!

COUNT [*taking his wife's hand*]. Such skin! So soft, so silky! The Countess's hand isn't half as smooth to the touch!

COUNTESS [*aside*]. That's all you know!

COUNT. Or her arms as firm, as shapely. Or her fingers as pretty and elegant and teasing.

COUNTESS [*imitating* SUZANNE's *voice*]. So love...?

COUNT. Ah, love is the tale of a heart and pleasure drives its story. It's pleasure which has brought me here to worship at your feet...

COUNTESS. Don't you love her any more?

COUNT. I love her a great deal. But after three years, marriage becomes so respectable.

COUNTESS. What did you look for in her?

COUNT [*stroking her hand*]. What I find in you, my sweet.

COUNTESS. But what exactly?

COUNT. I'm not sure. More variety perhaps, and more spice in our life, a whiff of excitement, for her to say no sometimes, who knows? Wives think that they've done all they need to once they've decided they love us. Once they've said they're in love, deeply in love (supposing they are), they become so endlessly accommodating, so eternally, relentlessly agreeable that one fine evening a man is startled to find that he has achieved boredom, not the happiness he was looking for.

COUNTESS [*aside*]. I never knew!

COUNT. The fact is, Suzanne, I've often thought that if husbands look outside marriage for the pleasures which they don't find inside it, it's because wives don't think enough about how to keep our love alive, how to renew theirs, how to—what's the word?—renovate its pleasures by varying them.

COUNTESS [*indignant*]. So wives must do it all?

COUNT [*laughing*]. And husbands nothing? Should we try to change nature? Our function is to catch them; theirs...

COUNTESS. Theirs?

COUNT ... is to keep us. People forget that.

COUNTESS. I won't.

COUNT. Nor me.

FIGARO [*aside*]. Nor me.

SUZANNE [*aside*]. Nor me.

COUNT [*taking his wife's hand*]. There must be an echo here. Let's keep our voices down. There's no need to worry your pretty head about it. You're exciting and beautiful and made for love! With a touch of contrariness you could be the most tantalizing creature in the world! [*He kisses her on the forehead*] Sweet Suzanne, a Castilian is always as good as his word. Here, as agreed, is the money to redeem the right I no longer have to the exquisite moment you promised to grant me. But since you have been so gracious about saying yes, I will add this diamond. Wear it for love of me.

COUNTESS [*curtseys*]. Suzanne accepts everything you offer.

FIGARO [*aside*]. You can't get more brazen than that.

SUZANNE [*aside*]. Oh how the money rolls in!

COUNT [*aside*]. So she can be bought, that's all to the good.

COUNTESS [*looking towards the park*]. I can see torches.

COUNT. It's the preparations for your wedding. Shall we slip into one of these pavilions until they've gone past?

COUNTESS. But there's no light.

COUNT [*leading her gently*]. We won't need light. We shan't be doing much reading.

FIGARO [*aside*]. She's going with him! I knew it!

[*He steps forward*

COUNT [*raises his voice as he turns*]. Who's that skulking there?

FIGARO [*furious*]. I'm not skulking, I'm bursting in!

COUNT [*whispers to the* COUNTESS]. It's Figaro!

[*He runs off*

COUNTESS. I'll follow you.

[*She goes into the pavilion on the right as the* COUNT *disappears into the trees*

SCENE 8

FIGARO, SUZANNE, *in the dark*

FIGARO [*trying to see what has happened to the* COUNT *and the* COUNTESS, *whom he still thinks is* SUZANNE]. I can't hear anything now. They'll have gone in, and I'm out here. [*In a calmer voice*] There are lots of blundering husbands who pay spies to snoop, and spend months worrying about a suspicion they can never prove. They should take a leaf out of my book. From the very start, I followed her around, kept my ears open, and always knew what was going on the moment it happened. That's the way. No doubts. You know where you stand. [*Pacing restlessly*] It's just as well I don't care. The fact that she's gone behind my back doesn't bother me. But I've got them at last!

SUZANNE [*who has been creeping forward in the dark, mutters*]. I'll make you pay for suspecting me! [*Imitating the* COUNTESS'*s voice*] Who's there?

FIGARO [*raving*]. Who's there? Someone who wishes to God he'd been strangled at birth!

SUZANNE [*in the* COUNTESS's *voice*]. Why, it's Figaro!

FIGARO [*looks hard then says quickly*]. Your Ladyship!

SUZANNE. Keep your voice down.

FIGARO [*urgently*]. Oh Madame, you've come at just the right time, thank God. Where do you think his Lordship is at this moment?

SUZANNE. Why I should care about that ungrateful man?

FIGARO [*more insistently*]. And Suzanne, my bride to be, where do you think she is?

SUZANNE. I said keep your voice down!

FIGARO [*more insistently still*]. Suzanne, who I thought so pure, who seemed so good and demure! The pair of them are in there. I'm going to rouse the...

SUZANNE [*stops his mouth with her hand but forgets to disguise her voice*]. Don't rouse anybody.

FIGARO [*aside*]. It's Suzanne! God damn!

SUZANNE [*in the* COUNTESS's *voice*]. You seem very tense.

FIGARO [*aside*]. The sly minx! She's playing games with me!

SUZANNE. Figaro, we can't let them get away with it.

FIGARO. Are you really serious about that?

SUZANNE. I'd be letting my whole sex down if I weren't. But men have many ways of getting even.

FIGARO [*confidently*]. No one here is extra to requirements. Women's ways are much more effective.

SUZANNE [*aside*]. Ooh, I could slap his face!

FIGARO [*aside*]. It would be a laugh if, just before the wedding...

SUZANNE. But what kind of revenge would it be if there were no love to give it point?

FIGARO. There might be no visible sign of love but, believe me, it lives and breathes behind this façade of respect.

SUZANNE [*stung*]. I don't know if you really mean that, but it could have been put more eloquently.

FIGARO [*kneels with a comic show of passion*]. Oh, your Ladyship, I worship the ground beneath your feet! Think of this moment, this place, these circumstances, and let your resentment add the polish so wanting in my poor words!

SUZANNE [*aside*]. My hand is itching.

FIGARO [*aside*]. My heart is racing.

SUZANNE. But sir, have you reflected...

FIGARO. Yes, Madame, I have.

SUZANNE. ... that anger and love...

FIGARO. Time and tide wait for no man! Your hand, Madame!

SUZANNE [*in her own voice, as she slaps his face*]. Here, take it.

FIGARO. Ow! *Demonio!* What a wallop!

SUZANNE [*slaps him again*]. Call that a wallop? Then try this one for size!

FIGARO. What's going on? Hell's teeth! What do you think I am? A gong?

SUZANNE [*with a slap for each phrase*]. I'll give you gong! It's me, Suzanne. This is for being suspicious, this is for wanting to get your own back, for your infidelities, your ruses, your insults, your scheming! Isn't this what they call love? That's what you called it earlier on.*

FIGARO [*laughs as he straightens up*]. Santa Barbara! Yes, it's love. It's wonderful! It's marvellous! Figaro is the happiest man in the world! Wallop away, my sweet, as hard as you like. But when you've turned me black and blue all over, Suzanne, spare a kindly glance for the most fortunate mortal ever walloped by a woman.

SUZANNE. 'Most fortunate mortal'! You two-faced hyena! Not fortunate enough to stop you trying it on with her Ladyship, which you did with such cheeky, sneaky words that I forgot I wasn't me. I weakened, yes, but at the time I was her.

FIGARO. You don't really think I was fooled? I recognized your angel voice.

SUZANNE [*laughing*]. You knew it was me? Oh, I'll make you pay for that!

FIGARO. You lay it on thick with the wallops but you still have it in for me—how like a woman! But tell me, what lucky star must I thank for finding you here, when I thought you were with him? And what about these clothes which took me in but now convince me you're innocent?

SUZANNE. It's you who're the innocent, coming here and falling into a trap which was meant for someone else. Is it our fault if we set out to muzzle a fox and end up catching two?

FIGARO. Who caught the other one?

SUZANNE. His wife.

FIGARO. His wife?

SUZANNE. Yes, his wife.

FIGARO [*howls*]. Oh Figaro! You should be shot for not seeing it coming! His wife! Women! Of all the sly, underhand, brilliantly clever... And the kisses I heard in the dark...?

SUZANNE. ... were given to her Ladyship.

FIGARO. And who did the page kiss?

SUZANNE [*laughing*]. His Lordship!

FIGARO. And this morning, behind the chair?

SUZANNE. Nobody.

FIGARO. Are you sure?

SUZANNE [*laughing*]. Still want more wallops, Figaro?

FIGARO [*kisses her hand*]. Wallops from such pretty hands. Not like the one I got from the Count. He really meant it.

SUZANNE. Come, man of pride, eat your humble pie.

FIGARO [*acting out his words*]. You're right. I kneel, I bow my head, prostrate I cringe, I grovel.

SUZANNE [*laughing*]. Ha ha ha! Poor Count! And he went to such trouble!

FIGARO [*gets to his knees*]. ... to seduce his own lawful wedded wife!

SCENE 9

The COUNT *enters and makes straight for the pavilion on the right of the stage.* FIGARO, SUZANNE

COUNT [*to himself*]. She's not in these woods, I've looked everywhere. Maybe she went in here.

SUZANNE [*whispers to* FIGARO]. It's him!

COUNT [*opening the door*]. Suzanne, are you there?

FIGARO [*whispers*]. He's looking for her. But I thought...

SUZANNE [*whispers*]. He didn't recognize her.

FIGARO. Shall we go for the kill? Ready?

[*He kisses her hand*

COUNT [*turns and sees*]. A man down on his knees to the Countess! Damn! I haven't got my sword with me!

[*He moves closer*

FIGARO [*gets to his feet, disguising his voice*]. Forgive me, Madame, for not realizing that this usual meeting-place of ours had been chosen for the wedding.

COUNT [*aside*]. It's the man who was hiding in the dressing-room this morning!

[*He strikes himself on the head*

FIGARO. But let it not be said that so trifling an obstacle stood in the way of our amours.

COUNT [*aside*]. Curses! Death and damnation!

FIGARO [*whispers to* SUZANNE *as he leads her to the pavilion*]. He's swearing. [*Aloud*] Let's not waste a moment, Madame, but make up for the time we lost this morning when I jumped from your window.

COUNT [*aside*]. Aha! Truth will out!

SUZANNE [*outside the pavilion, stage left*]. Before we go in, look and see if we've been followed.

[FIGARO *kisses her on the forehead*

COUNT [*cries*]. Vengeance!

[SUZANNE *runs into the pavilion already occupied by* FANCHETTE, MARCELINE, *and* CHERUBIN

SCENE 10

FIGARO, *the* COUNT, *who seizes him by the arm*

FIGARO [*pretends to quake with terror*]. It's the Master!

COUNT [*recognizes him*]. Oh it's you, you villain! Hello there! Is anybody there?

SCENE 11

PEDRILLO, *the* COUNT, FIGARO

PEDRILLO [*in riding-boots*]. Your Lordship, at last I've found you.

COUNT. Excellent, it's Pedrillo. Are you alone?

PEDRILLO. Just got back from Seville. Rode my horse into the ground.

COUNT. Right, come here and shout for all you're worth.

PEDRILLO [*shouts very loudly*]. No trace of the page anywhere. Here's the packet.*

COUNT [*pushes him away*]. Oh, you blithering idiot.

PEDRILLO. Your Lordship told me to shout.

COUNT [*still holding* FIGARO]. I meant for help. Hello-oh! Anybody there? If you can hear me, come here—and hurry!

PEDRILLO. Figaro's here, and me, that makes two. Nothing's can happen to you with the pair of us around.

SCENE 12

Cast as before, plus BRID'OISON, BARTHOLO, BAZILE, ANTONIO, GRIPPE-SOLEIL, *and all the wedding guests, who arrive carrying torches*

BARTHOLO [*to* FIGARO]. There! The moment we heard your signal...

COUNT [*points to the pavilion on the left of the stage*]. Pedrillo. Guard that door.

[PEDRILLO *obeys*

BAZILE [*whispers to* FIGARO]. Did you catch him with Suzanne?

COUNT [*points to* FIGARO]. And you men, surround the prisoner and guard him with your lives—or you'll all answer to me.

BAZILE. Ha ha ha!

COUNT [*furious*]. Silence! [*Icily, to* FIGARO] Now my fine buckeroo, are you going to answer my questions?

FIGARO [*coolly*]. I suppose so. I can't see anyone with the authority to rule that I don't have to, sir. You're in control here of everything—except yourself.

COUNT [*holding himself back*]. Except myself!

ANTONIO. That's telling him!

COUNT [*furious again*]. Rubbish! But if there's one thing that could make me more furious than I am already, it's the way you pretend to be so cool and collected.

FIGARO. Are we soldiers to kill and get killed for causes we know nothing of? Personally I like to know what I'm angry about.

COUNT [*beside himself*]. This is an outrage! [*Controls himself*] Well, man of principle, you say you don't know anything, but will you at least be good enough to tell us who is the lady you showed into that pavilion?

FIGARO [*deliberately pointing to the other*]. That one?

COUNT. This one.

FIGARO [*coldly*]. That's quite different. A young lady who honours me with her most particular friendship.

BAZILE [*astounded*]. Aha!

COUNT. You heard him, gentlemen?

BARTHOLO [*astounded*]. We heard.

COUNT [*to* FIGARO]. And does this young lady have any other friend-ships you know of?

FIGARO [*coldly*]. I know a noble lord was taken with her for a time. But either he lost interest in her or she likes me better than a man of more substance, but she has now swung in my favour.

COUNT [*angry*]. Favour! [*Controls himself*] At least he's candid, for what he has just admitted, gentleman, I assure you I myself have heard from his accomplice in person.

BRID'OISON [*astonished*]. His aaa-accomplice!

COUNT [*furious*]. Since the dishonour is public, so must my ven-geance be also.

[*He goes into the pavilion*]

SCENE 13

Cast as before, except the COUNT

ANTONIO. 'Tis only right.

BRID'OISON [*to* FIGARO]. So which mer-man took the other one's wer-wife?

FIGARO [*laughing*]. Nobody's had that pleasure!

SCENE 14

Cast as before, the COUNT, CHERUBIN

COUNT [*talking into the pavilion and dragging out someone we cannot identify*]. It's no use struggling. You are lost, Madame, your hour has come! [*He comes out without looking back*] We must be thankful that so hateful a union was not blessed with issue...

FIGARO [*exclaims*]. Cherubin!

COUNT. My page?

BAZILE. Ha ha ha!

COUNT [*beside himself, mutters*]. It's that damned page again! [*To* CHERUBIN] What were you doing in that pavilion?

CHERUBIN [*timidly*]. Keeping out of your way like you told me to.

PEDRILLO. Hardly seems worth killing a horse for.

COUNT. Antonio, go in and bring out the unworthy creature who has dishonoured me so that she may face her judge.

BRID'OISON. Is it her ler-Ladyship you're looking for in there?

ANTONIO. Ha! there be a God in 'eaven! You done similar often enough round 'ere yourself in the past...

COUNT. Inside!

[ANTONIO *goes inside*

SCENE 15

Cast as before, except ANTONIO

COUNT. You will observe, gentlemen, that the page was not alone.

CHERUBIN [*timidly*]. My fate would have been too hard to bear if its bitter sting had not been drawn by some tender-hearted person.

SCENE 16

Cast as before, ANTONIO, FANCHETTE

ANTONIO [*dragging by the arm a person we cannot yet identify*]. Come along, yer Ladyshipness, don't make us have to arsk you twice to get you come out 'cos we all knows very well that you went in.

FIGARO [*exclaims*]. It's my little cousin!

BAZILE. Ha ha ha!

COUNT. Fanchette!

ANTONIO [*turns and exclaims*]. Oh! Dang me! Must be your Lordship's idea of a joke, choosin' me to show all the company as how it's me own daughter wot's been the cause of all these goins-on.

COUNT. Who would have believed she was in there?

[*He is about to go in*

BARTHOLO [*steps forward*]. If your Lordship will allow me. All of this is far from clear. I am calm and perfectly composed.

[*He goes in*

BRID'OISON. A most bee-bewildering ber-business.

SCENE 17

Cast as before, MARCELINE

BARTHOLO [*talking to a person he has in tow*]. Don't be afraid, Milady, you'll come to no harm. You have my word. [*He turns and exclaims*] Marceline!

BAZILE. Ha ha ha!

FIGARO [*laughing*]. Oh, this is crazy! Now my mother's in it too!

ANTONIO. Each one's worse than the one before!

COUNT [*furious*]. I'm not interested in her. It's the Countess...

SCENE 18

Cast as before, plus SUZANNE, *who appears holding a fan in front of her face*

COUNT. ... Ah! She's coming out now! [*He grasps her arm tightly*] Well, gentlemen, in your view what should we do with this odious...

[SUZANNE, *head bowed, throws herself at his feet*

COUNT [*protests*]. No, no!

[FIGARO *drops to his knees beside her*

COUNT [*protests more loudly*]. No, no!

[MARCELINE *kneels*

COUNT [*protesting*]. No, no!

[*All kneel down to him, except* BRID'OISON

COUNT [*beside himself*]. No, not if there were a hundred of you!

SCENE 19

Cast as before. The COUNTESS *steps out of the pavilion*

COUNTESS [*drops to her knees*]. At least I can add one to the number.

COUNT [*looks at the* COUNTESS *then at* SUZANNE]. What's this?

BRID'OISON [*laughing*]. Good Lord! It's her ler-ler-Ladyship!

COUNT [*helps the* COUNTESS *to her feet*]. You mean... it was you, Countess? [*In a contrite voice*] Only your forgiveness, your generous forgiveness...

COUNTESS [*laughing*]. If you were me now, you'd say 'No, no!' But you're not, and for the third time today I forgive you unconditionally.

[*She rises*

SUZANNE [*rises*]. So do I.

MARCELINE [*rises*]. So do I.

FIGARO [*rises*]. So do I. It's that echo again.

[*All rise*

COUNT. An echo! I thought I had them dancing to my tune, and they've treated me like a child!

COUNTESS [*laughing*]. My Lord, you must have no regrets.

FIGARO [*dusting his knees with his hat*]. A day like today is excellent training for a diplomat.

COUNT [*to* SUZANNE]. But the note fastened with a pin?

SUZANNE. Was dictated by her Ladyship.

COUNT. She is owed an answer.

[*He kisses the* COUNTESS*'s hand*

COUNTESS. Everyone shall receive their due.

[*She gives the purse to* FIGARO *and the diamond to* SUZANNE

SUZANNE [*to* FIGARO]. Another dowry.

FIGARO [*weighing the purse in his hand*]. That makes three—though this one took some arranging.

SUZANNE. Like our wedding.

GRIPPE-SOLEIL. What about the bride's wedding garter, then? Who's going to get it? Me?

COUNTESS [*takes the ribbon she has kept all day next her heart and throws it on the ground*]. Her garter? It was in her dress. There it is.

[*The* PAGE-BOYS *present for the wedding start squabbling for it*

CHERUBIN [*quicker than the rest, snatches it up*]. Anyone who wants it is going to have to fight me for it.

COUNT [*laughing, to the page*]. For someone who's so sensitive, what did you think was so funny about having your jaw punched a while back?

CHERUBIN [*takes one step back and half-draws his sword*]. Me, Colonel? Punched?

FIGARO [*comically angry*]. It was on my jaw he got punched. That's how our betters hand out justice!

COUNT. Your jaw? Ha ha ha! [*To the* COUNTESS] What do you say to that, my dear?

COUNTESS [*lost in thought, she recovers and says sincerely*]. Oh, yes, my dear! For the rest of my life, and nothing can alter that, I swear.

COUNT [*clapping the judge on the shoulder*]. What about you, Brid'-oison? What do you make of it all now?

BRID'OISON. Of all I've seen, your Lordship?... Well, from my per-point of view, I don't know quite what to make of it. That's my per-point of view.

ALL TOGETHER. Spoken like Solomon!

FIGARO. I was poor and people looked down on me. I showed some brains and people hated me. Now, with a pretty wife and money...

BARTHOLO [*laughing*]. People will rush to be your friend.

FIGARO. They will?

BARTHOLO. I know them.

FIGARO [*turns to the audience*]. Wife and wealth apart, I should be truly honoured and very happy if you would.

The music of the same ritournelle *strikes up again*

First verse. BAZILE:

> Triple dowry, pretty spouse
> Essential items for a house.
> Of a noble and a beardless page
> Only a fool's consumed by jealous rage.
> But as the Latin adage once did state,
> A clever man is author of his fate

FIGARO. I've always known that. [*Sings*] Let those rejoice who were born with brains—*Gaudeant bene nati…*

BAZILE. That's not it. [*Sings*] *Gaudeant bene wealthy*.

Second verse. SUZANNE:

If a husband unfaithful be
He will boast and others laugh with glee.
But should it be the wife who strays,
He will ask a judge to make her mend her ways.
It is not fair, it is not just:
I'll tell you why, for tell I must:
Laws are written by the strong,
Laws are written by the strong.

Third verse. FIGARO:

A jealous husband, meek and mild,
Wanted both wife and ease of mind.
He bought a dog to act as guard
And kept it always in his yard.
But a fearful fuss broke out one night.
Up sprang the dog and bit him
—But not the lover who had sold it him,
—But not the lover who had sold it him.

Fourth verse. COUNTESS:

Take this wife who's all ice and pride
For whose spouse all love has died.
Take this other, with a roving eye,
Who swears she'll love hers till she die.
Which one is smarter than these both?
She who acquiesces but is loth
To trust her mate to keep his marriage oath,
To trust her mate to keep his marriage oath.

Fifth verse. COUNT:

Take this wife from out of town:
Who wears grim duty like a crown.
Now no one likes a melancholic
So let's have girls who frolic.

They're like coins or specie and
Fit the pocket of a married man
—But also pass from hand to hand,
—But also pass from hand to hand.

Sixth verse. MARCELINE:

All present here know the name of she
Who gave him life and vitality.
The rest's a mystery,
Love's secret and love's history.

FIGARO [completes the verse]:

That secret shows how a son, if bold,
Though sired by one who's dull and old,
May yet be worth his weight in gold,
May yet be worth his weight in gold.

Seventh verse.

By the lottery of fate that's birth
Nature makes us king or serf.
Our lot's decreed by luck and chance,
Only wit can make a difference.
Twenty kings may wear a crown,
But death deprives them of their renown,
While Voltaire's name will be forever known,*
While Voltaire's name will be forever known.

Eighth verse. CHERUBIN:

Woman, who with flighty ways
Casts gloom upon our salad days!
We may throw mud at your wicked tricks,
Yet observe how little of it sticks!
You're like the theatre's fickle pit:
Those who claim most to scold it
Are those who do most to court it,
Are those who do most to court it.

Ninth verse. SUZANNE:

If our play of the Follies of a Day,
Has something serious to say,

It is that folly must have its season
To give a human face to reason.
For nature works with measure
To lead us at her leisure
To do her bidding through our pleasure,
To do her bidding through our pleasure.

Tenth verse. BRID'OISON:

And so our comic course is rer-run.
You ask if there is sense behind the fun?
I believe it paints the hope and fear
Of all who are foregathered here.
When good people are oppressed too long
They kick and shout, for they are ser-strong.
But all will end not in tears but ser-song
    All dance as the curtain falls.

The New Tartuffe*

or,

THE GUILTY MOTHER

A Prose Drama* in Five Acts

First performed in Paris on 26 June 1792
at the Théâtre du Marais*

Families are always well served when the
troublemaker is shown the door

(*The play's last words*)

CHARACTERS

COUNT ALMAVIVA, *a Spanish nobleman, a proud aristocrat but with no trace of arrogance*

COUNTESS ALMAVIVA, *his most unhappy wife, a woman of angelic piety*

CHEVALIER LEON, *their son, a young man in love with freedom, as are all ardent spirits of the new age*

FLORESTINE, *ward and god-daughter of Count Almaviva, a young woman with a feeling heart*

MAJOR BÉGEARSS, *an Irishman, a Major of Spanish Infantry, formerly secretary to the Count during his time as ambassador; a devious man, a great schemer, and an accomplished troublemaker*

FIGARO, *valet, surgeon, and confidant to the Count; a man shaped by events and his experience of the world*

SUZANNE, *personal maid to the Countess, wife to Figaro, devoted to her mistress, and cured of the illusions of youth*

MONSIEUR FAL, *notary to the Count, a man of exact habits and thoroughly honest*

GUILLAUME, *Bégearss's German valet, a man too good for such a master*

The action takes place in Paris, in the house occupied by the Count's family, at the end of 1790

ACT I

An elaborately furnished drawing-room

SCENE 1

SUZANNE, *alone, with an armful of dark-coloured flowers which she is making up into a bouquet*

SUZANNE. Her Ladyship can wake up now and ring, it's done. Such a dismal job. [*She sits down dejectedly*] It's not nine o'clock yet and I'm already feeling exhausted... The last thing she said to me as I was getting her ready for bed stopped me sleeping all night... 'Tomorrow, Suzanne, as soon as it's light, send for lots of flowers and arrange them in my rooms.' And she told the porter: 'If anyone asks for me, I'm not at home all day.' 'I want you to make me up a bouquet of black and dark red blooms around a single white carnation.' There, it's ready. Her poor Ladyship, she was crying... Who can this motley offering be intended for? If we were in Spain, we'd be celebrating the saint's day of her son... [*mysteriously*] and of someone else who's dead. [*She stares at the flowers*] The colours of death and mourning. [*She sighs*] Her heart is broken and it'll never mend. I'll tie them up with black ribbon. Depressing, but that's how her sad fancy takes her.

[*She ties the bouquet*

SCENE 2

SUZANNE, FIGARO, *looking around mysteriously. The scene should be played very quickly*

SUZANNE. Come right in, Figaro! You look like a man who's strayed into your wife's boudoir on the off-chance of...

FIGARO. Is it safe to speak?

SUZANNE. Yes, as long as the door stays open.

FIGARO. Why do we need to go to such lengths?

SUZANNE. Because you know who might just walk in at any moment.

FIGARO [*stressing the name*]. You mean the right Honoré-Tartuffe Bégearss?

SUZANNE. I agreed to meet him here. You really must stop this habit of adding insults to his name. It's the sort of thing that gets out and it could spoil your plans.

FIGARO. His name really is Honoré!

SUZANNE. But not Tartuffe.

FIGARO. More's the pity!

SUZANNE. You sound very cross.

FIGARO. Furious [*She stands*] You've not forgotten our agreement? Let's be clear: are you going to help me prevent a catastrophe? You don't intend to go on letting him fool you? He's a very wicked man.

SUZANNE. No, but I don't think he trusts me. He never speaks to me any more. I'm really afraid that he believes we've patched things up between us.

FIGARO. Maybe, but we'll still go on pretending.

SUZANNE. But what have you found out that's put you in such a bad temper?

FIGARO. First, let's run through the situation so far. Ever since we've been in Paris and Monsieur Almaviva—we have to call him that because he won't allow anyone to call him his Lordship any more...

SUZANNE [*highly offended*]. A fine thing! And her Ladyship has taken to going out without her footman in livery. It makes us look the same as everybody else!...*

FIGARO. As I was saying, since he lost his oldest boy, a rakehell who got himself killed in a quarrel over cards, you know how completely everything has gone wrong for us and how grim and bitter the Count's become.

SUZANNE. You've turned rather tetchy yourself.

FIGARO. How he doesn't seem able to stand the sight of his other son.

SUZANNE. It's very noticeable.

FIGARO. How unhappy her Ladyship has been.

SUZANNE. It's a crime the way he carries on with her.

FIGARO. How he's got a good deal fonder recently of his ward Florestine. And especially how hard he's trying to turn his assets into cash.

SUZANNE. Hold on, Figaro, you must be losing your grip. I know all that, so why are you telling me it all again?

FIGARO. Because we must have everything clear in our minds so that we understand each other. We are agreed, aren't we, that the wily Irishman, that blot on the family landscape, was his Lordship's secretary whose job was to encode official embassy papers, and that in the process he somehow managed to get his hands on all their secrets. That the cunning weasel talked them into leaving Spain, where everything was peaceful, and come to this country which has been turned upside down, hoping that here he'd be better placed to exploit their disagreements, detach the husband from the wife, marry the ward, and get his hands on the family fortune which is already in a parlous state.

SUZANNE. What's my role to be? What can I do about it?

FIGARO. Don't let him out of your sight and keep me posted on every move he makes...

SUZANNE. But I tell you everything he says.

FIGARO. What he says isn't always the same as what he means. Watch out for words that slip out when he's talking, those tiny gestures, the way he moves: it's the key to a man's character. There's something wicked afoot. It's obvious he believes nothing can stop him, because to me he seems... craftier, wilier, more smug—in fact he's like these imbeciles here in France who start cheering before the battle's been won! You must try and be as devious as he is: butter him up, tell him what he'd like to hear, and whatever he wants, don't say no.

SUZANNE. That's asking a lot.

FIGARO. It will all go well and everything will turn out fine provided I'm informed as soon as anything happens.

SUZANNE. Should I tell the mistress?

FIGARO. It's too soon for that. They're all under his thumb. She wouldn't believe you and you'd sink us without saving them. Follow him around, be his shadow. Meanwhile, I'll keep an eye on him when he's out of the house.

SUZANNE. Listen, I told you he doesn't trust me, and if he finds us together... That's him coming downstairs... Not a word!... Make it look as if we're arguing—good and loud.

[*She puts the bouquet on the table*

FIGARO [*raising his voice*]. And I'm not standing for it! Just let me catch you once more...

SUZANNE [*raising her voice*]. What if you do? You don't scare me!

FIGARO [*pretending to hit her*]. Oh don't I! Well take that, you brazen trollop!

SUZANNE [*pretending to have been hit*]. Ow! He hit me! And in her Ladyship's room too!

SCENE 3

Major BÉGEARSS, FIGARO, SUZANNE

BÉGEARSS [*in uniform, wearing a black armband*]. What's all this noise? I could hear you arguing from my room. It's been going on for an hour.

FIGARO [*aside*]. An hour!

BÉGEARSS. I come down and find a woman in tears...

SUZANNE [*pretends to cry*]. The brute raised his hand to me!

BÉGEARSS. That's despicable! Monsieur Figaro! Since when did a gentleman strike a lady?

FIGARO [*brusquely*]. Dammit sir! I'll thank you to keep out of this. I am not a gentleman and this woman is no lady—she's my wife. She shows no respect, she's got her nose poked into something, and she thinks she can get the better of me because there are people in this house who always back her up. I intend to teach her...

BÉGEARSS. How can you be so boorish?

FIGARO. Listen, if I wanted someone to judge the way I treat her, you'd be the last person I'd ask. And you know very well why.

BÉGEARSS. I shall report you to your employer. You forget yourself, sir!

FIGARO. Me, forget myself? I'd rather forget you!

[*He goes out*

SCENE 4

BÉGEARSS, SUZANNE

BÉGEARSS. My dear child, I can't believe it. What on earth has made him so furious?

SUZANNE. He came looking for an argument. He said all sort of horrible things about you. He said I wasn't to see you or dare talk to you again. I stood up for you, things got out of hand and came to blows... It's the first time he ever hit me. That's the end, I want a separation. You saw him...

BÉGEARSS. Let's not go into that now. A faint shadow of doubt was beginning to cloud my faith in you, but this quarrel has removed it.

SUZANNE. Is that all the comfort you can offer?

BÉGEARSS. Don't you fret. I shall make it my business to see he doesn't get away with it. It's high time I repaid you for all you've done for me, my poor Suzanne. To begin with, I'll tell you a secret... But is the door shut? Better make sure. [*As* SUZANNE *goes to check, he mutters*] If I could have just a few minutes alone with the Countess's jewel-case, the one with the secret compartment I had specially made for her, where those important letters are hidden...

SUZANNE [*returns*]. Well, what's this big secret?

BÉGEARSS. I'm your friend. You help me and your future's made. I'm going to marry Florestine. It's all arranged. Her father is all for it.

SUZANNE. Who do you mean, her father?

BÉGEARSS [*laughing*]. You can't be that naive, surely? Listen, if anything's certain, it's this: when an orphan girl appears in a family, whether as ward or god-daughter, she's always the child of the husband. [*Decisively*] Anyway, I'm going to marry her... provided you can talk her into it.

SUZANNE. Oh, but Leon is head over heels in love with her!

BÉGEARSS. Their son? [*Coldly*] I'll soon put his fire out!

SUZANNE [*taken aback*]. Oh? But she's also very much in love with him.

BÉGEARSS. With him?

SUZANNE. Yes.

BÉGEARSS [*coldly*]. I'll cure her of that.

SUZANNE [*amazed*]. Oh? But her Ladyship knows how they feel and is all in favour of the match.

BÉGEARSS [*coldly*]. Then we'll have to change her mind for her.

SUZANNE [*dumbfounded*]. Her too? But what about Figaro? As far as I can tell, he has Leon's confidence...

BÉGEARSS. He's the least of my worries. Wouldn't you be pleased to be free of him?

SUZANNE. As long as he comes to no harm.

BÉGEARSS. Really! The very idea is offensive to anyone with an ounce of moral principle. Once they are all told where their best interests lie, they will change their minds as a matter of course.

SUZANNE [*doubtingly*]. If you can manage to do that...

BÉGEARSS [*insistent*]. I shall. You do realize that love does not enter into any of this? [*Suavely*] You're the only woman I've ever loved.

SUZANNE. But if Madame had been prepared...

BÉGEARSS. I would have consoled her, of course. But she turned me down. Such arrogance!... According to the plan the Count has worked out, she's to be packed off to a convent.

SUZANNE [*fiercely*]. I won't be involved in any scheme to harm her!

BÉGEARSS. What are you talking about? He's only doing what she wants. You're always saying what a saint she is, I've heard you...

SUZANNE. So she is, but is that any reason to persecute her?

BÉGEARSS [*laughing*]. No. But it is a reason for moving her to a place which is closer to heaven, home of the angels, from which she has stepped down temporarily... And given the fact that these new, far-seeing laws have made divorce possible...*

SUZANNE [*surprised*]. Are you saying the Count wants a separation?

BÉGEARSS. If he can arrange it.

SUZANNE [*angrily*]. Men are such brutes! They deserve to be throt-tled, the lot of them!

BÉGEARSS [*laughing*]. I hope you don't include me in that!

SUZANNE. Oh do you? I wouldn't count on it.

BÉGEARSS [*laughing*]. You're wonderful when you're angry! It shows just what a kind heart you have. As to languishing Leon, the Count has decided to send him abroad to see the world... for a long, long time. Figaro, as an experienced traveller, will go with him and be his keeper. [*He takes her hand*] Now this is what happens to us. The Count, Florestine, and I will go on living here, and you, dear Suzanne, from whom we will all have no secrets, shall run the house and manage everything. Goodbye husband, goodbye wife-beating, goodbye domineering bully—a future spun with silk and gold, a life of pure bliss!

SUZANNE. I suppose these inducements mean you want me to lend a hand with Florestine?

BÉGEARSS [*suavely*]. To be honest, I'm counting on you. You're a pearl among women, always were! The rest of it I can manage. It's just that part of it I hand over to you. [*Quickly*] For example, there's something crucial you can do for us at once... [SUZANNE *looks at him intently.* BÉGEARSS *checks himself*] I use the term 'crucial' because he thinks it is very important. [*Coldly*] In fact it's quite trivial. For some reason, the Count has decided that when the wedding contract is signed, he will give his daughter a diamond necklace identical to the one the Countess has. He doesn't want anyone to know.

SUZANNE [*surprised*]. Ah!

BÉGEARSS. Actually, it's a rather good idea. Expensive diamonds have a way of creating happy endings. Now, he may ask you to fetch him his wife's jewel-case, so that he can compare his jeweller's design with the original.

SUZANNE. But why must it be identical to Madame's? It seems a very odd idea to me.

BÉGEARSS. He wants to be certain it's just as fine as hers... Personally, as you can imagine, I couldn't care less. Watch out. Here he comes.

SCENE 5

The COUNT, SUZANNE, BÉGEARSS

COUNT. Ah, Monsieur Bégearss, I was looking for you.

BÉGEARSS. Before reporting to you, sir, I called in to tell Suzanne that you were intending to ask her to get you that jewel-case...

SUZANNE. Unless your Lordship feels...

COUNT. Stop! You're not to say 'your Lordship'! Didn't I give orders, when I came to this country...

SUZANNE. To my mind, sir, your orders undermine our status.

COUNT. That's because you see things more in terms of vanity than of respect for self and others! If you decide to live in another country, you don't go against the way things are done there.

SUZANNE. Well, at least will you give me your word of honour...

COUNT [*arrogantly*]. Since when have I ever behaved without honour?

SUZANNE. All right, I'll go and get it for you. [*Aside*] Well, Figaro did say I wasn't to refuse them anything.

SCENE 6

The COUNT, BÉGEARSS

COUNT. I think that sorts out an issue that seemed to be bothering her.

BÉGEARSS. There's another, sir, which concerns me a great deal more. I sense that you are far from happy...

COUNT. Can I be frank with an old friend? I thought my son's death was the worst thing that could happen to me. But now something even more painful has reopened the wound and makes life not worth living.

BÉGEARSS. If you hadn't ordered me never to mention the matter, I would point out that your other son...

COUNT [*quickly*]. Other son? I haven't got another son!

BÉGEARSS. Don't get excited, sir. Let's think calmly. The loss of the son you loved so much may be making you act unfairly towards this other boy, your wife, and yourself. Are such things best decided on the basis of mere suspicion?

COUNT. Suspicion? Oh, there is absolutely no doubt in my mind. My only regret is that I don't have proof. As long as my poor son was alive, I never thought about it. He was heir to my name, my public functions, my fortune... why should I spare that other creature a second thought? Icy indifference to him, a footling title, the Cross of Malta,* an allowance—that should have been enough to settle my account with his mother and him! But can you imagine my despair when I lose the son I loved only to see a stranger who not only inherits his rank and titles but, to add insult to injury, turns up every morning and addresses me by the odious name of 'father'?

BÉGEARSS. Sir, I'm afraid to antagonize you further by trying to placate you, but surely your wife's saintly life...

COUNT [angrily]. Just one more insult to add to the list! She buries her guilty past by leading a life of exemplary virtue!... For twenty years she has enjoyed admiration and respect from every quarter, and for all that time, with her canting ways, she has made damned sure that I get blamed for the consequences of my so-called obsession... Just thinking about it makes me loathe the pair of them more!

BÉGEARSS. But how did you expect her to behave, even assuming she were guilty? Is there any crime under the sun which twenty years of repentance cannot redeem? Were you entirely blameless yourself? And what about young Florestine? You call her your ward and care far more for her...

COUNT. And it is through her that I intend to be avenged! I shall sell everything I own, and all the money will go to her. The three millions in gold that have already been transferred from Veracruz will be her dowry, which means I'm giving it to you. All I ask is that you help me keep my gift a secret. Take the money, and when you ask for her hand, make up some tale about a will, a legacy from some distant relative.

BÉGEARSS [pointing to his armband]. As you see, in accordance with your wishes I am already in mourning.

COUNT. As soon as I have obtained royal authorization to complete the conversion of all my Spanish estates into coin of this realm, I'll find a way of making sure that all the money goes legally to both of you.

BÉGEARSS [with a show of reluctance]. I can't agree to this! Do you think that on the basis of a suspicion—as yet unconfirmed—I would have any part in the complete and utter ruin of the heir to your family's name, a young man who has many qualities, for surely you can see he has...

COUNT [losing patience]. More qualities than my son? Is that what you mean? That's what everybody keeps saying and it makes me hate him even more!

BÉGEARSS. Even assuming that your ward agrees to marry me and that you set aside the three millions from Mexico from your considerable fortune as a dowry for her, I still could not accept the money. I should agree only if the marriage contract stipulated that I would make her a gift of it, as a natural expression of my love for her.

COUNT [*embracing him*]. You are a good and honest friend! I could not hope to find a better husband for my daughter!

SCENE 7

SUZANNE, *the* COUNT, BÉGEARSS

SUZANNE. I've brought the jewel-case, sir. Don't keep it too long. I must put it back before I wake Madame.

COUNT. As you go, leave word that no one is to come in here unless I ring.

SUZANNE [*aside*]. Figaro's got to be told about this.

[*She leaves*

SCENE 8

The COUNT, BÉGEARSS

BÉGEARSS. Why do you want to examine the case? What do you have in mind?

COUNT [*takes a diamond-studded bracelet from his pocket*]. I don't intend to keep you in the dark any longer about how my wife wronged me, so listen. A certain Leon d'Astorga, who used to be my page and was known as Cherubin...

BÉGEARSS. I knew him. We both served in the same regiment in which, thanks to you, I was promoted to major. But he's been dead these twenty years...

COUNT. That's what gives me grounds for my suspicions. He had the audacity to fall in love with my wife. I thought she was in love with him. I sent him far away from Andalusia, by giving him a commission in my regiment. A year after the birth of my son, who has now been taken from me by that accursed duel... [*he wipes his eyes with his hand*] I was due to leave for Mexico as the new viceroy. Instead of staying in Madrid or at my palace at Seville or settling into Aguas-Frescas, which is such a lovely place, where do you suppose, my dear fellow, my wife decided to go? To a miserable chateau at Astorga,* on a run-down estate I'd bought from the page's parents. That's where she chose to live for the entire three years I was away. And that's where, after nine, ten months, I'm not sure, she gave birth to the worthless boy who is the image of his worthless father! Many years ago, when I was having my portrait done for the miniature that was part of the Countess's bracelet, the artist was struck by the page's looks and said he would like to paint him. It's one of the finest pictures in my collection.

BÉGEARSS. Yes... [*He looks away*] So fine that your wife...

COUNT [*interrupting*]. Won't ever look at it? Well, from that painting I've had this miniature done, to go into a second bracelet, identical in every detail to hers, made by the jeweller who mounts all her diamonds. I shall substitute this other bracelet for the one with my portrait in it. If she says nothing, you will agree that I have my proof. If she does mention it, then whatever tale she spins I shall cross-examine her and have the whole shameful business out with her.

BÉGEARSS. If you want my opinion, sir, I can't say I approve of what you're doing.

COUNT. Why not?

BÉGEARSS. These are hardly the methods of a gentleman. Now, if by some stroke of luck, for good or ill, certain facts had come your way, I could understand if you wanted to investigate further. But setting traps! Springing surprises! I ask you, would any decent man wish to place even his worst enemy at such a disadvantage?

COUNT. I've gone too far to stop now. The bracelet has been made and the page's picture has been set into it.

BÉGEARSS [*takes the jewel-case*]. Sir, think of your honour...

COUNT [*takes the bracelet from the case*]. Ah! Here it is—my portrait. It has always meant so much to me! At least I shall have the pleasure of putting it on my daughter's wrist. She's so much more worthy to have it.

[*He replaces it with the second bracelet*

BÉGEARSS [*pretends to try to stop him. They both pull at the case.* BÉGEARSS *neatly opens the secret compartment and exclaims angrily*]. Ah! now it's broken!

COUNT [*examines the case*]. No it's not. It's just a secret compartment that's sprung open while we were arguing. There are letters inside!

BÉGEARSS [*with a show of opposition*]. I sincerely hope you don't intend to take advantage...

COUNT. A moment ago you said: 'If some stroke of luck put certain facts my way, you would understand my wanting to investigate further...' Well, fate has obliged and I intend to take your advice.

[*He removes the papers roughly*

BÉGEARSS [*with fervour*]. As I live and hope, I will have no part in such a disgraceful proceeding! Put the papers back, sir, or else allow me to withdraw.

[*He takes several steps back. The* COUNT *holds the papers and reads.* BÉGEARSS *watches him furtively and rejoices in secret*

COUNT [*in a rage*]. I don't need to read any more. Put the rest of the letters back. I shall keep this one.

BÉGEARSS. No. Whatever it says, you are too honourable a man to stoop to...

COUNT [*proudly*]. Stoop to what? Finish your sentence, man! Say it! I think I can stand it.

BÉGEARSS [*bowing low*]. Sir, you are my patron. Forgive me and attribute my misplaced outburst to my deep concern.

COUNT. Far from holding it against you, you have gone up in my estimation. [*He throws himself into a chair*] Ah, Rosine, you betrayed me! For despite my philandering, she is the only woman

I ever... The other women were easy conquests. I know by how angry I feel, how much my contemptible affection... I hate myself for loving her!

BÉGEARSS. For the love of God, sir, put the letter back. It's poison.

SCENE 9

FIGARO, *the* COUNT, BÉGEARSS

COUNT [*gets to his feet*]. Who said you could barge in here? What do you want?

FIGARO. I came because you rang.

COUNT [*furious*]. I did no such thing. A servant has no business...

FIGARO. Ask your jeweller. He heard it too.

COUNT. My jeweller? What does he want with me?

FIGARO. He said he had an appointment. Something to do with a bracelet he's made.

[BÉGEARSS *realizing* FIGARO *is trying to see the jewel-case which is on the table, does his best to block his view*

COUNT. Oh!... Tell him to come back some other time.

FIGARO [*pointedly*]. But since you have Madame's jewel-case open, sir, perhaps now might be a suitable moment...

COUNT [*furious*]. Stop meddling! Get out, and if you breathe one word of this...

FIGARO. Just the one? I'd need a lot more than that. I don't do things by halves.

[*He glances at the jewel-case and the letter the* COUNT *is holding, glares contemptuously at* BÉGEARSS, *and goes out*

SCENE 10

The COUNT, BÉGEARSS

COUNT. We'd better close up her miserable jewel-case. I've got the proof I wanted. I have it and all I feel is devastation... Why did I have to find it? Oh God! Here, read it, my dear Bégearss.

BÉGEARSS [*pushing the letter away*]. And become privy to such secrets? God forbid that I should ever be accused of such a thing!

COUNT. What sort of friend are you if you won't listen when I try to confide in you? I see that the only troubles we ever feel truly sorry for are our own.

BÉGEARSS. Why? Just because I won't read the letter? [*Quickly*] Hide it: here comes Suzanne.

[*Hurriedly, he closes the secret compartment. The* COUNT *puts the letter inside the front of his coat; he looks dazed*

SCENE 11

SUZANNE, the COUNT, BÉGEARSS

SUZANNE [*runs in*]. The case! the case! Madame has rung.

BÉGEARSS [*hands it to her*]. As you see, Suzanne, it's exactly as it was.

SUZANNE. What's wrong with the Master? He looks very upset.

BÉGEARSS. It's nothing. Just got rather cross with your lumbering husband who ignored his orders and blundered in here.

SUZANNE [*ingenuously*]. But I told him quite plainly. I'm certain he knew exactly what I meant.

[*She leaves*

SCENE 12

LEON, *the* COUNT, BÉGEARSS

COUNT [*he is about to leave when he sees* LEON]. Here's the other pest!

LEON [*diffidently, he goes to embrace the* COUNT]. Good morning, father. I trust you slept well?

COUNT [*coldly, repulsing the gesture*]. Where were you last night, sir?

LEON. I was invited to attend a distinguished gathering, father.

COUNT. Where you gave a reading?

LEON. I was asked to read an essay I wrote on the scandal of monastic vocations and the right each person has to be released from his vows.*

COUNT. And does that include Knights of Malta?

BÉGEARSS. I hear it went down very well?

LEON. Some allowance was made for my age, sir.

COUNT. So, instead of making arrangements for your imminent departure to frustrate the Turk in the Levant, and in so doing to serve your noble order, you go about making enemies? You have ideas, you write. It's all the rage nowadays. Soon nobody will be able to tell a gentleman from a bookworm.

LEON [*diffidently*]. But father, it will be easier to tell an ignoramus from an educated man, a free man from a slave.

COUNT. Spoken like a fanatic! I can see which way your mind is working.

[*He makes to leave*

LEON. Father!...

COUNT [*scornfully*]. I'll thank you to leave such vulgar language to tradesmen and labourers in the streets. People of our rank speak with more refinement. Does anyone say 'Father' at court? Call me

'Sir'! You reek of the rabble. Father! Really! [*He leaves.* LEON *follows with a glance at* BÉGEARSS, *who responds with a sympathetic gesture*] Come, Bégearss, come along!

ACT II

In the COUNT's *library*

SCENE 1

The COUNT, *alone*

COUNT. Now that I'm alone at last, I can read this astounding letter—I can hardly believe the sheer luck that brought it my way. [*He takes the letter from his coat and reads, weighing each word*] 'Rash, unfeeling man! We have reaped what we have sown! The rashness with which you came creeping to me at night, in the chateau where you grew up and knew every creak of every stair; the violence of what followed... The crime of which you were guilty—as was I... [*he stops*] as was I—has received the punishment it deserves. This day, the feast of Saint Leon, patron saint of this place, and yours too, I have been delivered of a son who is my shame and my despair. Thanks to the joyless precautions I have taken, honour is safe, but I can no longer speak of virtue. I am condemned to a lifetime of unquenchable tears and know they can never wash away a crime... of which the evidence is all too alive. Never try to see me again... Such is my irrevocable wish. Despairingly, Rosine... who will never again dare sign by any other name.' [*Still holding the letter, he puts both hands to his forehead and walks up and down*] Who will never again dare sign by any other name!... Oh Rosine! where are our happy times now?... How could you stoop so low?... [*He paces restlessly*] A wicked woman could not have written a letter like that! The scoundrel forced himself on her... But wait, the reply is written on the letter itself. [*He reads*] 'Since I must never see you again, life has become an odious burden and I shall gladly end it in a dangerous assault on a fort for which I shall volunteer. I return your reproaches, the sketch I made of you, and the lock of your hair which I stole. The friend who will deliver this when I am dead may be trusted implicitly. He has seen me in the depth of my despair. Should the death of a man so unworthy kindle a last shred

of pity in you, then among the names that will be given to the heir...
of one more fortunate than myself... might I hope that the name
Leon may sometimes remind you of the unhappy wretch... who
dies still loving you and signs, for the last time, Cherubin Leon
d'Astorga.' Then, written in blood: 'I am wounded and it is fatal. I
have reopened the letter and in my blood, write this—my aching,
eternal farewell. Remember...' The rest has been obliterated by
tears. [*He paces restlessly*] And that's not something a wicked man
could have written either! Was it a moment of madness? [*He sits,
lost in thought*] I don't know what to think.

SCENE 2

BÉGEARSS, *the* COUNT

As BÉGEARSS *enters, he stops and bites his finger as though in two
minds*

COUNT. Ah, my dear fellow, do come in. You find me at rock
bottom.

BÉGEARSS. A most alarming sight, sir. I didn't dare stir from the
door.

COUNT. I've just read the letter. No, they were neither deceitful nor
depraved, but what they themselves say: two unfortunate young
people who lost their heads.

BÉGEARSS. Like you, I had assumed as much.

COUNT [*gets up and walks about*]. These wretched women who let
themselves be seduced have no idea what troubles they are storing
up for us!... They just carry on and on... the betrayals accumu-
late... and the public, always unfair and superficial, lays the
blame on the husband, who must nurse his sorrows in secret. He is
accused of being heartless, of being deficient in feeling because he
refuses to love the child born of his wife's culpable adultery!...
Our philandering scarcely leaves a mark on them, nor does it strip
them of the certain knowledge that they are the mothers of their
children, nor deny them the incalculable gift of motherhood!
Whereas their smallest whims, a passing fancy, a thoughtless lapse
can destroy a man's happiness... the happiness on which his life

is based: the certainty that he is a father. Ah, it is no accident that so much importance has always been given to the fidelity of wives! The good of society, and its ills too, are determined by how they behave. Whether a family is heaven or a living hell will always depend on the impression women give of themselves.*

BÉGEARSS. Calm yourself. Here's your daughter.

SCENE 3

FLORESTINE, the COUNT, BÉGEARSS

FLORESTINE [wearing a posy at her waist]. Sir, they said you were so busy that I didn't dare knock and say good morning. I thought you'd be cross.

COUNT. I was busy on your behalf, my dear! My dear daughter! I can call you that because I've looked after you since you were born. The man your mother married managed his affairs very badly and left nothing when he died. During her final illness, she put you in my charge. I gave her my word and I shall honour it, dearest girl, by finding you a fine, upstanding husband. I can speak freely in the presence of our friend, for he loves us both. Look around you. Choose. Isn't there anyone here who is worthy of your love?

FLORESTINE [kisses his hand]. No one but you, sir. But since you ask my opinion, my answer is that I would be happiest by remaining as I am. When your son marries—for it seems unlikely he can continue as a member of his celibate Order in these changed times—when he marries, he may well leave home and you. Oh, won't you let me be the one who will look after you when you grow old? It would be my duty, sir, but I would do it so gladly!

COUNT. Let's have no more of this 'sir' business. It's what we say to people we don't much care for. No one would think twice to hear such a grateful daughter call me by a more loving name. Say 'father'.

BÉGEARSS. You need have no secrets from her: she is worthy of your utmost trust... Come, young lady, won't you embrace the tender, loving man who raised you? You are deeper in his debt than you realize. To act as your guardian was no more than his duty. He was your mother's closest... most intimate friend... and, to put it in so many words...

SCENE 4

FIGARO, *the* COUNTESS *in a morning dress*, FLORESTINE, BÉGEARSS

FIGARO [*announcing*]. The Countess.

BÉGEARSS [*glares in fury at* FIGARO *and mutters to himself*]. Damn that man's eyes!

COUNTESS [*to the* COUNT]. Figaro said you weren't well. I was worried. I came at once, but now I see...

COUNT. ... that this interfering busybody has spun you yet another yarn.

FIGARO. Sir, I saw you pass by and you did not seem at all yourself... I'm relieved to see that there's nothing wrong.

[BÉGEARSS *inspects him closely*

COUNTESS. Good morning, Major Bégearss... There you are Florestine. You look lovely... Such a bloom to her cheek, so radiant, don't you think? If the good Lord had blessed me with a daughter, I would have wanted her to be just like you in looks and personality. You shall have to take her place. Would you like that, Florestine?

FLORESTINE [*kisses her hand*]. Oh, Madame!

COUNTESS. Who has given you flowers so early in the day?

FLORESTINE [*happily*]. No one gave them to me. I made the posies myself. Isn't it Saint Leon's Day?

COUNTESS. You are a sweet girl, you never forget anything. [*She kisses her on the forehead. The* COUNT *reacts angrily but* BÉGEARSS *restrains him. The* COUNTESS *turns to* FIGARO] Since we're all present, inform my son that we shall be taking our chocolate here.

FLORESTINE. While they're getting it ready, godfather, won't you let us see the fine bust of Washington* which they say you keep in your room?

COUNT. I've no idea who sent it. I didn't ask to have it. It's probably for Leon. A remarkable piece. I keep it upstairs in my collection. Come along, we'll all go.

[BÉGEARSS *is the last to leave. Twice he turns and glares at* FIGARO *who responds in kind: it is an exchange of unvoiced threats*

SCENE 5

FIGARO, *alone*

FIGARO [*setting the table with the breakfast cups*]. Reptile! The gaze of Medusa,* eh? You can measure me for size, you can look pure poison, but I'm the one with the eyes that kill!... But where does he collect his post? There's never anything for him among the letters that are delivered to the house. Was he alone when he slithered up from hell? There must be another fiend who writes to him... but I've no way of finding out...

SCENE 6

FIGARO, SUZANNE

SUZANNE [*runs in and whispers urgently to* FIGARO]. He's the one the girl's going to marry—he has the Count's word on it. He'll cure Leon of loving Florestine. He'll turn Florestine against Leon. He'll persuade Madame to give her consent. He'll see to it that you are kicked out of the house. He'll pack Madame off to a convent until such time as the Master can divorce her. He'll cheat Leon out of his inheritance and make me belle of the ball. That's today's news—so far.

[*She hurries away*

SCENE 7

FIGARO, *alone*

FIGARO. No, Major, if you don't mind, we're going to have this out between us first. I'll teach you that it's not only sinners who prosper. Ariadne in the shape of Suzanne has given me the thread that will help me negotiate the labyrinth and slay the Minotaur.* I will entangle you in snares and unmask you* so completely that... There must be something he wants very much indeed if he can make such a careless error by letting the cat out of the bag to her. Is he really that sure of himself?... A foolish man and vanity go together like a horse and carriage. My scheming Major talks too much: he's blabbed. And he's blundered!

SCENE 8

GUILLAUME, FIGARO

GUILLAUME [*with a letter*]. Herr Mayorr Pésharrs? Ach, I see he iss not here.

FIGARO [*setting the table*]. You can wait for him. He won't be long.

GUILLAUME [*recoiling*]. Mein Gott! I vill not for der Mayorr wait in same room with you. My Meister, he not vish it, dem sure he don't.

FIGARO. Forbids it, does he? In that case, give me the letter. I'll see he gets it when he comes back.

GUILLAUME [*recoiling*]. Not letters gif you neither! Dem me! I soon order of der poot get!

FIGARO [*aside*]. Let's seen what this clown knows. [*Aloud*] You've just come from the post office, is that it?

GUILLAUME. Dem me, no. I am not from post comink.

FIGARO. I expect it's a letter from the gentleman, the Irish relative who has left him some money? You know all about that, don't you, Guillaume old man?

GUILLAUME [*with a snigger*]. Letter from man who ded iss! No, if you blease! Not from him, I sink! More bossible iss from other man. Bossible it come of one of mans... not content mans, over dere.

FIGARO. You mean from some malcontent?

GUILLAUME. Ja, but diss I not say.

FIGARO [*aside*]. It's not unlikely. He's got a finger in all sorts of pies. [*Aloud*] We could look at the stamp. Then we'd know.

GUILLAUME. Diss I not say. Why? Letters to house of Herr O'Connor comink. Also I am not knowing vat iss stemp.

FIGARO [*quickly*]. O'Connor? The Irish banker?

GUILLAUME. Iss same!

FIGARO [*collects himself and proceeds more coolly*]. Lives near here, in the street behind this house?

GUILLAUME. His haus ver' nice, dem me! Peoples iss ver', allow me, blenty tchenerous.

[*He wanders to one side of the stage*

FIGARO [*aside*]. I can't believe my luck!

GUILLAUME [*returns*]. You say nottink of diss penker, not to nobody, you unnerstend? I make mistake to say it... Dem me!

[*He stamps the floor with his foot*

FIGARO. Of course, I wouldn't dream of it. You needn't worry.

GUILLAUME. Mein Meister, he say, you dem clever men and I not clever men. So he iss right, I tink? But I feel mebbe not right to tell you diss gnowlitch...

FIGARO. Why?

GUILLAUME. Diss I not know. The valet who zegrets tells, mebbe? Iss sinful to be like dat. Iss nesty, wile, not like a men.

FIGARO. That's true. But you didn't say anything.

GUILLAUME [*grief-stricken*]. Mein Gott! Mein Gott! Diss I not know: vot I ken say, vot I kennet say... [*He turns away with a sigh*] Aaah!

[*He wanders over to a bookcase and stares blankly at the books*

FIGARO [*aside*]. Now we're getting somewhere. I thank my lucky star! [*He gets out his notebook*] But I must work out why our devious Major makes use of a cretin like him... Just as footpads fear streetlights... Yes, but a moron is like a lantern: the light shines clean out of him. [*He speaks aloud what he writes*] 'O'Connor, Irish banker.' My discreet investigations have to start there. As methods go, it's not entirely constitutional. *Ma per dio*, but it's effective— and I can think of lots of precedents. [*He writes*] Four or five gold louis for the servant who collects the post, so that he can stop at a tavern and open any letters with the right Honoré-Tartuffe Bégearss's handwriting on the envelope... Ah, honourable and hypocritical, but not for much longer. A deity has put me on your tracks. [*He closes his notebook*] Chance, the hidden god! The Ancients used to call you destiny. Nowadays, we've got another name for you...

SCENE 9

The COUNTESS, *the* COUNT, FLORESTINE, BÉGEARSS, FIGARO, GUILLAUME

BÉGEARSS [*notices* GUILLAUME *and speaks to him sharply as he takes the letter*]. Why can't you deliver all correspondence to my rooms?

GUILLAUME. I thought diss rooms iss same as.

[*He leaves*

COUNTESS [*to the* COUNT]. Sir, the bust is quite admirable. Has your son seen it?

BÉGEARSS [*holding the letter which he has opened*]. Ah! A letter from Madrid! It's from the Minister's private secretary. There's something here that concerns you. [*He reads*] 'Please inform Count Almaviva that the King's authorization for the transfer of all his estates will be included in the mail due to leave tomorrow.'

[FIGARO *listens and, without speaking, nods knowingly to himself*

COUNTESS. Figaro, tell my son we are all having breakfast in here.

FIGARO. Madame, I will go and let him know.

[*He leaves*

SCENE 10

The COUNT, *the* COUNTESS, FLORESTINE, BÉGEARSS

COUNT [*to* BÉGEARSS]. I must write to the buyer to inform him.
Have tea sent to me in my study.

FLORESTINE. Dear Papa, I shall bring it myself.

COUNT [*whispers to* FLORESTINE]. Think seriously about the matter
I touched on with you.

[*He kisses her on the forehead and leaves*

SCENE 11

LEON, *the* COUNTESS, FLORESTINE, BÉGEARSS

LEON [*disconsolately*]. When I come in, my father leaves the room.
He's always so curt with me...

COUNTESS [*sharply*]. Leon, why do you say such things? Am I to be
eternally vexed by people who jump to the wrong conclusions?
Your father went out because he has to write to the man who is
buying his estates.

FLORESTINE [*gaily*]. You're sorry he's not here? We're sorry too.
But he knows it's your birthday and he asked me to give you this
posy.

[*She gives a deep curtsey*

LEON [*while she pins it to his lapel*]. He couldn't have asked anybody
who could make me more grateful for all his kindness.

[*He embraces her*

FLORESTINE [*pretending to struggle*]. Did you see, Madame? You can never tease him because he always takes advantage.

COUNTESS [*with a smile*]. Well it is his birthday, so I think we needn't be too hard on him.

FLORESTINE [*lowering her eyes*]. As a punishment, Madame, make him read out his speech which by all accounts was a great success at the meeting last night.

LEON. If my mama decides I was in the wrong, I'll go and get my penance.

FLORESTINE. Madame, do say he must!

COUNTESS. Very well, bring us your speech. I shall fetch my needlework. It will help me to concentrate while I listen.

FLORESTINE [*gaily*]. Obstinate mule! You're overruled! I shall hear it even though you're not willing to...

LEON [*tenderly*]. Me, unwilling, when it's you who gives the orders? Oh Florestine, I defy you to show that your wish is not my command.

[*The* COUNTESS *and* LEON *leave, each their separate way*

SCENE 12

FLORESTINE, BÉGEARSS

BÉGEARSS [*in a whisper*]. Now, young lady, have you guessed who is to be your husband?

FLORESTINE [*overjoyed*]. Dear Major Bégearss! You are such a good friend to all the family that I shall speak all my thoughts aloud to you. Who is there for me to look at—my godfather did say: 'Look around you, choose'? I now see the full extent of his kindness: he can only mean Leon. But I haven't a penny to my name and can hardly expect...

BÉGEARSS [*in a terrifying voice*]. Who? Leon? His son, who is also your brother?

FLORESTINE [*gives a shriek of distress*]. Oh, sir!

BÉGEARSS. Didn't he say: 'call me father'? Open your eyes, my dear girl, and abandon a misguided dream which could have the most terrible consequences.

FLORESTINE. Yes, terrible for both of us!

BÉGEARSS. You realize that a secret like this must stay buried forever in your heart.

[*He leaves, with his eyes fixed on her*

SCENE 13

FLORESTINE, *alone, in tears*

FLORESTINE. Dear God! He is my brother, and my feelings for him... Exposed to the harsh light of day! I was living in a dream: but this is such a cruel awakening.

[*Overcome, she collapses into a chair*

SCENE 14

LEON, *holding a paper,* FLORESTINE

LEON [*gives a start of delight and says to himself*]. Mama's not back yet and Major Bégearss has gone away. Let's make the most of the opportunity. [*Aloud*] Florestine, you look as perfect and lovely this morning as you always do. And just now you seemed so happy and said such kind and sunny things that my hopes revived.

FLORESTINE [*despairingly*]. Oh, Leon!

[*She sinks back*

LEON. Oh my God! You're crying, and the awful look on your face tells me that something dreadful has happened!

FLORESTINE. Truly dreadful. Oh Leon! Dreadful things are all I have to look forward to.

LEON. Florestine, don't you love me any more? My feelings for you...

FLORESTINE [*categorical*]. Your feelings? You must never speak to me of them again.

LEON. What? The purest love...

FLORESTINE [*in despair*]. Stop this, it's too cruel, or else I must leave.

LEON. Good God! What on earth has happened? Major Bégearss spoke to you. I want to know what that man said!

SCENE 15

The COUNTESS, FLORESTINE, LEON

LEON. Mama, I need your help. I don't know what to think. Florestine doesn't love me any more!

FLORESTINE [*through her tears*]. Oh Madame, not love him any more? My godfather, you, and he, the three of you are my only reason for living.

COUNTESS. I don't doubt it for one moment, my dear. You have a kind heart and I trust it utterly. But what can have upset you like this?

LEON. Mama, you do approve of the strength of my feelings for her?

FLORESTINE [*throwing herself into the* COUNTESS*'s arms*]. You must tell him to stop! [*Weeping*] If he doesn't, I shall die! It's agony!

COUNTESS. My dear girl, I don't understand you. I am just as puzzled as he is... I can feel her trembling. Did he do something you didn't like?

FLORESTINE [*takes a step back*]. Madame, I don't dislike him. I love and respect him like a brother. But he must never expect any more than that.

LEON. You hear her, Mama? Look, you unfeeling girl, just say what you mean!

FLORESTINE. Leave me alone, let me be, or you'll have my death on your conscience.

SCENE 16

The COUNTESS, LEON, FIGARO *who arrives with the breakfast tray,* SUZANNE *who enters from the opposite side of the stage carrying the* COUNTESS's *needlework.*

COUNTESS. Take everything away, Suzanne. There won't be any breakfast and there won't be any reading. Figaro, you can serve the Master's tea. He's in his study, writing. And you, Florestine, come to my room: I am your friend and you can put my mind at rest. My dear children, you both have a special place in my heart. Why do you seem to take it in turns to make me worry so? There's something going on here and I need to get to the bottom of it.

[*They leave*

SCENE 17

SUZANNE, FIGARO, LEON

SUZANNE [*to* FIGARO]. I don't know what all this is about, but I'd lay good money that it's Bégearss up to no good. I'm going to make absolutely sure that the Mistress is fully in the picture.

FIGARO. Hold your fire until I've investigated further. We'll meet tonight and decide what to do. But there is one thing I've discovered...

SUZANNE. And you'll tell me then?

[*She leaves*

SCENE 18

FIGARO, LEON

LEON [*dejected*]. Oh God!

FIGARO. Well, what's been going on, sir?

LEON. I honestly don't know. I'd never seen Florestine so bright and cheerful. I knew she'd had a talk with my father, I left her alone with Major Bégearss for a couple of moments, and when I got back she was here, by herself, crying her eyes out and saying I was never to have anything more to do with her. What can he have said to her?

FIGARO. If I weren't afraid you'd take matters into your own hands, I'd tell you certain things you really should know. But at this point we need to tread very warily, and it would only take an angry outburst from you to wreck all the watching and waiting I've done over the last ten years.

LEON. Ah, if wary walking is all that's involved... But what do you think he said to her?

FIGARO. That she's got to marry Honoré Bégearss and that it's all settled between your father and him.

LEON. Between my father and Bégearss? The swine's going to have to kill me first!

FIGARO. If you carry on like that, sir, the swine won't kill you but he will marry Florestine and pocket your inheritance too.

LEON. Very well. I'm sorry. You always were a friend. So tell me what I've got to do.

FIGARO. Guess the riddle of the Sphinx or expect to be eaten alive.* I'll rephrase that: stay cool, let him say his piece, and take care he doesn't suspect you're on to him.

LEON [in a rage]. Me, keep cool!... All right, I'll be cool. But inside I'm incandescent! So he thinks he can take Florestine from me! Aha! Here he comes. I'll have it out with him... coolly.

FIGARO. Keep a grip on your temper or you'll ruin everything.

SCENE 19

BÉGEARSS, FIGARO, LEON

LEON [barely controlling himself]. Major, Major Bégearss, could I speak to you for a moment? If you care for your own good, you

will answer me directly. Florestine is extremely upset. What did
you say to her?

BÉGEARSS [*icily*]. And who said I said anything to her? Can't she be
upset without my being the reason for it?

LEON [*sharply*]. Don't prevaricate, sir. One moment she was in the
best of spirits. After she'd spoken to you, I saw her in tears.
Whatever caused her troubles, I share them because I love her.
Now, you will tell me the cause or I shall require satisfaction.

BÉGEARSS. People less arrogant than you invariably find me very
amenable. I never submit to threats.

LEON [*in a rage*]. Very well, you swine! On your guard! It's your life
or mine!

[*He reaches for his sword*

FIGARO [*comes between them*]. Come, Major. Not your closest
friend's son? In his house? Where you're his guest?

BÉGEARSS [*controlling himself*]. I don't need you to tell me what my
obligations are... I will have this out with him. But I want no
witnesses. So get out and give us some privacy.

LEON. Go, Figaro. He can't get out of this now. Let's not give him
any excuses.

FIGARO [*aside*]. I must tell his father at once.

[*He leaves*

SCENE 20

LEON, BÉGEARSS

LEON [*bolting the door*]. Perhaps it would suit your purpose better to
fight than talk. The choice is entirely yours. But I will not agree to
any other way of proceeding.

BÉGEARSS [*coldly*]. Leon! A gentleman does not spill the blood of
his best friend's son. Did you really want me to discuss a most
delicate matter in front of a miserable servant, an upstart who's

got so above himself that he seems to think he knows better than his master?

LEON [*sits*]. Your point, sir. I'm waiting.

BÉGEARSS. You will regret your outburst. It was quite uncalled for.

LEON. We shall see soon enough.

BÉGEARSS [*assuming a cool, solemn tone*]. Leon, you are in love with Florestine. I've been aware of it for some time... While your brother was alive, I saw no point in encouraging your unfortunate feelings, for they could never come to anything. But after the terrible duel which cost him his life and made you the heir, I was vain enough to believe I had sufficient influence to talk your father into letting you marry the girl you love. I did everything I could to persuade him, but all my efforts ran into a solid wall of resistance. Grieving to see him reject an arrangement which, as I thought, would make everyone happy... I'm sorry, my dear boy, but what I am about to tell you will hurt you. But I have to say it now if you are to be spared a lifetime of misery. Summon up all your fortitude, you're going to need it. I pressed your father to break his silence and take me into his confidence. In the end he said: 'My dear, dear friend! I know that my son loves Florestine. But how can I let him marry her? Everyone thinks she is my ward. In fact, she's my daughter: she is his sister!'

LEON [*recoils in horror*]. Florestine... my sister?

BÉGEARSS. That is the awful truth which it was my sorry duty... Oh, I had to tell each of you. By saying nothing, I could have ruined both your lives. Well, Leon, do you still want to cross swords with me?

LEON. You are a true friend and I am an ungrateful, unfeeling wretch! I was mad! Can you forget my anger?

BÉGEARSS [*pure Tartuffe*]. Yes, but only on condition that this terrible secret goes no further... It would be infamous if your father's shame were to be made public.

LEON [*throwing himself into* BÉGEARSS's *arms*]. Ah, never!

SCENE 21

The COUNT, FIGARO, LEON, BÉGEARSS

FIGARO [*hurrying in*]. They're in here! There they are!

COUNT. With their arms around each other's necks? Have you lost your grip?

FIGARO [*stunned*]. By God, sir, a man could lose his grip over a lot less than this.

COUNT [*to* FIGARO]. Are you going to explain the meaning of this charade?

LEON [*trembling*]. I think I'm the one who should explain, father. I feel so foolish I could die. Over some quite trivial matter, I allowed myself to behave... unpardonably. But the Major is a generous man. He has not only made me see sense, but has been good enough to excuse my rash outburst and forgive me. I was expressing my thanks when you arrived.

COUNT. This is by no means the first time you have had cause to thank him. Indeed, we are all in his debt.

> [FIGARO *says nothing but strikes his forehead with his fist.*
> BÉGEARSS *notices and smiles*

COUNT [*to his son*]. I think you'd better go. The fact that you admit to such appalling behaviour makes me very angry.

BÉGEARSS. But the incident's closed, sir, forgotten.

COUNT [*to* LEON]. Go away and reflect on how deeply you have wronged your friend, my friend, the most decent man that ever was!

FIGARO [*furious, to himself*]. More like a pack of demons inside a coat and breeches!

SCENE 22

The COUNT, BÉGEARSS, FIGARO

COUNT [*in* BÉGEARSS's *ear*]. Come, my friend, let's finish what we started. [*To* FIGARO] As for you, you stupid clod, you and your wild suspicions... Fetch me the three million in gold which you were responsible for bringing from Cadiz. There were sixty bearer bonds. I said I wanted them numbered.

FIGARO. It's done.

COUNT. Get me the portfolio case they're in.

FIGARO. What are in? The three millions?

COUNT. Of course. Well, what's keeping you?

FIGARO [*meekly*]. Me, sir? I haven't got them.

BÉGEARSS. What do you mean, you haven't got them?

FIGARO [*loftily*]. No, sir, I haven't.

BÉGEARSS [*sharply*]. What have you done with them?

FIGARO. When my master asks the questions, I must account for my actions to him. But I don't have to tell you anything.

COUNT [*angrily*]. Don't be impertinent. Now, what did you do with them?

FIGARO [*coolly*]. I gave them to your notary, Monsieur Fal, for safekeeping.

BÉGEARSS. On whose instructions?

FIGARO [*loftily*]. Mine. I always follow my own instructions.

BÉGEARSS. I'd wager there's no truth in this story.

FIGARO. Seeing that I have his signed receipt, it more than likely that you'd lose your stake, sir.

BÉGEARSS. Or if he does have the money, he'll be using it to speculate on the market. People of that sort are all in it together.

FIGARO. You should be more civil when you speak of a man who has served you well.

BÉGEARSS. I don't owe him a thing.

FIGARO. I'll take your word for it. But when a man has just inherited forty thousand Spanish doubloons*...

COUNT [*growing angry*]. I suppose you've got something to say about that too?

FIGARO. Who, me, sir? I'm just puzzled by it. I knew the relative who has left Major Bégearss the money. A somewhat wild young gentleman, who gambled, threw his money about, and liked fighting. Short on self-restraint and decency, a man of no character, who had nothing of his own—even the vices that killed him were borrowed. The ill-advised duel which...

[*The* COUNT *stamps his foot*

BÉGEARSS [*angrily*]. Never mind that, are you going to say why you deposited the money with the notary?

FIGARO. Simple, sir. So that it wouldn't be my responsibility any more. It could have been stolen, who knows? Shady characters often worm their way into a house like this.

BÉGEARSS [*angrily*]. That's all very well, but your Master insists on having it back.

FIGARO. Well, my Master could send someone round to get it.

BÉGEARSS. But is the notary going to release it if he doesn't see the receipt?

FIGARO. I'll go and get it now and give it personally to the Master. My duty will have been done, so if anything goes wrong, he won't be able to put the blame on me.

COUNT. I'll be waiting in my study. Bring it to me there.

FIGARO. I must advise you that Monsieur Fal will only hand the money over on production of the receipt. Those were my instructions.

[*He leaves*

SCENE 23

The COUNT, BÉGEARSS

BÉGEARSS. That's the rabble for you! Give them everything they ask for and see what happens! In all honesty, sir, I am your friend but I have to say this: you place too much trust in that man. He has worked out what we're planning. He was a barber and horse doctor and you made him your steward and secretary, a kind of general factotum. Everybody knows that he has lined his pockets at your expense.

COUNT. I have absolutely no doubts about his honesty. But it is true that he has got very above himself...

BÉGEARSS. There's one way you can get him off your back and reward him at the same time.

COUNT. That's something I've often wanted.

BÉGEARSS [*confidentially*]. When you send your son to Malta, you'll probably need someone you can trust to keep an eye on him. That troublemaker will be only too pleased to be thought worthy of your confidence and will certainly agree to go. That way, you'll be rid of him for a good long time.

COUNT. My friend, you're right. I also hear that he gets on very badly with his wife.

[*He leaves*

SCENE 24

BÉGEARSS, *alone*

BÉGEARSS. Another obstacle out of the way! Oh, of all the self-righteous, prying...! Was there ever such a clown? The old family retainer, intent on preventing me getting my hands on the money and calling me names, as if this were some play. Tartuffe Bégearss, is it? Well, thanks to me you'll find out how uncomfortable it is when you come face to face with the Turk. You won't be meddling in my affairs any more!

ACT III

The COUNTESS's *drawing-room. There are flowers everywhere*

SCENE 1

The COUNTESS, SUZANNE

COUNTESS. I haven't been able to get any sense out of her, only tears and sobs. She is convinced she's done something to offend me. Keeps asking me to forgive her. Says she wants to take the veil. If I put all that together with the way my son is acting, I can only conclude that she blames herself for responding to his feelings and encouraging him to hope, because she thinks she hasn't enough money to be a suitable wife for him. Such charmingly delicate sentiments, though she is rather overdoing things. Apparently Major Bégearss said something to her about it, with the result that she now feels very sorry for herself. He is a man of the highest principles, but he has such a prickly sense of what is right that sometimes he goes too far and imagines trouble where other people see none.

SUZANNE. I have no idea what's making her so miserable. But there's something very peculiar going on here, as if a curse has been put on the whole house. The Master couldn't be more grim and keeps us all at arm's length. You're permanently in tears. Mademoiselle Florestine sobs all day and your son is inconsolable. That leaves Major Bégearss, as unmoved as God in his heaven, who doesn't seem bothered by anything, and watches you all going through the mill as though he didn't care.

COUNTESS. But, my dear, he feels for us in his heart. Indeed, without him to give comfort and soothe our hurts, without his wisdom to give us strength, reconcile our differences, and pacify my irascible husband, we would all be a great deal worse off than we are.

SUZANNE. I sincerely hope you're right, Madame.

COUNTESS. I can remember a time when you weren't as hard on

him. [SUZANNE *glances away*] Be that as it may, only he can put my mind at rest about that boy. Go and ask if he would be good enough to come down to see me.

SUZANNE. No need. Here he is. I shall see to your hair later.

[*She leaves*

SCENE 2

The COUNTESS, BÉGEARSS

COUNTESS [*dejectedly*]. Oh, my poor Major Bégearss! What on earth is going on here? Are we finally approaching the awful moment which I've been dreading for so long as I watched the storm clouds gather? The Count's aversion for my unfortunate son seems to grow with every day that passes. Do you think he suspects? Has he heard something?

BÉGEARSS. I don't think so, Madame.

COUNTESS. Since the death of my older son, which was a punishment for my sins, I have observed a profound change in the Count. Instead of approaching our ambassador in Rome with a view to having Leon released from his vows, I have seen him grow more determined to send him to Malta. I am also aware, Major, that he has sold his estates, and intends to leave Spain for good and settle in this country. The other day at dinner, in the presence of thirty guests, he spoke of divorce in terms which sent shivers down my spine.

BÉGEARSS. I was there, I recall it only too well.

COUNTESS [*weeping*]. I'm so sorry, but you're such a good friend. I wouldn't cry like this in front of anyone else.

BÉGEARSS. You may confide your worries to a man who understands.

COUNTESS. Tell me then, was it he or you who broke Florestine's heart? It was always my wish that she should marry Leon. She was born without expectations, I know. But she is noble, beautiful, and pure. She grew up as one of the family, and now that my son has become heir, surely he will have enough money for both of them?

BÉGEARSS. Too much, perhaps. And that's the root of the problem.

COUNTESS. But it's as if heaven has waited all this time to punish me more savagely for a mistake which I have always bitterly regretted. Now all at once everything seems to be conspiring to shatter my hopes. My husband hates my son... and now Florestine won't marry him. I don't know what's got into her, but she has made up her mind to have no more to do with him. It will kill the poor boy! I know it will! [*She puts her hands together*] God of vengeance! Have you let me live through twenty years of tears and repentance only to make me suffer the horror of seeing my sin brought into the open? Oh God, grant that I alone shall suffer and I shall not complain. But do not let my son pay for a crime he did not commit! Major Bégearss, can you see any way through all these troubles?

BÉGEARSS. Yes. You are a pearl among women! I can dispel your fears: that's exactly why I've come. When we are afraid, all we can see is the awful, terrible thing that we dread. Whatever we say or do, fear poisons our every waking moment. But I have the key to the mystery. You can still be happy again.

COUNTESS. How can I be happy when I am filled with remorse?

BÉGEARSS. It is not the case that your husband has been avoiding Leon, for he has no grounds to suspect the secret of his birth.

COUNTESS [*eagerly*]. Major Bégearss!

BÉGEARSS. His moods and words which you took to be hate are merely the outward expression of his own uneasy conscience. I shall put your mind completely at rest.

COUNTESS [*fervently*]. Dear Major Bégearss!

BÉGEARSS. A great weight will be lifted from you when you've heard what I am about to say. But you must never breathe a word of it to anyone. Your secret is the truth about Leon's birth. His secret is the truth about Florestine's! [*He lowers his voice*] He is her guardian... but also her father...

COUNTESS [*clasping her hands*]. God in his infinite goodness has shown me mercy!

BÉGEARSS. So you can imagine how he felt when he realized his two children were in love! He could neither tell the truth nor allow a lasting affection to develop between them by remaining silent. Hence his sombre moods and strange behaviour. And if he is determined to send his son far away, it's because he believes that his prolonged absence and the vows he has taken will, if anything can, put an end to a regrettable attachment which he knows he can never permit.

COUNTESS [*praying with great fervour*]. Oh God, fount of all mercies! You have granted me the means of redeeming in some degree the unintentional sin of which a headstrong young man was once the cause! You have also opened my eyes to something which I in turn can forgive in the husband whom I have so gravely wronged! Oh, Count Almaviva, my heart was dead, withered by twenty years of sorrow, but it shall live again for you! Florestine is your daughter! She shall be as dear to me as though she were my own child. Can we not simply forgive each other and leave the rest unsaid? Oh, Major Bégearss, what else do you have to say?

BÉGEARSS. Dear lady, I have no wish to cut short the rejoicing of a nature as good as yours. It is the heart that is sad, not the heart that is glad, that leads us into danger. But for your own peace of mind, hear me out.

COUNTESS. I will. You are a generous friend and I owe you everything. Go on.

BÉGEARSS. Your husband, trying to find a way of saving his darling Florestine from committing what he believed would be incest, suggested that I might marry her. But independently of the deep and hopeless affection which, out of respect for your sorrows...

COUNTESS [*grieving*]. Ah, my dear friend, you wish to spare my feelings...

BÉGEARSS. We must not speak of that. When the subject was first raised with Florestine, a few ambiguously turned words made her think that the Count was referring to Leon. She's only a girl, and her face lit up. Just then, a servant announced that you were coming. At that point, I did not attempt to explain what her father had in mind. But later I had a word with her, reminding her of the proper relationship of brother and sister, and it was that which provoked her outburst and the horrified reaction for which neither your son nor you could find an explanation.

COUNTESS. The poor boy had no inkling of the truth.

BÉGEARSS. Now that you know what has been proposed, do you agree that we should go ahead with a marriage which would undo all the harm that's been done?

COUNTESS [enthusiastically]. Absolutely. The ways I both feel and think coincide on this point, and I shall make it my business to see that it happens. This way, the secret of their birth will remain hidden, far from the reach of prying eyes. We have suffered torment for these past twenty years, and now at last we can look forward to happier times—and it is you, old friend, that my family can thank for it.

BÉGEARSS [raising his voice]. To be quite certain that their troubles are over, there is one more sacrifice that has to be made, and you have the strength to make it.

COUNTESS. You have only to say what it is.

BÉGEARSS [sternly]. The letters and papers of a certain unfortunate man who is dead must be reduced to ashes.

COUNTESS. Ah, God!

BÉGEARSS. When my friend was dying and asked me to deliver them to you, his last wish was that your reputation should be protected and that no trace should remain which might harm your good name.

COUNTESS. God! God!

BÉGEARSS. It's been twenty years, and I have never managed to persuade you to let go of those sad reminders which keep you in perpetual mourning. Even leaving aside the misery they've brought you, surely you can see the risk you are running?

COUNTESS. Why? What's there to be afraid of?

BÉGEARSS [*looking around to see if anyone can hear him, he whispers*]. I don't suspect Suzanne. But a maid who knows you still have those letters might very well decide one day that they could make her a fortune! If just one of them were to find its way into your husband's possession—and he might well be prepared to pay a lot of money for it—you would find yourself in serious trouble.

COUNTESS. No, Suzanne is too good-hearted for that.

BÉGEARSS [*firmly, raising his voice*]. Dear lady, you have paid your debt to love, to grief, to duty in many forms. If you are satisfied with the way I acted as your friend, then I think I am entitled to something in return. You must burn all those papers, destroy the memory of an indiscretion for which you have atoned many times over! But so that we need never return again to so painful a subject, I insist that you make the sacrifice here and now.

COUNTESS [*trembling*]. Surely this the voice of God himself! As though He were ordering me to forget him and cast off the mourning veil which has shrouded my life since the day he died. Yes, my God! I will obey the good friend Thou hast given me. [*She rings*] What he asks in Thy name is no more than what my conscience has long urged me to do: only my own weakness stayed my hand.

SCENE 3

SUZANNE, *the* COUNTESS, BÉGEARSS

COUNTESS. Suzanne! Bring me my jewel-case. No, I'll get it myself. You'd have to go for the key...

SCENE 4

SUZANNE, BÉGEARSS

SUZANNE [*anxiously*]. What's happening, Major Bégearss? Has everyone gone mad? It's bedlam in this house! The Mistress never has a dry eye and Mademoiselle Florestine is sobbing her heart out. Young Leon says he's going to drown himself and the Master has locked his door and won't see anybody. Why is everyone so interested in this jewel-case all of a sudden?

BÉGEARSS [*one finger on his lips, signalling the need for discretion*].
Hush! This is no time for questions. You'll know soon enough...
Everything's going as planned... We've accomplished as much
today as... Shh!

SCENE 5

The COUNTESS, SUZANNE, BÉGEARSS

COUNTESS [*holding the jewel-case*]. Suzanne, bring us some hot coals
from the brazier in my dressing-room.

SUZANNE. If it's for burning papers, the night-light is still lit in its
bracket on the wall.

[*She brings it*

COUNTESS. Stand by the door and see that no one comes in.

SUZANNE [*aside*]. But first, I'll run and tell Figaro.

SCENE 6

The COUNTESS, BÉGEARSS

BÉGEARSS. How often have I longed for this moment to come, for
your sake!

COUNTESS [*sobbing*]. Dear friend, do you realize what day we've
chosen to make the final sacrifice? The anniversary of the birth of
my unhappy son! Every year I have devoted this day to these
letters, asking for God's forgiveness and finding solace in my tears
as I read them again. For I at least persuaded myself that what we
did was more waywardness than sin. Oh! Must I burn every scrap
of what I have left of him?

BÉGEARSS. Yes, unless you are determined to destroy the son who is
your living link with him! Don't you owe it to him to make this
sacrifice so that he may be spared the countless, terrible consequences? You owe it to yourself! Your own security for the rest
of your life may well depend on this momentous act.

[*He opens the secret compartment and takes out the letters*

COUNTESS [*surprised*]. Why Major, you are better at opening it than I am!... Let me read them one last time!

BÉGEARSS [*severely*]. No, I cannot allow it!

COUNTESS. Just the last one, where he bids me farewell in the blood he shed for me and provides a lesson in the courage I myself need to show at this moment.

BÉGEARSS [*opposing her*]. If you start reading them now, we'll never burn anything.* You must make a sacrifice which is total, courageous, unforced, and free of human weakness! Or if you dare not do the deed yourself, then I must be strong for you. There, into the flames they go!

> [*He throws the packet of letters into the night-light*

COUNTESS [*quickly*]. Major Bégearss! Must a good friend be so cruel? That's my whole life you are burning there! Let me have one small remnant to keep!

> [*She tries to snatch the burning letters but* BÉGEARSS *restrains her forcibly*

BÉGEARSS. I will scatter the ashes to the four winds!

SCENE 7

SUZANNE, *the* COUNT, FIGARO, *the* COUNTESS, BÉGEARSS

SUZANNE [*running in*]. The Master's coming, hard on my heels. It's Figaro's doing, not mine.

COUNT [*surprising* BÉGEARSS *with his arms around the* COUNTESS]. What is the meaning of this, Madame? Is there a reason for such behaviour? What are you doing with fire, your jewel-case, and those letters? Why have you been arguing? Why are you crying?

> [BÉGEARSS *and the* COUNTESS *maintain an embarrassed silence*

COUNT. Well? Have you nothing to say?

BÉGEARSS [*recovering, says in a pained voice*]. Sir, I hope that you will not insist on thrashing this matter out here, in front of the servants. I do not know your reasons for wishing to take Madame by surprise like this. For my part, I am determined to behave as I always do, by telling nothing but the truth, whatever it may be.

COUNT [*to* FIGARO *and* SUZANNE]. Get out, the pair of you!

FIGARO. But first sir, at least be fair to me by acknowledging that I have given you the notary's receipt for that business we were discussing earlier.

COUNT. That I do gladly. I admit I was wrong. [*To* BÉGEARSS] You may be assured, Major, that this is the receipt.

[*He returns it to his pocket.* FIGARO *and* SUZANNE *leave on opposite sides of the stage*

FIGARO [*aside to* SUZANNE *as they go off*]. I can't see him wriggling out of this...

SUZANNE [*aside*]. He's trickier than a bag of monkeys.

FIGARO [*aside*]. I've got him now!

SCENE 8

The COUNTESS, *the* COUNT, BÉGEARSS

COUNT [*solemn*]. Madame, we are alone.

BÉGEARSS [*still shaken*]. I shall speak for both of us. I will answer your questions, every one. Have you ever known a single occasion, sir, when I did not tell the truth?

COUNT [*curtly*]. Sir, did I suggest any such thing?

BÉGEARSS [*fully himself again*]. Although I cannot possibly approve of what I regard as an improper inquisition, I have given my word and will repeat what I said to Madame when she asked my advice: 'Whoever has been entrusted with a secret must never keep any documents likely to compromise the friend, now dead, who gave them to us to look after. It may grieve us to destroy them and we may have good reasons to keep them. But respect for the dead is a sacred duty and comes before all else.' [*He gestures to the* COUNT] Isn't it possible that through some unexpected mishap they might fall into the wrong hands? [*The* COUNT *tugs his sleeve to prevent him developing the point any further*] In my place, sir, would you have said anything different? Anyone who wants cautious advice or tepid, spineless reassurance had better not come to me! You both have had good cause to know that this is so, especially you, your Lordship. [*The* COUNT *repeats his signal*] That is what led me, when I was asked to do so by Madame, and without enquiring what the papers might contain, to give advice which, I could see, she had not the strength to follow to the letter. I had such strength and did not hesitate to use it to overcome her reluctance, which I judged very irresponsible. That is why were arguing. Others will make of it what they will, but I do not regret what I said or did. [*He raises both arms*] What is the sacred bond of friendship? No more than an empty word unless we are prepared to discharge the solemn duties which go with it. Now if you would allow me, I shall withdraw.

COUNT [*exalted*]. O most excellent man! No, you shall not withdraw. Madame, he is shortly to be even more closely allied to us. I have decided that he shall marry Florestine.

COUNTESS [*warmly*]. Sir, you could not make a better use of the legal rights you have over your ward. Your choice has my full approval, should you think it necessary, and the sooner it happens the better.

COUNT [*hesitating*]. Very well... Tonight... A simple ceremony... your almoner will perform the service...

COUNTESS [*fervently*]. Excellent! Since I have always been like a mother to her, I shall now go and prepare her for her solemn nuptials. But surely you won't stand by and let your friend be the only one to behave generously to our dear boy Leon? I would like to think that the opposite was true.

COUNT [*embarrassed*]. Ah Madame... please believe...

COUNTESS [*overjoyed*]. Oh sir, I do believe you... Today is my son's birthday. The conjunction of these two events shall give this day a special place in my heart.

[*She leaves*]

SCENE 9

The COUNT, BÉGEARSS

COUNT [*watching her leave*]. I can't get over my astonishment. I was expecting endless arguments and objections, and I find that she is fair, kind, and generous to my daughter. 'I've always been like a mother to her', she said... No, this is no wicked woman! There is a dignity about her which impresses me deeply... something in her voice which deflects the most damning criticism. But, old friend, I myself am not above reproach for allowing my surprise to show when I saw the letters being burnt.

BÉGEARSS. Personally, I wasn't at all surprised, seeing who it was you came in with. I imagine that snake Figaro had hissed in your ear that I was there to betray your secrets? Scurrilous slurs are powerless against a man such as myself: I observe them from a great height. But in any case, sir, what were those letters to you? Hadn't you already, against my advice, taken what you wished to keep? Ah, if only she had come to me earlier, you would not now have overwhelming evidence against her!

COUNT [*anguished*]. Yes, overwhelming! [*Animated*] I can't stand keeping it here, inside my coat: it's as though my chest were on fire.

[*He takes the letter from inside his coat and puts it in his pocket*

BÉGEARSS [*continues in a kindly tone*]. Perhaps I should make more progress with you if I spoke up for the young man who by law is your son. After all, he's not to blame for the tragic circumstances which brought him so close to you.

COUNT [*his anger returning*]. Him! Close? Never!

BÉGEARSS. Nor is he in any way to blame for loving Florestine. Still, as long as he stays near her here, how can I marry her? She may love him too, and will consent only out of respect for you. Wounded feelings...

COUNT. I take your meaning, old friend. The point you make convinces me that I must send him away immediately. Yes, and I will feel happier once that grim reminder of all he stands for is out of my sight. But how can I raise the matter with the Countess? Will she agree to be parted from him? I suppose there will have to be a confrontation?

BÉGEARSS. A confrontation, no. But divorce is now accepted in this headstrong country. You might wish to consider that as a way forward.

COUNT. What, and make my private life public knowledge? A number of spineless wretches have done it. It's the lowest point to which our degenerate age has yet sunk. It means disgrace and shame, and I leave both to those who behave so scandalously and those who push them into it!

BÉGEARSS. With both the Countess and yourself I have always tried to do what is right and honourable. I am not in favour of using violence, especially where a son is concerned...

COUNT. Say 'a stranger', whose departure I shall bring forward.

BÉGEARSS. And not forgetting that insolent valet.

COUNT. I'm too sick of him to want to keep him here. Now you, my friend, go straight to my notary, show him my receipt which I have here, and bring me back the three millions in gold which he has been keeping for me. That way you can be genuinely magnanimous in the marriage contract which I want signed and sealed today... for now you truly are the possessor of a fortune... [*He gives him the receipt, takes him by the arm, and they leave*] And tonight, at midnight, quietly, in the Countess's private chapel...

[*We do not hear the rest*

ACT IV

The COUNTESS's *drawing-room, as before.*

SCENE 1

FIGARO, *alone. He paces restlessly and keeps glancing around him*

FIGARO. 'Come to her Ladyship's drawing-room at six,' she says, 'it's the safest place to talk...' I rush to get through all I had to do and arrive here in a lather: so where is she? [*He walks up and down, mopping his brow*] Ah no, I didn't imagine it, I really did see them walk out of here, him and his Lordship arm in arm... So it's a setback, but that doesn't mean throwing in the towel. Politicians don't turn tail and rush from the platform just because they've had their argument killed under them. The man is loathsome—and such a smooth operator! [*Indignantly*] He manages to burn Madame's letters so that she doesn't realize they're not all there, and then he manages to wriggle out of it when he's called upon to explain himself... He is as black as the hell Milton described.* [*In a bantering tone*] I was right a while back, when I was so angry: Honoré Bégearss is the demon the Jews called Legion.* And if you take a close look, you'll see Old Nick himself, he of the cloven hoof which my old mother used to say is the only part of them devils can't hide! [*He laughs*] Ha ha ha! I do believe I'm getting my old sparkle back! First on account of the fact that I've handed the Mexican millions to Fal for safekeeping, which gives us some time. [*He slaps one hand with a letter*] And second... Doctor of Advanced Hypocrisy, Major in the Tartuffian brigade! Thanks to Chance which directs all, to the brilliance of my tactics, and to a handful of well-spent golden coins, I have in my hand a note which promises me a letter of yours in which, I am informed, you let your mask fall in such a way as to leave no room for doubt! [*He opens the note and reads*] Surely the scoundrel who has read it can't really want fifty louis? Ah well, he shall have the money if the letter is worth it. It'll be a year's wages well spent if I can undeceive a master to whom we all owe so much... But where are you Suzanne, to share the fun? *O che piacere!**... It'll have to wait till tomorrow, then. I can't see that anything disastrous will be happening tonight. Still, why waste time? Whenever I have in the past, I've always regretted it. [*With suddenly energy*] No shilly-shallying: I'll go and plant the bomb. Then I'll sleep on it, see if I've come up with anything else in the morning, and tomorrow we'll see which of us, him or me, blows the other into small pieces!

SCENE 2

BÉGEARSS, FIGARO

BÉGEARSS [*with mocking irony*]. Well I never, it's brother Figaro! Such a charming room—and all the more so for seeing you in it, sir.

FIGARO [*responding in kind*]. If only for the pleasure of having me kicked out of it one more time.

BÉGEARSS. That was nothing, and surely not worth fretting over? Still, it's most considerate of you to keep it in mind: we all have our own little ways.

FIGARO. And yours is putting the case for Bégearss only behind closed doors?

BÉGEARSS [*clapping him on the shoulder*]. A clever man like yourself doesn't have to hear absolutely everything, because he can work it all out for himself.

FIGARO. We all have to use whatever small talents heaven has bestowed on us.

BÉGEARSS. And how much does our master plotter believe he stands to gain with those he is currently deploying?

FIGARO. Since I've not bet on the game, I shall win the lot... provided I make sure my opponent loses.

BÉGEARSS [*stung*]. We shall have to see how you play your hand.

FIGARO. There won't be any brilliant moves, the sort that send the gallery wild. [*Adopts a half-witted look*] But as good King Solomon said: 'It's every man for himself and God for us all.'

BÉGEARSS [*smiling*]. Neatly put. But did he not also say: 'The sun shines for everyone'?*

FIGARO [*defiantly*]. Yes, by lighting up the snake that's about to bite the unsuspecting hand that feeds it.

[*He leaves*

SCENE 3

BÉGEARSS, *alone*

BÉGEARSS [*watching him go*]. He doesn't even try to hide what he's up to any more! Defiant, is he? It's a good sign: it means he has no inkling of what I'm planning. He'd laugh on the other side of his face if only he knew that come midnight... [*He searches hurriedly through his pockets*] Damn! What did I do with that piece of paper? Ah, here it is. [*He reads*] 'Received from Monsieur Fal the sum of three millions in gold as per the schedule attached. Paris, the date, Almaviva.' Excellent! I've got the girl and I've got the money! But it's not enough. The Count is ineffectual and will never find a proper use for the rest of his fortune. The Countess has him where she wants him: he's afraid of her, he still loves her. She'll never go into a convent unless I set them against each other and force them to have it out... with no holds barred. [*He paces up and down*] Yes, but I can't afford to have a squalid confrontation tonight! Try to hurry things along and you get carried away in the rush. There'll be plenty of time for that tomorrow, after I've tied the marriage knot so tight that they'll never be free of me! [*He puts both hands to his chest*] Damn this feeling of exultation! It's like a swelling, here. Control yourself!... It has a power of its own, and if I don't let it settle down while I'm alone here, it will either kill me or make me look a fool. Oh, they're so unworldly, so naive, they'd believe anything, such as a bridegroom who is going to hand over a huge dowry! Tonight I shall marry Florestine against her wishes! [*He rubs his hands with glee*] Bégearss! Well played, Bégearss!... But why say Bégearss when you're already more than half way to becoming Count Almaviva? [*Sinister*] Just one more step, Bégearss, and you'll be there! But first, you must... Figaro is the fly who can get into the ointment. He was the one who made the Count come. The smallest thing that goes wrong now, and I'm done for... That valet is bad news... The villain's got eyes in the back of his head... So get on with it: he's got to go, and his knight-errant with him.

SCENE 4

BÉGEARSS, SUZANNE

SUZANNE [*running in and giving a cry of surprise on seeing a man who is not* FIGARO]. Oh! [*Aside*] It's not him!

BÉGEARSS. You sound surprised. Who were you expecting to find here?

SUZANNE [*recovering*]. No one. I thought I was alone.

BÉGEARSS. Since I've got you here, I'd like a word before the committee meets.

SUZANNE. Committee? What do you mean? Oh really, for the last two years I haven't understood a word of the way people talk in this country.*

BÉGEARSS [*with a sardonic laugh*]. Ha ha! [*He rummages for a pinch of snuff in his snuffbox, looking pleased with himself*] By committee, I mean a meeting between the Countess, her son, our young ward, and myself to discuss an important matter—you know what I mean.

SUZANNE. After the scene I witnessed, surely you're not still hoping?

BÉGEARSS [*smugly*]. Not hoping, no. It's rather that... I'm marrying the girl tonight.

SUZANNE [*quickly*]. But she loves Leon!

BÉGEARSS. Don't be silly. Didn't you say to me: 'If you can manage to do that, sir...'*

SUZANNE. Oh! Who'd have thought...

BÉGEARSS [*taking his pinch of snuff in series*]. But tell me, what are they saying? Are they talking? You've got your feet under the table here, they speak frankly to you: do they have a good opinion of me? That's what interests me.

SUZANNE. And what interests me is what sort of magic it is that enables you to make people do what you want. The Master goes round singing your praises, the Mistress thinks the sun shines out of you, her son has pinned all his hopes on you alone, our ward has put you on a pedestal...

BÉGEARSS [*smugly, shaking snuff from his shirt-front*]. And you, Suzanne, what do you say?

SUZANNE. I'll be honest, sir, I admire you. In the middle of the awful troubles you've stirred up here, you're the only one who stays calm and unruffled. It's as if one of those djinns had been let out of his bottle and was making everything move just as he pleases.

BÉGEARSS [*very conceited*]. My dear, there's nothing to it. To start with, there are just two things that make the world go round: morality and politics. Morality, a very footling thing, means being fair and honest. It is, so they say, the basis of a number of rather boring virtues...

SUZANNE. And politics?

BÉGEARSS [*exalted*]. Ah! Politics is the art of making things happen, of leading people and events by the nose: it's child's play. Its purpose is self-interest, its method intrigue. Always economical with the truth, it has boundless, dazzling possibilities which stand like a beacon and draw you on. As deep as Etna, it smoulders and rumbles for a long time before finally erupting into the light of day. By then nothing can stop it. It calls for superior talents and is threatened by only one thing: honest principles. [*He laughs*] That's the key to all the deals that are ever made!

SUZANNE. Morality may leave you cold, but on the other hand, you obviously find politics very exciting.

BÉGEARSS [*suddenly wary, recovers*]. Oh, it's not politics, it was you, comparing me with djinns who make the world turn as they please. Leon's coming. You better go.

SCENE 5

LEON, BÉGEARSS

LEON. Major Bégearss! I don't know which way to turn!

BÉGEARSS [*protectively*]. Dear boy, what's happened?

LEON. My father has just told me, in his bluntest manner, that I have just two days in which to get myself ready to leave for Malta. No servants, he said, only Figaro, who is to act as my companion, and a man who will go on ahead to prepare the way.

BÉGEARSS. His behaviour would certainly look very odd to anyone unaware of the skeleton in his cupboard. But we know the truth, and our first duty is to see things from his point of view. This journey is the response to fears which are all too understandable! Malta and the Order are just an excuse. The real reason is the nature of the love you feel.

LEON [*sorrowfully*]. But, Major, now that you are going to marry her...

BÉGEARSS [*confidentially*]. You're her brother, and if you think there's anything to be gained by delaying your unfortunate departure... I can see only one way...

LEON. Major! Tell me what it is!

BÉGEARSS. It would mean your mother overcoming the timidity which prevents her from having any opinion of her own when she's with him. Her being so docile does you considerably more harm than if she were a stronger character. Let's suppose a father had been given to understand something which turned him against his son: who has more right than a mother to make him see reason? Persuade her to try... not today... tomorrow, and say she must be strong.

LEON. Major Bégearss, you're right. His real motive is the fear you mentioned. And of course, only my mother can make him change his mind. Here she is now, with a person... who... I cannot, must not love any more. [*Greatly distressed*] Ah! I ask you as a friend: make her happy!

BÉGEARSS [*tenderly*]. That I will, by talking to her about her brother every day.

SCENE 6

The COUNTESS, FLORESTINE, BÉGEARSS, SUZANNE, LEON

COUNTESS [*her hair dressed, richly turned out, wearing a red and black gown and holding flowers of the same colours*]. Suzanne, my diamonds.

[SUZANNE *goes to fetch them*

BÉGEARSS [*with a show of dignity*]. Madame, and you, Mademoiselle, I shall leave you with my young friend. I will vouch here and now for everything he tells you. I do not say this lightly, but you must not give a second thought to the satisfaction I should feel at becoming a member of your family. You must think only of your own happiness. I shall contribute to it only in the way you shall determine. But whether this young lady accepts my proposal or not, let me say now that the entire fortune I have just inherited I intend her to have, either by way of the marriage contract or in my will. I shall go now and have the papers drawn up. It is for Mademoiselle Florestine to decide which she prefers. After what I have just said, it would be inappropriate if my continuing presence here should in any way influence a decision which she alone must make, and of her own free will. But whatever the outcome may be, rest assured that I shall consider it sacred. I shall accept it without demur.

[*He bows deeply and leaves*

SCENE 7

The COUNTESS, LEON, FLORESTINE

COUNTESS [*watching him go*]. He is an angel sent by heaven to set all our troubles to rights.

LEON [*passionate in his despair*]. Oh Florestine, we must resign ourselves. When we realized we could not belong to one another, the shock and unhappiness made us swear we would never belong to any one else. This pledge I will carry out for both of us. It does not mean that I shall be losing you entirely, for although I had hoped to gain a wife, I have found a sister. We can go on being fond of each other.

SCENE 8

The COUNTESS, LEON, FLORESTINE, SUZANNE, *who enters carrying the jewel-case*

COUNTESS [*as she speaks, she puts on her earrings, rings, and bracelet, without examining any of them*]. Florestine, marry Bégearss. His civilized behaviour makes him a worthy candidate for your hand. And since marrying him would make your guardian happy, you must do it today.

[SUZANNE *leaves, taking the jewel-case with her*

SCENE 9

The COUNTESS, LEON, FLORESTINE

COUNTESS [*to* LEON]. My son, it is best not to enquire into those things we are not meant to know. Florestine, you're crying.

FLORESTINE [*weeping*]. Have pity on me, Madame! Oh, how can one person bear so many blows in a single day? I no sooner learn who I really am than I have to surrender my new freedom and give myself to... I feel sick with misery and dread. I can find no reasons for rejecting Major Bégearss, yet my heart sinks at the thought that he will be my... Yet I have no choice. I must sacrifice myself for the good of the brother I love, for the sake of his happiness which will not now be mine to make. You say that I'm crying! I could not do more for him if I were to lay down my life for his sake! Mama! Pity us! Give your children your blessing, for we are very unhappy!

[*She kneels.* LEON *does likewise*

COUNTESS [*placing her hands on their heads*]. I bless you both, my children. Florestine, you are my daughter now. If only you knew how very dear to me you are! You shall be happy, my child, happy in the knowledge that you have done what is right. It will more than compensate for any other form of happiness.

[*Both stand*

FLORESTINE. But do you really believe, Madame, that my devotion to duty will reconcile the Count with his son Leon? Because we must not deceive ourselves. His unfounded hostility can sometimes seem more like hatred.

COUNTESS. My dear girl, I have every hope.

LEON. Major Bégearss certainly thinks so. He told me. But he also said that only Mama could work such a miracle. Will you have the courage to speak to him on my behalf?

COUNTESS. I have often tried to, my son, but without any noticeable result.

LEON. You are so good, Mother, but your goodness has worked against me! Your fear of antagonizing him has prevented you from using the rightful influence to which your own good heart and the respect of all have entitled you. If you were to speak to him firmly, he couldn't refuse.

COUNTESS. You really think so, son? I shall try, and you shall be there when I do. Your rebuke distresses me almost as much as his unfairness. But so that your presence does not undermine all the good I shall say of you, wait in my dressing-room. From there, you will hear me put your rightful case. You will no longer have grounds for accusing your mother of lacking firmness when she defends her son. [*She rings*] Florestine, you cannot stay, it wouldn't be proper. Go to your room and pray Heaven that I succeed, so that I can at last make peace among my beleaguered family.

[*Florestine leaves*

SCENE 10

SUZANNE, *the* COUNTESS, LEON

SUZANNE. You wanted something, Madame? You rang.

COUNTESS. Go to the Count, from me, and ask if he would step in here a moment.

SUZANNE [*alarmed*]. But Madame! You're frightening me! Mercy, what will come of it? I don't understand. The Master never comes here without...

COUNTESS. Just do what I say, Suzanne, and don't worry about the rest.

[SUZANNE *leaves, raising her hands to heaven in fear*

SCENE 11

The COUNTESS, LEON

COUNTESS. You are about to find out, my son, if your mother is weak in defending your interests. But give me a moment to collect myself in prayer and gather my thoughts for what I shall say: so much depends on it.

[LEON *goes into his mother's dressing-room*

SCENE 12

The COUNTESS, *alone*

COUNTESS [*kneeling by her chair*]. The Last Judgement cannot be more terrible than this moment of truth! The blood has almost stopped flowing in my veins!... O God! grant me the strength to reach into my husband's heart! [*Lowers her voice*] Thou alone dost know why I have never spoken out! Ah, if it were not that my son's happiness was at stake, Thou knowest, Lord, that I would never ask anything for myself! But if what a wise friend has told me is

true—that a sin regretted for twenty years may earn Thy generous pardon—then, O Lord, grant me the strength to reach into
my husband's heart!

SCENE 13

The COUNTESS, *the* COUNT, *with* LEON *concealed*

COUNT [*curtly*]. Madame, I am informed you wished to see me?

COUNTESS [*meekly*]. I thought, sir, that we should be freer to talk
here than in your rooms.

COUNT. Well here I am, Madame. Speak.

COUNTESS [*trembling*]. Let us sit down, sir, I beg you, and listen to
me carefully.

COUNT [*impatient*]. No, I shall stand to hear what you have to say.
You know I cannot stay still when I'm talking.

COUNTESS [*sits with a sigh and says in a whisper*]. It's about my son,
sir.

COUNT [*sharply*]. Your son, Madame?

COUNTESS. What other subject could overcome my reluctance to
raise a topic which you invariably refuse to discuss? But I have just
seen him in a state that would melt the hardest heart—bewildered
and stunned by your decision to send him away at once, but above
all by the callousness with which you have ordered him into exile.
Oh, what did he ever do to get so far on the wrong side of so just a
fa... man? Ever since an untimely duel robbed us of our other
son...

COUNT [*presses his hands to his face, the picture of grief*]. Ah!

COUNTESS. ... this boy, who ought never have known what such
unhappiness means, could not have been more caring or done
more in his efforts to make our cross easier to bear.

COUNT [*pacing slowly*]. Ah!

COUNT. His brother's headstrong character, disorderly habits,
extravagant tastes, and dissolute behaviour were often a cause of

worry to us. In depriving us of our son, perhaps heaven, strict but wise in its judgements, has spared us even greater anxieties that lay in the future.

COUNT [*grieving*]. Ah!

COUNTESS. But tell me, has our remaining boy ever been anything but a dutiful son? What did he ever do that deserved any sort of rebuke? He is an example to all young men of his age and is respected by all and sundry. He is well liked, popular, and his opinions are valued. There is only one person, his fa... famous protector, my husband, who seems blind to his many qualities which are all too visible to everyone else. [*The* COUNT *walks faster, without speaking. The* COUNTESS, *taking heart from his silence, continues in a firmer tone and, by degrees, raises her voice*] On any other topic, sir, I should be only too happy to bow to your superior judgement and make my sentiments and my humble opinion conform to yours. But I am talking... of a son... [*The* COUNT *grows agitated as he paces*] As long as he had an older brother, and while pride in so great a name prevented him, as a younger son, from marrying, then his destiny was to join the Order of Malta. At the time, no doubt custom and practice masked the unfairness of making such a distinction between two sons [*fearfully*] having equal rights.

COUNT [*growing more agitated. Aside, in a half-strangled voice*]. Equal rights!

COUNTESS [*a little louder*]. But over the last two years, ever since that horrible event transferred all those rights to him, is it not astounding that you have done nothing to have him released from his vows? It is common knowledge that you only left Spain so that you could dispose of your estates either by sale or transfer. If your purpose was to prevent them going to him, then you could not have treated him more shabbily if you hated him! Now you intend to send him away, as though you wished to banish him from the house where his fa... family lives! Please allow me to point out that there is no rational explanation for the strange way you have treated him. What did he do to deserve it?

COUNT [*stopping suddenly; in a terrifying voice*]. What did he do?

COUNTESS [*alarmed*]. I did not intend, sir, to offend you.

COUNT [*louder*]. What did he do, Madame! You dare put that question to me?

COUNTESS [*losing her composure*]. Sir! Please! You are frightening me!

COUNT [*in a fury*]. Since you have deliberately gone out of your way to open the box of resentments which until now I have kept firmly shut out of fear of what people would say, you shall hear the fate I have decided for you and for him.

COUNTESS [*dismayed*]. Ah, sir! Sir!

COUNT. You wanted to know what he did.

COUNTESS [*raising her arms*]. No, sir, don't say a word!

COUNT [*beside himself*]. Think back and remember what you, my unfaithful wife, did yourself! How you took your lover to bed and introduced into my house the child of another man which you had the gall to call my son!

COUNTESS [*despairingly she tries to stand*]. Please, let me leave.

COUNT [*pinning her to the chair*]. No, you shall not leave. You shall not escape the verdict of guilty which hangs over you. Now, [*brandishing the letter*] do you recognize the writing? It is your own culpable hand! And these words scribbled in blood which are the reply...?

COUNTESS [*at the end of her tether*]. Any more of this and I shall die!

COUNT [*forcefully*]. Oh no you won't! You shall hear the words I have underlined. [*He reads in a wild voice*] 'Rash, unfeeling man! We have reaped what we have sown!... The crime of which you were guilty, as was I, has received the punishment it deserves. On this day, the feast of Saint Leon, patron saint of this place, and yours too, I have been delivered of a son who is my shame and my despair.' [*He puts the letter aside*] And that child was born on Saint Leon's Day, more than ten months after I left for Veracruz!

[*While he continues to read very loudly, we hear the* COUNTESS, *who is distraught, speak in a broken, semi-delirious voice*

COUNTESS [*praying, with hands clasped*]. Lord God of all! Thus it is that Thou dost not allow even the most hidden sins to go unpunished for ever!

COUNT. ...And now the words of the seducer: [*He reads*] 'The friend who will deliver this after I am dead may be trusted implicitly.'

COUNTESS [*praying*]. Strike me dead, O God! For it is what I deserve!

COUNT [*reads*]. 'Should the death of a man so unworthy kindle a last shred of pity in you, then among the names that will be given to the heir... of one more fortunate than myself...'

COUNTESS [*praying*]. Accept my horrible sufferings as the expiation of my sin!

COUNT [*reads*]. ... might I hope that the name Leon...' [*He puts the letter aside*] And the boy was called Leon!

COUNTESS [*distraught, with her eyes closed*]. My God! My sin must have been very great indeed to deserve such punishment! May Thy will be done!

COUNT [*louder*]. And though you carry the indelible mark of shame, you dare ask me to explain why I detest him?

COUNTESS [*still praying*]. Who am I to oppose Thy will when Thine arm reaches out to strike me down?

COUNT. And even as you plead for the child of this depraved man, you wear my portrait on your wrist!

COUNTESS [*looks at it as she removes the bracelet*]. Here, sir, I return it to you. I know that I am not worthy to keep it. [*Suddenly frantic*] My God! What is happening to me? I must be going out of my mind! My guilty conscience has made me see ghosts... It is a foretaste of eternal damnation... I see what cannot be... This portrait is not of you but of him, and he is making signs for me to follow him, to join him in the grave!

COUNT [*alarmed*]. What do you mean? No, it's not what...

COUNTESS [*delirious*]. Horrible phantom! Get away from me!

COUNT [*anguished*]. It's not what you think!

COUNTESS [*throws the bracelet onto the floor*]. Wait... Yes, I shall do as you say...

COUNT [*concerned*]. Madame, listen to me...

COUNTESS. I will come... I obey... I am dying...

[*She faints away*

COUNT [*alarmed, he picks up the bracelet*]. I went too far... She's really ill... O God! I must go and get help.

[*He rushes out. Her body shaken by convulsions of grief, the* COUNTESS *sinks to the floor*

SCENE 14

LEON, *running in, the* COUNTESS *in a faint*

LEON [*urgently*]. Mother! Oh Mother! You're dying and I'm entirely to blame! [*He picks her up and sits her back on her chair, still in a faint*] Why didn't I just go away, without asking anything of anyone! I could have prevented all these terrible things happening.

SCENE 15

The COUNT, SUZANNE, LEON, *the* COUNTESS *still in a faint*

COUNT [*as he enters, he exclaims*]. Her son is here too!

LEON [*beside himself*]. She's dead! Ah! I will not live without her!

[*He holds her in his arms and cries out*

COUNT [*alarmed*]. Smelling salts! Smelling salts! Suzanne, a million if you save her!

LEON. Oh my most unhappy mother!

SUZANNE. Madame, smell this bottle. You support her, sir, and I'll try to unlace her bodice.

COUNT [*beside himself*]. Snap the fastenings, tear her clothes!... Ah! I should not have been so hard on her.

LEON [*calling out deliriously*]. Dead! She's dead!

SCENE 16

The COUNT, SUZANNE, LEON, *the* COUNTESS *unconscious*, FIGARO

FIGARO [*running in*]. Who's dead? Her Ladyship? Will everybody stop shouting! All this din you're making is enough to kill her! [*He holds her wrist*] No, she isn't dead. It's just a faint, the blood rushing suddenly to the head. We've got to ease the pressure and there's not a moment to be lost. I'll go and fetch what's required.

COUNT [*beside himself*]. Run like the wind, Figaro! All I have shall be yours!

FIGARO [*sharply*]. I don't need your promises: I know Madame's life is in danger!

[*He runs off*

SCENE 17

The COUNT, LEON, *the* COUNTESS *unconscious*, SUZANNE

LEON [*holding the bottle under her nose*]. If only we could make her breathe in! O God, please give my unhappy mother back to me!... She's starting to come round...

SUZANNE [*weeping*]. Madame, that's it, Madame...

COUNTESS [*coming round*]. Ah! It is not an easy thing to die!

LEON [*beside himself*]. No, Mama, you shall not die!

COUNTESS [*distracted*]. God most high! Those who stand in judgement over me...! My husband and my son!... know everything... and I have wronged them both [*She drops to the floor and prostrates herself*] You may each take your vengeance! There can be no forgiveness for me now! [*Suddenly appalled*] A guilty mother! A faithless wife! One moment of madness meant ruination for us all! I have brought abomination upon my family. I lit the flame of internecine war between a father and his children! God who is just! It was right that my crime should be found out! May my death be counted as the expiation of all my sins!

COUNT [*desperate*]. No! You mustn't say that! Seeing you suffer like this is tearing me apart! Let's sit her down. Leon!... Give me a hand, my boy! [LEON *gives a violent start*] Suzanne, help us to sit her in the chair.

[*They help her into the chair*

SCENE 18

Cast as before, and FIGARO

FIGARO [*running in*]. Has she come round yet?

SUZANNE. Oh God, I think I'm going to faint too.

[*She begins to unlace her bodice*

COUNT [*shouting*]. Figaro! Help us!

FIGARO [*panting*]. Just a minute! Calm down, she's not in such a bad way as all that. I was out but, by God, I came back just in time!... She gave me the fright of my life! Come on, Madame, chin up!

COUNTESS [*praying, with her head leaning back in her chair*]. Oh merciful God, please let me die!

LEON [*making her comfortable*]. No, Mama, you shall not die and we will right all the wrongs that we have done. Sir—I shall never offend you again by addressing you in any other way—sir, take back your titles and your money. I had no right to either, though that I did not know. But for pity's sake do not publicly humiliate this unfortunate lady who was once your... for it would kill her... By what definition of justice can a mistake paid for by twenty years of contrition be still considered a crime? My mother and I shall not stay under your roof a moment longer.

COUNT [*impassioned*]. No! You shall never leave here!

LEON. She will withdraw to a convent and I, under my own name of Leon, shall don the uniform of a private soldier and fight to defend the freedom of our new Republic. I shall have no identity, and will either die for France or live to serve the nation as a zealous citizen.*

[SUZANNE *weeps in one corner;* FIGARO *is absorbed in his own thoughts in another*

COUNTESS [*speaking with difficulty*]. Leon! My own dear son! Your courage gives me back the will to live. I can go on because my son has a good heart and does not hate his mother. Such noble pride in adversity shall be your inheritance. The Count married me without a penny to my name* and we shall ask nothing of him now. I shall eke out a miserable existence by the labour of my own two hands while you will be fighting for your country.

COUNT [*in despair*]. No, Rosine! Never! I am the guilty person here! And I was about to reject your loving kindness and leave myself with nothing to look forward to but a miserable old age.

COUNTESS. You will be surrounded by love and kindness. You'll still have Florestine and Bégearss—and is not Florestine your daughter, who is so dear to your heart...?

COUNT [*taken aback*]. What!... Where did you hear that? Who told you?

COUNTESS. Sir, give her your entire fortune. My son and I will raise no objection. Her happiness will be our consolation. But before we go our separate ways, may I ask one favour? Will you tell me how you came by a letter which I thought had been burned with the rest? Did someone betray me?

FIGARO [*calling out*]. Yes! It was that fiend Bégearss! I caught him in the act earlier on, I saw him giving it to the Master.

COUNT [*speaking quickly*]. No, I came by it by accident. This morning, he and I were examining your jewel-case together for a quite different reason. We had no idea that it had a secret compartment. As we talked, he was holding it and suddenly the compartment sprang open in his hand, taking him completely unawares. He thought he'd broken the mechanism.

FIGARO [*shouting louder*]. A secret compartment took him unawares? The man's an ogre! It was he who had it made!

COUNT. Is this possible?

COUNTESS. It's only too true.

COUNT. We saw some papers inside. He had no idea they were there, and when I tried to read them to him he refused even to look at them.

SUZANNE [*calling out*]. He's read them often enough with Madame!

COUNT. Is that true? Did he know what they said?

COUNTESS. He was the man who brought them to me. He was in the army and delivered them after a certain officer was killed.

COUNT. Was he the trusty friend, who knew everything?

FIGARO
COUNTESS } [*together*]. It was him!
SUZANNE

COUNT. Such infernal devilry! How cleverly he led me on! But now I know everything.

FIGARO. Are you sure?

COUNT. I know exactly what he's up to. But so that I'm absolutely certain, let's see if we can get to the bottom of the mystery. Now, who told you about my Florestine?

COUNTESS [*quickly*]. He told me in confidence, no one else.

LEON [*quickly*]. He told me and said I was never to repeat it.

SUZANNE [*quickly*]. He told me too.

COUNT [*horrified*]. The man's a monster! And I was about to let him marry Florestine and give him everything I own!

FIGARO [*quickly*]. He'd have got more than a third of it already if I hadn't taken your three millions in gold without telling you and left it all for safekeeping with Monsieur Fal. You were about to make the money over to him. Fortunately I suspected as much. I gave you the receipt...

COUNT [*quickly*]. The swine has just been and collected it. And he's gone to get the whole sum.

FIGARO [*glumly*]. I deserve to have my neck wrung! If that money is handed over, all my hard work will have been for nothing! I shall go round to Monsieur Fal's as quick as I can. You'd better pray that it's not too late!

COUNT [*to Figaro*]. The villain can't have got there yet.

FIGARO. If he's stopped off somewhere on the way, we've got him. I'll hurry!

[*He is about to leave*

COUNT [*detains him, insistent*]. Remember Figaro, you must not breathe one word about the awful secret you've just been told.

FIGARO [*with great feeling*]. Oh sir! For twenty years it has been safe with me, and for the last ten I've been trying to stop an evil man turning it to his own advantage. Be sure you wait until I get back before you do anything.

COUNT [*quickly*]. Do you think he'll try to talk his way out of this?

FIGARO. There's nothing he won't try. [*He takes a letter from his pocket*] But here's what we counter-attack with. Read what this infernal letter says: it's as if the jaws of hell itself were speaking. You'll be grateful for all the trouble I took to get my hands on it. [*He gives him* BÉGEARSS's *letter*] Suzanne! Madame must have her drops. You know how I administer them. [*He gives her a small bottle*] See that she lies down on her ottoman, and make sure she has absolute quiet. Sir, you won't start again, will you? Otherwise she could just slip away from us.

COUNT [*impassioned*]. Start again? If I did, I could never think of myself without loathing!

FIGARO [*to the* COUNTESS]. Hear that, Madame? He's back to his old self again. Yes, that's my Master talking. One thing I've always said, and it fits him: a kindly man who is quick to anger is also quick to forgive.

[*He hurries off. The* COUNT *and* LEON *help the* COUNTESS *and all leave*

ACT V

The main drawing-room of the house, as in Act I

SCENE 1

The COUNT, *the* COUNTESS *with her cheeks unrouged and her clothes still dishevelled,* LEON, SUZANNE

LEON [*supporting his mother*]. Mama, it was far too hot up there in your room. Suzanne, bring that armchair here.

[*They help the* COUNTESS *into the chair*

COUNT [*very attentive, arranging the cushions*]. Are you comfortable like that? What's this? You're not still crying?

COUNTESS [*distraught*]. Don't stop me. Tears help. All these sordid disclosures have used up the last of my strength, especially that abominable letter.

COUNT [*very indignant*]. He has a wife in Ireland and was about to marry my daughter! And if every penny I have had been deposited with a London bank, it would have kept his entire villainous gang in luxury until every last one of us is dead.* And by God, who knows what methods he would have used to...

COUNTESS. Poor man! Don't take on so! But it's high time Florestine was told she can come down. She was dreading the fate that was in store for her! Go and get her, Suzanne, but don't mention what's been happening.

COUNT [*gravely*]. What I told Figaro, Suzanne, was meant as much for you as for him.

SUZANNE. Sir, anyone who has watched Madame weep and pray these last twenty years has been too grieved by all she's been through to want to make things worse.

[*She leaves*

SCENE 2

The COUNT, *the* COUNTESS, LEON

COUNT [*genuinely solicitous*]. Oh, Rosine! Dry your tears! God rot anyone who tries to make you unhappy ever again!

COUNTESS. Leon, my son, you should get down on your knees to a protector who has been so kind to you. And thank him for your mother's sake.

[*He is about to kneel*

COUNT [*raises him to his feet*]. Let us forget what has been, Leon. We shall never mention the subject again, nor shall we give your mother any further reason to worry. Figaro said she should have absolute quiet. Very well, but let's also remember how young Florestine is and be careful not to tell her the real reasons why Madame is unwell.

SCENE 3

FLORESTINE, SUZANNE, *and the cast as before*

FLORESTINE [*running in*]. Heavens above! Mama, what has happened?

COUNTESS. Only something that you'll be very relieved to hear. Your guardian will explain.

COUNT. I'm sorry, dear Florestine, but I shudder to think of the danger to which I was about to put you in—you who are so young! Thank the Lord, who unmasks the unrighteous, you shall not marry Bégearss! No, you will never be the wife of that vile, ungrateful man!

FLORESTINE. Oh, merciful heaven! Leon!

LEON. Dear sister, he tricked us both!

FLORESTINE [*to the* COUNT]. He called me sister!

COUNT. He tricked us all. He used us, playing one off against the other. You were the prize, the reason for all his squalid duplicities. I am going to turn him out of my house.

COUNTESS. Your instinct told you to fear him and it served you better than all our experience put together. You must thank God, my sweet child, who has saved you from a terrible fate.

LEON. Sister, he took us all in.

FLORESTINE [*to the* COUNT]. Sir, he keeps calling me his sister!

COUNTESS [*jubilant*]. Yes, Florestine, you are one of the family! That is our most treasured secret. This is your father, this is your brother, and I shall be your mother for as long as I live. Be sure you never forget. [*She extends her hand to the* COUNT] Almaviva, it is true, isn't it, that she is my daughter?

COUNT [*jubilant*]. As true as he is my son! These are our two children!

[*They all embrace*

SCENE 4

FIGARO, MONSIEUR FAL *the notary, and the cast as before*

FIGARO [*running in and casting off his coat*]. It's no good! He's got the money. I saw the swine walking off with it as I got to Monsieur Fal's.

COUNT. Monsieur Fal, weren't you rather quick off the mark?

M. FAL [*quickly*]. Not at all, sir, the very opposite. He was with me for an hour and stayed until I finalized the contract, including the clause which is in fact a deed of gift. Then he returned my receipt to me, with yours appended to it, and said the money was his, a family bequest which he'd given to you in confidence for safekeeping.

COUNT. The scoundrel! He's thought of everything!

FIGARO. Except to fear for his future!

M. FAL. Given his explanation, how could I refuse to hand over the

money he had come for? To wit, a draft for three millions payable
to the bearer. If you stop the wedding now and he decides to keep
the money, there's virtually nothing you can do to avoid disaster.

COUNT [*vehemently*]. I'd throw away all the gold in the world if I
could get shot of him!

FIGARO [*tossing his hat onto a chair*]. I'll be hanged if he keeps a
penny of it. [*To* SUZANNE] Suzanne, stand by the door and keep
watch.

[*She leaves*

M. FAL. Do you have any way of making him admit, in front of
reliable witnesses, that he got the money from the Count? If not, I
don't see how he can be made to surrender it.

FIGARO. If he finds out from his German valet what's been going on
here, he'll never set foot in the house again.

COUNT [*quickly*]. So much the better! That's all I ask! He can keep
all the rest!

FIGARO [*quickly*]. What, let him keep your children's inheritance
out of pique? That's not being virtuous, I call that being feeble.

LEON [*angrily*]. Figaro!

FIGARO [*louder*]. I won't take my words back. [*To the* COUNT] How
do you reward loyalty, if that's how you treat disloyalty?

COUNT [*losing his temper*]. But if we try to stop him and fail, all we'll
do is to make absolutely sure he wins hands down.

SCENE 5

Cast as before, SUZANNE

SUZANNE [*appears at the door and calls out*]. Major Bégearss is coming back.

[*She leaves*

SCENE 6

Cast as before, except SUZANNE

COUNT [*beside himself*]. Ah! The back-stabbing, two-faced...

FIGARO [*very quickly*]. There's no time to agree on a plan now. But if you just listen to me and back me up, so that he's lulled into a false sense of security, we'll get the better of him, I'll stake my life on it!

M. FAL. Are you going to raise the matter of the money and the contract?

FIGARO [*very quickly*]. Certainly not. He's far too wily a customer for me to bring up the subject out of the blue. We've got to go the long way round and bring him to the point where he admits everything of his own accord. [*To the* COUNT] Make out you're going to dismiss me.

COUNT [*puzzled*]. Eh? But... for doing what?

SCENE 7

Cast as before, SUZANNE, BÉGEARSS

SUZANNE [*running in*]. Major Bégeaaaaaaarss!

[*She stands beside the* COUNTESS, BÉGEARSS *appears to be very surprised*

FIGARO [*exclaims as he sees* BÉGEARSS]. Major Bégearss! [*Meekly*] Well, this is just one more humiliation to add to the rest. [*To the* COUNT] Since you make the forgiveness I seek conditional on a full confession of my faults, I hope the Major here will be no less generous.

BÉGEARSS [*taken aback*]. What's going on? Why is everyone here?

COUNT [*sharply*]. To turn an unprincipled rogue out of doors.

BÉGEARSS [*even more surprised when he sees the notary*]. Monsieur Fal too?

M. FAL [*showing him the contract*]. As you see, we've wasted no time, everything is going entirely according to your wishes.

BÉGEARSS [*surprised*]. Ah!

COUNT [*impatient, to* FIGARO]. Get on with it, I'm getting tired of this.

[*During this scene,* BÉGEARSS *eyes them all very closely, one by one*

FIGARO [*to the* COUNT, *as though asking his pardon*]. Since there's no point pretending any more, I'll just admit all my pathetic mistakes. Yes, I'm sorry to say again that to cause Major Bégearss trouble, I spied on him, followed him around, and generally made life difficult for him. [*To the* COUNT] For example, you hadn't rung, sir, when I barged in on you, because I wanted to know what the pair of you were doing with Madame's jewel-case which was in full view, wide open.

BÉGEARSS. Open it was, much to my consternation!

COUNT [*reacts with a gesture likely to give the game away; aside*]. The nerve of the man!

FIGARO [*bows low and pulls at his coat to warn him*]. Careful, sir!

M. FAL [*alarmed*]. Sir!

BÉGEARSS [*aside, to the* COUNT]. Stay calm, or we'll never find out anything.

[*The* COUNT *stamps his foot;* BÉGEARSS *stares at him*

FIGARO [*sighing, to the* COUNT]. It was also why, knowing that Madame was closeted with him to burn certain papers which I knew were important, I arranged for you to burst in on them suddenly.

BÉGEARSS [*to the* COUNT]. Didn't I tell you?

[*The* COUNT, *infuriated, bites his handkerchief*

SUZANNE [*whispers to* FIGARO *from behind*]. Come on, get it over with!

FIGARO. And then, realizing you all saw things the same way, I confess I did everything I could to provoke a confrontation between you and Madame, though it didn't turn out as I had hoped.

COUNT [*angrily, to* FIGARO]. How long do you propose to go on trying to excuse yourself?

FIGARO [*contrite*]. Regrettably, I've nothing more to say, for the confrontation I mentioned ended with Monsieur Fal being sent for to finalize the contract. The Major's lucky star has protected him against all my schemes and plans!... Sir, surely thirty years of loyal service...

COUNT [*brusquely*]. That's not for me to judge.

[*He begins to stride quickly up and down*

FIGARO. Major Bégearss!

BÉGEARSS [*his confidence restored, says ironically*]. Who? Me? But my dear fellow, I was hardly expecting to be told that I was so deeply obliged to you! [*Self-righteously*] What! Am I supposed to be in your debt because I now see that my happiness has been hurried along by the same sordid stratagems that were designed to thwart it? [*To* LEON *and* FLORESTINE] Let this be a lesson for both you young people. We must always step out honestly on the path of virtue. As you see, sooner or later the schemer always brings about his own downfall.

FIGARO [*utterly contrite*]. Yes! You're so right!

BÉGEARSS [*to the* COUNT]. Sir, forgive him one last time and then turn him out.

COUNT [*curtly, to* BÉGEARSS]. Is that your verdict? I shall abide by it.

FIGARO [*fervently*]. Major Bégearss! After what I've done, I deserve no better. But I see that Monsieur Fal is anxious to have his contract signed and sealed...

COUNT [*curtly*]. I have read every clause.

M. FAL. Bar this one. I shall read out the terms of the settlement which Major Bégearss intends to make... [*Looking for the clause*] Hon... Hono... Honor..., James-Honoré Bégearss,

Esquire... This is it! [*He reads*] 'And to offer his future wife an unequivocal mark of his regard for her, the aforementioned future husband, James-Honoré et cetera hereby gives and assigns to her all his worldly goods in their entirety, these consisting at this date, [*he stresses the next words*] as he has declared and vouched for in the presence of us, the notary undersigned, of three millions in gold, attached hereto, in secure bonds payable to the bearer.'

[*Still reading, he holds out his hand for the money*

BÉGEARSS. The bonds are here in this wallet. [*He gives the wallet to* MONSIEUR FAL] It's all there except for two thousand I held back to cover the wedding expenses.

FIGARO [*quickly, pointing to the* COUNT]. But the Master decided he would pay for everything. I have his written instructions here.

BÉGEARSS [*taking the bonds from his pocket and handing them to the notary*]. In that case, put these with the rest. Now the sum is there in full.

[FIGARO *turns away and puts his hand over his mouth to prevent himself laughing.* MONSIEUR FAL *opens the wallet*

M. FAL [*motioning to* FIGARO]. You, sir, can count the whole sum while we attend to the outstanding details.

[*He gives the open wallet to* FIGARO *who, seeing the contents, exclaims.*

FIGARO [*excitedly*]. Now I see that honest repentance is like any good deed: it brings its own reward.

BÉGEARSS. In what way?

FIGARO. I've been lucky enough to observe that there is not just one generous man here, but two! Ah, may heaven make all the wishes of two such excellent friends come true! We don't need to write anything down. [*To the* COUNT] These are your bearer bonds, oh yes, I recognize them. You and Major Bégearss have been competing to show which of you is the more generous! One of you gives everything he has to the groom; the other passes it on to his future bride. [*To* LEON *and* FLORESTINE] What a man, Mademoiselle

Florestine! Ah, a fount of munificence, and how you will love him!...
But what am I saying? I was carried away. I trust I've not been
indiscreet and offended anyone?

[*All remain silent*

BÉGEARSS [*at first disconcerted, he recovers then decides to speak*]. I
don't think anyone could be offended, provided my good friend
here does not deny his good action and puts my mind at rest by
allowing me to confirm that I did indeed receive the money from
him. A man of generous disposition is never offended by gratitude, and my satisfaction would be incomplete if I did not say how
grateful I am for his kindness. [*Points to the* COUNT] To him I owe
both my happiness and my good fortune. By sharing both with his
daughter, I am merely returning to him what is his by right. Give
me the wallet. All I want is the honour of laying it at her feet in
person, as we sign this auspicious contract.

[*He reaches for it*

FIGARO [*jumping for joy*]. Gentlemen, you heard that? You are witnesses and could testify if required. Sir, here's your money. Give it
to this man if in your heart you think he deserves to have it.

[*He gives the* COUNT *the wallet*

COUNT [*getting to his feet; to* BÉGEARSS]. By God! Give it to him?
Get out of my house, you cold-blooded villain! Hell itself is not as
foul as you! Thanks to this faithful old valet of mine, I have been
saved from the consequences of my folly. Now leave this house at
once!

BÉGEARSS. But old friend, you've been taken in again!

COUNT [*beside himself, strikes him on the cheek with an opened letter*]. And this letter, you blackguard! Have I been taken in by that
too?

BÉGEARSS [*realizes what the letter is, snatches it away, and reveals
himself in his true colours*]. Ah!... I've been outmanoeuvred! But
I shall have the last laugh!

LEON. You've made us all suffer horribly: it's time you left the
whole family in peace!

BÉGEARSS [*furious*]. You young fool! You will pay for the rest of them. I challenge you to cross swords with me.

LEON [*quickly*]. I'm ready and willing!

COUNT [*quickly*]. Leon!

COUNTESS [*quickly*]. My son!

FLORESTINE [*quickly*]. Brother!

COUNT. Leon! I forbid it... [*To* BÉGEARSS] Since your conduct proves you are no gentleman, you have no honour to satisfy. That is not the way men like you can hope to end their lives.

[BÉGEARSS *reacts with a fearsome gesture but does not speak*

FIGARO [*forcibly restraining* LEON]. No you don't, my boy! You can't do it! Your father is right. Duelling is abhorrent, it's madness, and people's attitudes to it have changed.* From now on, if men must fight, they can fight the enemies of France! Just leave him to choke on his own rage. And if he dares to attack you, defend yourself as you would if he were a common murderer. No one thinks it's wrong to put down a mad dog! But he won't dare try it! A man capable of doing as much wickedness as he has must be both despicable and a coward.

BÉGEARSS [*beside himself*]. You damned...!

COUNT [*stamping his foot*]. When are you going to get out? I find the very sight of you painful.

The COUNTESS *sits petrified in her chair.* FLORESTINE *and* SUZANNE *support her.* LEON *goes to help them*

BÉGEARSS [*between clenched teeth*]. Yes, by God, I'll go. But I have all the evidence I need to prove that you are guilty of the blackest treason! You only applied for his Majesty's authorization to sell your estates in Spain so that, at no risk to yourself, you could make trouble from this side of the Pyrenees.

COUNT. You swine! What are you saying?

BÉGEARSS. What I shall say when I denounce you in Madrid. On the strength of that life-sized bust of Washington in your study alone, I could have everything you own confiscated.*

FIGARO [*raising his voice*]. Yes, and you'd pocket the third of its value that informers always get.

BÉGEARSS. But to make sure you can't sell anything, I am going directly to our ambassador and tell him he must intercept his Majesty's authorization which is expected in today's mail.

FIGARO [*taking a package from his pocket, he exclaims*]. The King's authorization? Here it is. I got in first. I've already been to collect the packet, on your behalf, from the secretary at the Embassy. The mail from Spain had just arrived.

[*The* COUNT *reaches eagerly for the package*

BÉGEARSS [*furious, he strikes himself on the forehead, takes two steps as though he is about to leave, then turns*]. And so we part! A house of shame, a family with neither decency nor honour! You will now have the gall to conclude an immoral, degenerate marriage, by allowing a brother to marry his sister. But rest assured, the whole world will know the depravity into which you have sunk!

[*He leaves*

SCENE 8

Cast as before, except BÉGEARSS

FIGARO [*jubilant*]. Let him publish his allegations: slander is the last refuge of a coward! He's no danger now: exposed for what he is, his hand all played out, and not twenty-five louis to his name! Oh, Monsieur Fal! I would never have forgiven myself if he'd walked off with the two thousand louis he took from the pile! [*He continues on a more solemn note*] Besides, no one knows better than he does that, biologically and legally speaking, these two young people are not related: they are not kin but complete strangers to each other!

COUNT [*hugs him and cries*]. Oh Figaro!... Madame, he's right!

LEON [*very quickly*]. Oh God! Mama! Is there hope?

FLORESTINE [*to the* COUNT]. Does this mean, sir, that you are not...

COUNT [*overjoyed*]. My dear children, we will have to make enquir-ies.* We will use assumed names and consult lawyers who are dis-creet, open-minded, and utterly trustworthy. Listen both of you: the time comes when people of good will forgive each other for the wrongs they did and the mistakes they once made! When kindness and affection replace the unruly emotions which once set them at odds! Rosine—your husband gives you back your name—let us go and rest and recover from what has been a very trying day. Mon-sieur Fal, do stay with us. Come along, children, both of you! Suzanne, embrace your husband! And may the causes of all our quarrels be buried for ever! [*To* FIGARO] The two thousand louis he kept back are yours, an advance on the reward which you have well and truly earned.

FIGARO [*quickly*]. Me, a reward, sir? Thank you, but no. If I've been of some use to you, I'd hate to spoil it all by bringing money into it. The only reward I want is to be allowed to live out my life under your roof. When I was a young man, I often knew failure; let's hope today will make up for all that! Now I'm old, I can forgive my younger self: indeed, I take pride in the man I once was. In a single day our lives have been changed! No tyrant now to oppress us! No bare-faced hypocrite! We have all done our duty. Let's not worry too much if we've sometimes had our differences. Families are always well served when a troublemaker is shown the door.*

EXPLANATORY NOTES

THE BARBER OF SEVILLE

1 *Comédie Française*: the first performance, in five acts, was a failure. But the second, on 26 February, in four acts, was a triumph.

Act II: the quotation from *Zaïre* (1732), Voltaire's most frequently staged tragedy, is a joke Beaumarchais directs against himself. The initial reception given to his his long-awaited offspring had been an enormous embarrassment to him. But the second performance was such a triumph that he declares, with some exaggeration, that he can now 'die happy'.

5 *Queen Isabella*: Isabella of Castile (1451–1506), queen of Spain and wife of Ferdinand of Aragon.

(NO. 1): this and the numbers which follow refer to the score of *The Barber of Seville*, which was published separately. Some of the songs were by Beaumarchais himself, others perhaps by the composer Dezède. No. 5 was the work of Baudron, leader of the orchestra of the Comédie Française.

8 *how oft...*': a parody of a line from Voltaire's *La Henriade* (1723), ix. 45.

9 *your judges*: twenty-four hours were allowed for appeals to be lodged against court judgements.

11 *new dramas*: to Bartholo's old-fogeyish rejection of the *drame bourgeois* (of which Beaumarchais was a champion) are added other strands of the century's scientific, medical, and philosophical progress enshrined in the *Encyclopédie* (1751–72), edited by Diderot and D'Alembert.

13 *the Prado*: the Paseo del Prado was then a fashionable walk. The museum was built on the site in the nineteenth century.

19 *a hand*: the basins were intended to collect the blood which Figaro, as a barber-surgeon, was authorized to take from patients. The eye in the hand was part of the crest of the Royal Academy of Surgeons.

32 *Figaro's little girl*: nothing so far suggests that Figaro is a family man, a role for which he claims he is fitted (III.5). But his 'little girl' is never mentioned in the later plays.

awake her...: probably a popular tune of the day which has not been identified.

THE MARRIAGE OF FIGARO

80 *of the Play*: these notes, which reveal Beaumarchais's unusual interest in the staging of his work, were printed at the end of the preface to the first

edition. The actors named were members of the cast of the original production.

81 *in the preface*: there, she is described in these terms: 'Why should the maid Suzanne, quick-witted, resourceful, and cheerful, also have a claim on our attention? Because, being propositioned by a powerful nobleman who has more advantages than he needs to seduce a girl of her class, she does not hesitate to disclose the Count's intentions to the two people who have the most reason to keep a close eye on his behaviour: her mistress and her fiancé. And also because, throughout her entire role, which is almost the longest in the play, she does not speak one sentence, not one word, which does not express her sound good sense and devotion to duty. The only ruse she adopts is intended to help her mistress, to whom she is sincerely attached, and whose every desire is utterly honest.'

83 *in the margin*: in this translation, in a footnote.

87 *droit du seigneur*: the legendary right attributed to the medieval lord of the manor to spend the first night of her marriage with the bride of his serf. It had featured in a number of plays. Voltaire's *Le Droit du seigneur* (1762) had been restaged in June 1779, and another, by Desfontaines, Martini, and Laval, was performed at the Théâtre Italien in December 1783. Since neither play proved controversial, it was clearly not because Beaumarchais used the motif but the manner in which he treated it to symbolize feudal oppression that aroused opposition. Even so, the question was topical. In the 1770s there was a revival of the ceremony of the *rosière* during which the prettiest village girl was crowned Queen of the May. It received much bad publicity because it was believed to be open to the same kind of abuse as the *droit du seigneur*.

89 *your mule*: the mule treated by Figaro in *The Barber of Seville* (II.4).

90 *demean us*: from Voltaire, *Nanine* (1749), III.6.

92 *haven't forgotten*: on this debt, see *The Barber of Seville* (II.4). Bartholo had agreed to cancel it in the final scene of the last Act.

94 *when she was young*: Marceline was Bartholo's housekeeper in *The Barber of Seville* (II.4), though she does not make an appearance.

113 *her patch-box*: in the seventeenth century small pieces of black silk, or sometimes taffeta, were attached to the face with gum to heighten the required paleness of the complexion. The practice came into fashion again at court in the eighteenth century as an essential accompaniment of powdered hair. Patches were given names according to their position on the face: the *coquette* was worn on the lips, the *effrontée* (or bold) on the nose, on so on. They were kept in ornamental boxes equipped with a mirror.

114 *bluebird*: according to Beaumarchais's note on the costumes of the characters, Cherubin wears a short blue cloak worn over one shoulder, and a hat with feathers.

115 *Spanish Conversation*: the print, from the composition painted in 1755 by

Carle Vanloo (1705–65), was made by J. Beauvarlet in 1769. Beaumarchais here follows the recommendation made by the originator of the *drame bourgeois*, Diderot (who used *tableaux* in both his plays and his novels), that at certain moments the dramatic action should be frozen in a pictorial representation to allow the audience time to absorb its significance. See p. 116.

115 *Marlbroug*: John Churchill (1650–1722), Duke of Marlborough, fought against the French during the European wars of the first decade of the century. To an old tune were added satirical words which gave 'Marlbroug' lasting fame.

   SUZANNE: the first of Beaumarchais's indications of the 'nominal ranking' of the names of characters in the scene. See p. 84.

147 *God-damn*: what was believed to be the characteristic oath of Englishmen had been used as a general term of contempt for them since medieval times: Joan of Arc's soldiers called their opponents *godons*.

150 *song goes*: a line from the unpretentious old ballad which Alceste prefers to Oronte's modish sonnet in Molière's *The Misanthrope* (1666), I. 2.

157 *Otros Montes*: Voltaire had already mocked outlandish German and grandiose Spanish names in *Candide* (1759), chs. 1 and 13. Don Pedro's titles translate as 'Baron of High Places and Exalted Mountains and Other Hills'

158 *Cicero's finest*: Marcus Tullius Cicero (106–43 BC), a leading statesman and the foremost orator of ancient Rome. He was also a great wit, and his oration *Pro Murena* is remembered for its sustained humour.

159 *milled piastres*: the *piastre* was the currency of Turkey, but it was also minted in Spain and was later known as the Spanish dollar or peso. It was a silver, edge-rolled coin worth about 5 French livres.

   Thalestris: a queen of the Amazons who journeyed for thirty-five days to meet Alexander in order to raise children by the conqueror of Asia. The story is told by Quintus Curtius, *The History of Alexander the Great*, 5.5.

166 *wait and see*: according to Beaumarchais's friend, Gudin de la Brenellerie, this passage was cut in performance because it was considered too controversial. It echoes contemporary protests against the oppression of women. In an essay on women published in 1772, the Academician Thomas spoke of their 'slavery' in a male society. Restif de la Bretonne (*Les Gynographes*, 1777) offered them certain legal rights, and Laclos (*Essai sur l'éducation des femmes*, 1783) believed it would take a 'revolution' to free them. Figaro was right: in the economically depressed 1780s money to pay the military was short, and soldiers were set to work in the textile trades, traditionally the preserve of women.

168 *two loving women*: these last exchanges show that even Figaro is not immune from the sentimentalizing, exalted spirit of the *drame bourgeois*, which contrasts with his usual bustling, positive attitude to life. But it

confirms our impression that his streetwise effectiveness is ultimately guided by a belief in family values, honesty, and—in a word—Virtue.

179 *Panurge's sheep?*: in Rabelais's *Quart Livre* (chs. 7 and 8), Panurge throws a bleating ram into the sea and observes that the rest of the flock leap overboard after him, thus proving that sheep are the most stupid animals in the world, 'as Aristotle said'.

190 *in the pageant?*: that is, her 'small part as a shepherdess in the revels tonight': see I.7.

193 *as a vet*: see *The Barber of Seville*, I.2.

Barca: Barca, between the Gulf of Sidra and Egypt, had been a powerful Turkish province since the sixteenth century. Figaro's attack on censorship is directed less at Islam than against the power of the Catholic Church to censor free speech. Here, Beaumarchais appears at his most Voltairean.

net surplus: in the 1770s the expression was used by Quesnay and the 'Physiocratic' school of economists, who identified the true wealth of nations as the agricultural surplus.

is meaningless: this assertion of the freedoms and responsibilities of the press has appeared under the masthead of France's oldest surviving newspaper, *Le Figaro*, since 1866.

194 *free-market principle*: an echo of the laissez-faire principle recommended by contemporary liberal economists. But the market was evidently not free enough for Figaro, nor was it for Beaumarchais, the entrepreneurial businessman, who considered government intervention a constraint on trade.

at Faro: the word is derived from *pharaon*, the name given in certain card games to the king of hearts. Faro is a game of chance in which players place bets on the order in which cards appear. Gambling at cards, a fashion imported from England, was very popular in France in the late eighteenth century.

203 *earlier on*: see III.18.

206 *the packet*: the packet containing Cherubin's commission, which Pedrillo was given to deliver in the first scene of Act III.

215 *forever known*: this discreet homage to Voltaire is one of the most assertive political statements in the play. It reveals the depth of Beaumarchais's admiration for the modern, Voltairean values of tolerance, free speech, and rational enquiry.

THE GUILTY MOTHER

217 *The New Tartuffe*: the earliest version of Molière's comedy, *Tartuffe* was banned in 1663 as an attack on religious orthodoxy and was not finally authorized until 1669. Its appearance on the title page of his new play indicates both Beaumarchais's anti-authoritarian stance and underlines

his intentions: his target in 1792 is not the new political orthodoxy but the eternal hypocrisy of those who prey on the innocent.

217 *Prose Drama*: from the outset, Beaumarchais indicates that his play deals with matters more serious than those for which comedy was thought suitable.

Théâtre du Marais: the play was badly received, but was a success when restaged on 5 May 1797.

220 *everybody else!*: a few lines earlier, Almaviva is shown to be sufficiently in sympathy with the Revolution to respect the laws which abolished noble titles: see also I.5. Suzanne is clearly more jealous of social distinctions than her master. Her reaction was anticipated in Laclos's *Les Liaisons dangereuses* (Letter CVII), where Azolan is sent by Valmont to spy on Mme de Tourvel and resents having to wear an inferior livery.

225 *divorce possible*: an anachronism. Divorce was permitted by the law of 20 September 1792, though the play is set 'at the end of 1790'.

227 *Cross of Malta*: worn by members of the ancient Order of the Knights Templar. In the eighteenth century recruits included the impoverished younger sons of noble families for whom a role could not be found in the Church or the army. For novelists and playwrights it was a boon. From Des Grieux, narrator of Prévost's *Manon Lescaut* (1732), to Danceny in Laclos's *Les Liaisons dangereuses*, heroes who loved and lost were packed off 'to Malta' to escape the law and forget their sorrows, just as the Beau Gestes of popular fiction were later sent to join the Foreign Legion.

230 *at Astorga*: a town west of the city of Leon, in the province of that name.

234 *from his vows*: a reference to the decree abolishing monastic orders issued by the Constituent Assembly on 16 February 1790.

238 *of themselves*: this less than charitable estimate of women is in marked contrast to the views expressed in *The Marriage of Figaro* (III. 16).

240 *bust of Washington*: in France, George Washington, first president of the new United States, was identified with moderate, constitutional republicanism. Almaviva's admiration shows the distance separating him (and Beaumarchais) from the radical politics of the extremists.

gaze of Medusa: one of the three Gorgons of Greek mythology. She had serpents for hair and eyes which could turn living things to stone. She was finally overcome by Perseus, who cut off her head.

241 *slay the Minotaur*: Ariadne gave Theseus the clew (or thread) which guided him through the Cretan labyrinth and thus enabled him to kill the Minotaur, half-man, half-bull, who devoured an annual tribute from Athens of young men and girls.

unmask you: masks, borrowed from the Italian *commedia dell'arte*, had long been used to enable audiences to recognize staple comic types. Even after actors ceased to wear masks, the idea remained as a dramatic metaphor. The villain of Molière's *Tartuffe* is 'unmasked' by the revelation of his hypocrisy. Figaro resolves to expose Bégearss, the 'New Tartuffe', in the same way.

249 *eaten alive*: the Sphinx, which had the face of a woman, the feet and tail of a lion, and the wings of a bird, kept watch on the road to Thebes and devoured any of its inhabitants who failed to solve her riddle: what is four-footed, three-footed, and two-footed? When Oedipus gave the correct answer, 'Man', the Sphinx threw herself off the nearest mountain.

254 *Spanish doubloons*: Figaro counts in Spanish doubloons or pieces of eight. There were 10 livres to the écu, and eighty écus to the doubloon. Forty thousand doubloons was the equivalent of 3,200,000 livres, or just more that the Count's three millions.

263 *burn anything*: Bégearss cannot allow her to inspect the letters again, for she would know that Cherubin's last letter is missing: the Count has it.

268 *Milton described*: a place of 'sorrow, doleful shades' and 'darkness visible' (*Paradise Lost*, i. 59–69). Clearly Figaro's command of English has improved since the days when he knew only 'God-damn!'

called Legion: see Luke 8: 30.

269 *O che piacere!*: 'Oh what larks!' One of the Italian expressions which Figaro has always used, though he is Spanish.

270 *for everyone*: of course, neither of these proverbs is attributable to Solomon.

271 *in this country*: before about 1780, a *comité* was a small, social gathering. As the Revolution approached, it came to mean a group which met for political purposes. It was part of the new political vocabulary which arrived in France through the periodicals which took an interest in the English system of government, notably *Le Courier de l'Europe*, which Beaumarchais had edited. This is one of the few specific references the play makes to the Revolution.

to do that, sir: see I. 4.

284 *zealous citizen*: to the overheated, sentimental style of the *drame bourgeois*, Leon adds the melodramatic declamation of Revolutionary oratory.

285 *to my name*: because of Bartholo's 'maladministration of his ward's finances' (*The Barber of Seville*, V.8). The Count asked only for Bartholo's consent and did not pursue a claim against him.

288 *is dead*: Bégearss's motive is thus revealed to be money, which he channels to London, to finance a gang of thieves.

297 *have changed*: the *ancien régime* had enforced strict rules against duelling, which not only depleted royal armies but also threatened the king's authority: the duellist's honour was a form of natural law which took precedence over the laws of the realm. In the eighteenth century the unauthorized wearing of swords in public was banned, and after 1789 duelling, an aristocratic practice, was frowned on as a visible symbol of everything the hated *ancien régime* had stood for.

297 *everything you own confiscated*: anti-Washington feeling (see note to p. 242) was real enough to make this a serious threat, and it soon strengthened. In April 1793 the Girondin representative Genet was sent as minister-plenipotentiary to the United States, where he attempted to promote the more extreme French concept of republicanism. His activities were not well received, and within months he was ordered to leave.

299 *make enquiries*: Leon and Florestine are not related by blood and are brother and sister only by their upbringing: the Countess has admitted that he is her son by Cherubin and the Count acknowledge Florestine as his daughter by an unnamed woman. The charge of incest (a theme of many novels and plays of the period) has no basis, and the Count's caution is dictated by the need to avoid any whiff of scandal and steer clear of any legal threat to Leon's position as his heir. If Beaumarchais fails to produce a neat solution in the comic tradition, it was because the play is a *drame* which places the emphasis on the happiness of the family and its members. Even so, the Court's response seems unnecessarily defensive and is scarcely reassuring, for it undermines Figaro's confident belief, asserted in his final speech, that no tyrant or hypocrite can now harm the family.

shown the door: the Count's change of heart (which has restored his love for his wife, turned him into a kindly paterfamilias, and revived his regard for Figaro) has brought us close to the spirit of conciliation which defines the closing moments of *The Marriage of Figaro*. But his words, like Figaro's closing speech, can also be read as an appeal for unity addressed to the divided France of 1792.

The Oxford World's Classics Website

www.worldsclassics.co.uk

- Browse the full range of Oxford World's Classics online

- Sign up for our monthly e-alert to receive information on new titles

- Read extracts from the Introductions

- Listen to our editors and translators talk about the world's greatest literature with our Oxford World's Classics audio guides

- Join the conversation, follow us on Twitter at OWC_Oxford

- Teachers and lecturers can order inspection copies quickly and simply via our website

www.worldsclassics.co.uk

American Literature

British and Irish Literature

Children's Literature

Classics and Ancient Literature

Colonial Literature

Eastern Literature

European Literature

Gothic Literature

History

Medieval Literature

Oxford English Drama

Poetry

Philosophy

Politics

Religion

The Oxford Shakespeare

A complete list of Oxford World's Classics, including Authors in Context, Oxford English Drama, and the Oxford Shakespeare, is available in the UK from the Marketing Services Department, Oxford University Press, Great Clarendon Street, Oxford OX2 6DP, or visit the website at www.oup.com/uk/worldsclassics.

In the USA, visit www.oup.com/us/owc for a complete title list.

Oxford World's Classics are available from all good bookshops. In case of difficulty, customers in the UK should contact Oxford University Press Bookshop, 116 High Street, Oxford OX1 4BR.